Implementing Oracle API Platform Cloud Service

Design, deploy, and manage your APIs in Oracle's new API Platform

Andrew Bell
Sander Rensen
Luis Weir
Phil Wilkins

BIRMINGHAM - MUMBAI

Implementing Oracle API Platform Cloud Service

Acquisition Editor: Dominic Shakeshaft
Content Development Editor: Alex Sorentinho
Technical Editor: Gaurav Gavas
Project Coordinator: Suzanne Coutinho
Proofreader: Tom Jacob
Indexer: Tejal Daruwale Soni
Graphics: Tom Scaria
Production Coordinator: Nilesh Mohite

First published: May 2018

Production reference: 1310518

Published by Packt Publishing Ltd.
Livery Place
35 Livery Street
Birmingham
B3 2PB, UK.

ISBN 978-1-78847-865-6

www.packtpub.com

`mapt.io`

Mapt is an online digital library that gives you full access to over 5,000 books and videos, as well as industry leading tools to help you plan your personal development and advance your career. For more information, please visit our website.

Why subscribe?

- Spend less time learning and more time coding with practical eBooks and Videos from over 4,000 industry professionals

- Improve your learning with Skill Plans built especially for you

- Get a free eBook or video every month

- Mapt is fully searchable

- Copy and paste, print, and bookmark content

PacktPub.com

Did you know that Packt offers eBook versions of every book published, with PDF and ePub files available? You can upgrade to the eBook version at `www.PacktPub.com` and as a print book customer, you are entitled to a discount on the eBook copy. Get in touch with us at `service@packtpub.com` for more details.

At `www.PacktPub.com`, you can also read a collection of free technical articles, sign up for a range of free newsletters, and receive exclusive discounts and offers on Packt books and eBooks.

Foreword

At this point in time, tens of thousands of companies are exploring solutions for how to better design, build, and manage applications with the aim of improving their customer experience and growing their bottom line. The application development domain is vast, yet so elegant and simple, so long as fundamental principles of architecture are understood and adhered to. APIs form an essential principle that if incorporated into application design and architecture will help produce applications that are simple to develop, manage, and evolve. These benefits free organizations to allocate more of their development capacity to improving their user experiences, adding capabilities, optimization of experiences, and innovation of new experiences.

APIs as a concept were discovered, meaning that they exist whether they are consciously accounted for at the time of design, or if they are inadvertently created as a by product of service development. Like doors to a building, APIs can be specific considerations or an afterthought. Any person who has used a building where doors are explicitly designed for the needs of the user's interaction with the building appreciates the elegance and flow of maneuvering into and within the building. Consider how buildings used for different purposes, such as hotels, airports, personal homes, and retail stores, have vastly different use cases for their doors ranging from the main entrance, delivery docks for trucks, gates for airplanes, to the storage of valuables just to name a few examples. Also, consider how doors also play a major role in security ranging from crime prevention, privacy, fire prevention, and more. If one can appreciate the importance of doors in our society, one will realize the importance of API design and API management in the application development domain. For users to have the feeling of elegance when using or managing an application, proper API design and management must be done.

Tooling for API Design and Management has already become very mature, offering many capabilities to help development teams meet their goals in whichever circumstance they find themselves. While there is a continuing evolution in the tooling, which will continue for the time to come, the time to leverage the tooling is today. Thousands of companies, with tens of thousands more on the way, across all industries have already developed API initiatives and have incorporated industry tooling and best practices to launch successful internal and public APIs. For companies that have yet to start an explicit initiative for API Design and Management, the time is now.

This book will provide a specific perspective, using scenarios based on real-life use cases, on how to interpret and be successful with domain-specific concepts such as API first design, microservices-based backend implementation, API testing, monitoring, and more. For companies already well underway, this book will provide complementary information, which can be used to succeed with any industry standard tooling, but will use the Oracle API Platform Cloud Service as an example. Welcome to the API community!

Vikas Anand

Vice President Product Management,

Oracle Corporation

Contributors

About the authors

Andrew Bell works at Capgemini where he is a Senior Applications Consultant for the Oracle Practice. He has more than 30 years' experience in the IT industry covering a wide range of software products and industry verticals. He worked with Oracle products and toolsets for more than 25 years including 12 years working with Oracle SOA suite and Oracle BPM. He first started working in the SOA space 14 years ago, and has successfully delivered many challenging and complex Oracle Middleware projects for large blue-chip clients. In recent years, he has become involved with numerous SaaS-to-SaaS integration projects as well as API development and microservice architectures.

Andrew is well respected for his depth of knowledge in the areas of SOA, API design, and BPM. He has strong team lead and communication skills and a deep all round technical knowledge, which covers both the Oracle stack and Java.

> *I would like to thank my wonderful wife, Alison, for her patience and support while I spent many hours locked away working on this book, and my children James, Christopher, George, and Ella. I would also like to thank my good friend, Luis, for giving me the opportunity to write this book with him and the other authors. Thank you so much, Luis, Phil, and Sander, for your time and knowledge sharing; it was great working alongside you all. Very much appreciated.*

Sander Rensen has been involved in the integration space with over 12 years of experience in the IT industry. Sander started his career as a developer in migrating large sets of data, but his organizational and leadership skills were soon taken noticed, which he applied successfully across a variety of data migration projects. Sander soon turned his attention to focus on traditional SOA architecture to develop, design, test, and lead SOA implementations to a successful outcome for his clients. In Capgemini, Sander executes two roles. He is leading the Oracle UK PaaS Team and is a PaaS Architect with his current focus on API Management and adapting microservice architecture.

Outside his project responsibilities Sander has an eye for young talent, and as part of the Capgemini Apprentice and Graduate Program helps to find the right talent, and once hired, advise them in their careers and include them in some of the initiatives that he is running. Sander is also an alumni of one of the Capgemini pretentious Future Leaders Programs.

Sander is a passionate advocate of integration technologies and shares his knowledge and insights on social media, presented at the Oracle User Group Conference (UKOUG), and helps his local charity with a cost-effective website.

Outside his work, after his family, Sander is keen in sports that involves anything with a ball at present, mainly tennis and golf.

> *This book has been a great project. I am honored to be asked to help writing this book by innovators like Luis Weir and Phil Wilkins, and I am also honored by the learning from Andy Bell and the years of experience he has brought to the table. Thank you.*
>
> *This book would not have been possible for me without the support of my family in The Netherlands and the UK. First of all, my mum and dad in The Netherlands who have always given me the freedom to explore and find my ways to take on new adventures. Lastly, my wife, Siobhan and our kids, who are my true inspiration to continue to drive for perfection. My wife has taken up a lot of extra responsibility to look after the kids while I was stuck in the attic or a dark corner in the kitchen writing the book.*

Luis Weir is an Oracle Ace Director and a Thought Leader in PaaS technologies and SOA. With more than 15 years of experience implementing IT solutions across the globe, Luis has been exposed to a wide variety of business problems many of which he has solved by adopting traditional SOA architectures, API management, and now Microservice Architectures. As CTO of Capgemini's UK Oracle DU, his current focus is in setting up the strategic technology direction for the practice and also in assisting key client accounts define and implement strategic solutions using modern Oracle and open source technologies that can help realize business benefits.

Having always had a natural talent for software, computers, and engineering in general, Luis's career in software started from an early age. Even before starting university, Luis's entrepreneurial spirit led him to start several ventures, including one of the very first social media websites in his country of origin (Venezuela) as well as a small software development firm. Although none of these ventures turned into a multi-million corporation, the experience and knowledge gained during this period led him to develop the passion for distributed software computing that inevitable led to SOA.

Luis is the co-author of *Oracle API Management 12c Implementation* (2015, Packt Publishing), *Oracle SOA Governance 11g Implementation* (2013, Packt Publishing), as well as numerous articles and white papers. Luis is also a frequent speaker at industry events including Oracle OpenWorld, and most recently at Oracle Code London, Beijing, Sydney, and San Francisco. Luis holds an MS in Corporate Networks and Systems Integration from the Universitat Politecnica de Valencia (UPV) and a BS in Electronics Engineering from the Universidad Nueva Esparta.

I want to thank all co-authors and reviewers of this book, especially Phil Wilkins for being a crucial member of the implementation team and also for taking the initiative to write this title.

Most importantly, I want to thank my beautiful family—my wife, Elena, and gorgeous daughters, Helena, Clara, and Alicia for once again having to cope with daddy who was stuck in the computer, writing, instead of being outside playing in the park.

Phil Wilkins has spent over 25 years in the software industry with a breadth of experience in different businesses and environments from multinationals to software startups, and customer organizations including a global optical and auditory healthcare provider to specialist consulting. He started out as a developer on real-time mission critical solutions, and has worked his way up through technical and development leadership roles primarily in Java-based environments. Phil now works for Capgemini in a multi-award winning team (which includes his co-authors) specializing in cloud integration and API technologies and more generally with Oracle technologies.

Beyond his day job, Phil has contributed his knowledge and experience by providing input and support to the development of technical books (particularly with Packt Publishing), including co-authoring *Implementing Oracle Integration Cloud Service*. In addition to this, he has also had a number of articles published in technical journals in his own right as well as being an active blogger. Phil has presented a broad range of industry events from Oracle Open World in San Francisco to Special Interest Groups and Meetups, including running an Oracle Developer Meetup in London. Phil is also a member of the Middleware & Integration Special Interest Group Committee among others. Phil's expertise and contributions to the Oracle community have been acknowledged by Oracle by accrediting him as an Oracle Ace.

When not immersed in work and technology, he spends his downtime pursuing his passion for music and spending time with his wife and two boys.

Firstly, I'd like to thank my co-authors who have taken on the challenge of writing this book and those who have helped us with the development of the content such as Oracle's Product Management and The A-Team.

I would like to thank those who have offered the opportunities and encouraged and supported me over the years which has helped me to get to position to have this book become a reality.

Lastly, but most importantly to me, I would like to take this opportunity to thank my wife, Catherine, and our two sons, Christopher and Aaron, for tolerating the many hours that I have spent in front of a computer not only on this project, but the many that have proceeded and those that will surely follow.

About the reviewers

Ricardo Ferreira is a Principal Solution Architect at Oracle. He is part of a special division of Oracle's Engineering called The A-Team, a highly respected team within Oracle that has the responsibility of - succeed where all else failed - therefore helping Product Management, Sales, Consulting, and Support in their most complex challenges.

He has more than 20 years of experience, and throughout his professional career, he has held several technical roles, which goes from Software Engineering, Sales Consultancy, and ultimately Solution Architecture. Before joining Oracle in 2011, he worked for other technology vendors such as Red Hat, Progress Software, and IONA Technologies. His background has been particularly focused on Distributed Systems, specifically in the areas of Integration, APIs, Messaging, and In-Memory Computing.

Nowadays; Ricardo spends part of his time helping the Oracle API Platform Cloud Service product to evolve, by building needed features (he is the author of the REST 2 SOAP policy), helping the community inside and outside Oracle to address technical issues, being one of the Black Belt instructors for advanced classes of the product.

Arturo Viveros is an outstanding Mexican IT Professional currently based in Oslo, Norway. He is a certified Cloud Integration Architect with over 12 years of experience in the design, development, and delivery of software for a variety of customers and industries. Arturo is also a Developer Champion, Oracle ACE, and a published technology writer both in English and in Spanish. He also strives constantly to be involved with and support developer communities/user groups that focus on technologies such as Oracle, Cloud, Java, DevOps, Software Architecture, open source, and Blockchain. In his spare time, Arturo enjoys family life, reading, hiking, travelling, playing guitar, and practicing sports such as tennis, football, and skiing.

Thanks to Luis, Phil, and the rest of the crew for having me be a part of this awesome project; special thanks to my employer, Sysco, for supporting this kind of endeavor and particularly to my department manager, Jon Petter, who is always around my corner. As always, all my efforts are dedicated to my lovely wife, Jessica, and my beautiful family, Luly, Arturo, and Dany.

Rolando, with a passion of systems and applications integration, has spent most of his professional career working with customers to solve a common long time problem: Applications Integration.

Since his years in college he started to work with Hewlett Packard (Mexico), where he joined back in 2001. Even though his tenure with HP was short, he realized that his professional career should be focused on Applications Integration. He started to implement integration solutions with JAVA, XML, web services, EAI.

He graduated with honors and was the best qualified student of his generation (1997-2001) . He studied in Mexico at Universidad Iberoamericana.

An important event happened while he was working with HP. It was the HP and Compaq fusion. When that happened, a lot of changes occurred at HP and Rolando moved to Oracle. That pretty much changed his professional career to these days.

At Oracle, he was always focused in the Integration technology that Oracle had at that time. There were not too many products unlike today, but it was something to start with.

Then the Collaxa acquisition by Oracle happened, and that was the first step in this journey that has turned Rolando into one of the most respected professionals in the Oracle SOA space for the Latin-American market.

Rolando started to work with Oracle BPEL PM and had the opportunity to join the Oracle Product Management Team. He was the first PM for LAD in those days, covering from Mexico to Brazil.

From 2005 to 2010, he was a Principal Product Manager for the Latin-American region being in charge the whole Fusion Middleware stack. Those years were the ones when Oracle acquired most of the components that are the foundation of the current Middleware offering: BEA, Thor, SUN, Oblix, Tangosol, and so on. Rolando had to be proficient in the whole stack, which was a great challenge because of the extension of every product. All these had kept Rolando very busy in the whole region, and gave him the opportunity to work in the most important customer of the region. From Mexico to Argentina, Rolando collaborated with the different Oracle's subsidiaries to promote the usage of Fusion Middleware.

Then in 2010 he joined S&P Solutions. He joined as an associate. S&P Solutions is one of the most important Oracle partners in the Latin-American region. In S&P, Rolando has had the opportunity to implement most of the Oracle Fusion Middleware stack, with top companies in Mexico (telcos, financial institutions, retailers, manufacturing, and construction).

Currently, Rolando and his company have evolved into a modern development technology consulting firm. New wave development around Microservices, APIs, DevOps, Containers, Chatbots, Opensource technology are deployed on the cloud.

Rolando is both an Oracle ACE and Oracle Developer Champion, and is also one of the leaders of the ORAMEX Oracle Users Group in Mexico. He has a lot of articles and posts published at his blog (`oracleradio.blogspot.com`) as well as in the Oracle Tecnhology Network for the Spanish speaking community.

Rolando wrote, back in 2015, *Oracle API Management 12c Implementation* together with some other friends and colleagues. This has been one of his greatest achievements in his career.

I would like to thank my savor, Jesus Christ, for giving me the time, knowledge, and talent to do my work as good as I can.

I also would like to thank my wife, Cristina, and daughter, Constanza, for supporting me. They have always been with me and always help me move forward. I'd also like to thank my mom, dad, and brother. I'm blessed to be part of a great family. I'd also like to thank my company, S&P Solutions, my business partner and great friend, Ricardo González, and with special love to my friends, Leonardo González, Erik Sigg, and Paola Sánchez.

Packt is searching for authors like you

If you're interested in becoming an author for Packt, please visit `authors.packtpub.com` and apply today. We have worked with thousands of developers and tech professionals, just like you, to help them share their insight with the global tech community. You can make a general application, apply for a specific hot topic that we are recruiting an author for, or submit your own idea.

Acknowledgments by All Authors

Firstly, we would like to thank our employer, Capgemini UK, the Oracle DU and Colin Daly for supporting us in writing and promoting this book.

We would also like to thank our clients, specially Niklas Olsson, for entrusting on us the implementation of the Oracle API Platform CS, an experience which was very valuable to make the use cases of this book as close to reality as possible.

Special thanks to the Oracle API Platform CS Product Team, Vikas Anand, Darko Vukovic, Jakub Nesetril, Robert Wunderlich, Kathryn Lustenberger, and all other members, for creating such an amazing product and supporting us not just in writing this book but also implementing it for our clients. In addition to the Product Team, Oracle A-Team (Ricardo Ferreira, Andy Knight, Deepak Arora, and others) have been incredibly helpful and sharing with us their insights and tips and tricks. Also, thanks to Jürgen Kress who has been very supportive and engaging; enabling us as a partner and providing access and early sight of the product.

Last but not least, we would like to thank the Packt Publishing team, particularly Dominic Shakeshaft who took the time to help us get this project up and running.

Table of Contents

Preface

The ball game has changed for the IT industry. Organizations that today don't offer access to their products and services seamlessly through multiple channels, are not just considered outdated but are seriously seeing a decline in their market share. They are being disrupted.

This inflection point, arguably kick-started by the huge popularity of smartphones inevitably making mobile apps the benchmark for user experience, ended up introducing considerable pressure for businesses to modernize their IT landscape and therefore, keep up with the competition (digital giants and startups) and new demands of users in general (customers and employees):

The iPhone

Source: https://commons.wikimedia.org/wiki/File:Steve_Jobs_presents_iPhone.jpg

For digital giants such as Google, Apple, and Facebook, or even for a startup, this doesn't represent a real challenge. As many have said already, *such organizations were born digital* and therefore they are not directly exposed to such disruption, and if they were, they are ready to quickly respond to the challenge (that is, Snapchat vs Facebook, Waze vs Google Maps). For traditional organizations, on the other hand, which is the vast majority worldwide, this represents a huge challenge as they can't simply wipe their existing IT landscape and start from scratch.

Such organizations must carefully devise plans and strategies to modernize their business. They must make available considerable investments to digitally transform their operations and adapt to modern business models capable of engaging customers through digital channels in a more intimate and dynamic way.

But as organizations embark on the journey of digital transformation, it soon becomes evident that without reliable access to core information assets, delivering relevant and modern solutions that put the customer at the center is a real challenge.

What is an API?

Application Programming Interfaces (**APIs**) and the technologies and platforms that enable them, can bridge this gap. **APIs can act as doors** to previously locked information assets and key business functionality. APIs are already enabling millions of user experiences through a wide variety of devices such as smartphones, tablets, smart watches, bots to name just a few.

However, APIs are not new. APIs have been around for almost as long as there has been software development. In the early days of IT, APIs weren't anything like what we typically think of them today, but they have always embodied the same basic goals, namely a contract (explicit or implicit) that describes the data to be exchanged and an action. Today when we talk about APIs, we mostly refer to a specific type, **REST APIs** (also known as web APIs):

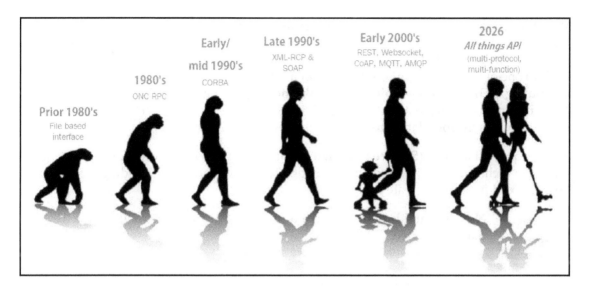

API evolution

In the days of **COBOL (Common Business-Oriented Language)** for example, the interface was often described through files containing structure definitions. As programming moved on to languages such as **C**, we saw interfaces become more explicit through things like header files.

As interface definitions developed within programming languages, the problem also needed to be addressed in distributed solutions. This resulted in the rise of frameworks like **CORBA (Common Object Request Broker Architecture)** where we saw contracts being defined with **IDL (Interface Definition Language)** combined with communications standards such as **GIOB (General Inter-Orb Protocol)** so information could be inter-exchanged among programs in distributed networks.

This type of rudimentary APIs had a problem, though. They either had aspects of the interface not clearly defined to understand the definition you had to interpret the actual code, or they were very restrictive in terms of the communications protocol, for example, **RMI (Remote Method Invocation)** for **Java** and **IIOP (Internet Iner-ORB Protocol)** for **CORBA**.

With the arrival of the Internet **HTTP (Hypermedia Transfer Protocol)**, the protocol that truly enabled the World Wide Web, it was not long before new and more open protocols emerged. The use of HTTP, combined with the **XML (Extensible Markup Language)**, gave birth to one of the most popular standards in modern distributed computing, **SOAP (Simple Object Access Protocol)**. Along with **WSDL (Web Service Description Language)** as an interface definition language, both would be used in combination as the foundation to define **web services**.

It at this point that **SOA (Service Oriented Architecture)** was conceived. A vendor-neutral and open architectural style based on the notion that services, as core building blocks, could be composed in order to create more flexible solutions.

 Note that at this point API as a term wasn't really used. Services was the main term used.

And the **Enterprise Service Bus (ESB)** was born. Introduced as the main mechanism to realize SOA, ESBs represented the evolution of traditional **EAI (Enterprise Architecture Integration)** tools. However, instead of using proprietary protocols, they used open web services standards. This made ESBs extremely popular to the point that most organizations worldwide still use ESBs to satisfy many of their integration needs.

ESBs delivered many good benefits, and for many years they satisfied common integration requirements. But as mentioned at the start, an inflection point would take the entire IT industry by surprise.

With the increased popularity of mobile apps and the wide availability of **cloud computing** (at this point becoming popular among large enterprises), **REST (Representational State Transfer)** is introduced as a much simpler and more efficient way to implement services. Only that they were not referred to as services but **web APIs**. Although not enforced by the REST specification itself, most REST implementers favor **JSON (JavaScript Object Notation)** over XML the format to send data in REST.

This new way to provide access proved to be much more lightweight and simpler to adopt than its SOAP/WSDL predecessor and quickly rocketed in popularity.

ESB/SOA vendors, while trying to keep up with new demands, quickly adapted their 1st generation SOA stacks and XML appliances to also support REST/JSON capabilities, giving the vendors at least some time to digest what was going on in the industry. These are known as 2nd generation API platforms; these are just adaptations of ESBs and XML appliances to support REST APIs:

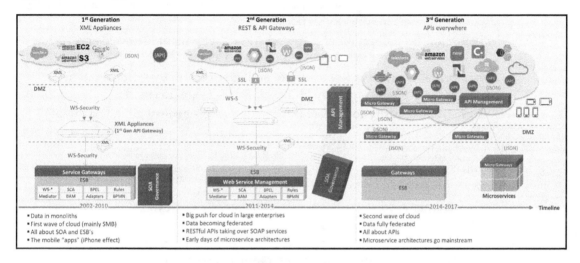

API platform evolution – from ESBs to micro-gateways

Some vendors, however, truly acknowledging that there had been a fundamental change in the industry, understood that just putting *lipstick on a pig* wouldn't do. They understood that information had become federated, that access via APIs had become the new standard; but most importantly a new way to construct services, a new kid in the block, had arrived to stay: **Microservices Architecture**.

3rd generation APIs

These few vendors understood that Microservices Architecture wasn't fundamentally different from SOA in terms of its principles. However, in terms of realization, the technologies used to implement microservices truly delivered to the promise of flexibility, scalability, and agility. Therefore, in order to deliver a modern 3rd generation API platform, they had to build a solution from the ground up with modern requirements in mind.

These vendors acknowledged that a 3rd generation API platform had to comply with at least the following requirements:

- Implement APIs anywhere (in any vendor's cloud or on-premises) without introducing an operations nightmare and huge costs
- Empower communities of developers by letting them discover and subscribe to APIs via a self-service developer portal
- Deliver seamless tooling for end-to-end API development life cycle and API-first so developers get the tools they need to design, create, and test their APIs
- Give information owners full visibility and control over their information by letting them decide how and by whom their assets are accessed
- Deliver strong security to protect information assets against all major threats (that is, OWASP top 10)
- Is lightweight, appliance-less/ESB-less, and suitable for Microservice Architectures
- Is elastic (that is, can scale easily)
- Is centrally managed regardless of the number of gateways, APIs, and their location
- Makes meaningful use of statistics so operations data can be used to gain business insight and not just to monitor and troubleshoot
- Is subscription-based, with no CPU-based licensing

 A recommended reading is *3rd-Generation API Management: From Proxies to Micro-Gateways,* http://www.oracle.com/technetwork/articles/soa/weir-3rd-gen-api-mgmt-3787102.html.

This brings us neatly to the **Oracle API Platform Cloud Service (Oracle APIP CS)** and the goal of this book.

The Oracle APIP CS is a 3rd generation API platform built from the ground up to satisfy digital requirements and therefore is capable of meeting modern API demands.

In this book, we will explore the capabilities of the product and take a hypothetical use case (which is underpinned with real-world considerations that the authors have had to address) to demonstrate how the platform can be applied.

We will also show how to set up the product, follow an API-first approach to implement a microservice, manage it with the Oracle APIP CS and subsequently streamline the entire development life cycle with even automated testing.

The book also has a chapter in explaining how customers that have adopted the previous (2nd gen) Oracle API management solution can migrate to this new platform.

What this book covers

This book will take the reader through the following chapters:

Chapter 1, *Platform Overview*, provides a full and comprehensive overview of the platform, introducing key concepts and the capabilities from the perspective of the management console.

Chapter 2, *Use Case*, describes a hypothetical use case in which we can then illustrate the different aspects of the API Platform Cloud Service. While the case maybe hypothetical, the underpinning needs come from real-world scenarios the authors have seen.

Chapter 3, *Designing the API*, goes through the process of designing APIs following an API-design first approach taking a use case. This includes using features such as API definition using the API blueprint, API mocking to test the API behavior, and Dredd to unit-test an API implementation.

Chapter 4, *Building and Running the Microservice*, show how the API definition produced can be realized using microservice technologies as APIs are natural partners. To demonstrate the microservice, we'll deploy the service on Amazon using Docker and into Oracle's Container Cloud.

Chapter 5, *Platform Setup and Gateway Configuration*, goes into the detail of instantiating APIP, configuring the cloud platform and then installing and configuring an API gateway including all pre-requisites. We first need to install and configure an API gateway to be able to manage the API for our microservice. This chapter deals with this topic.

Chapter 6, *Defining Policies for APIs*, will take you through the process of looking at the policies available to us, and defining the policies to be used with our APIs and then deploy them now that we have a gateway ready, an API definition set, and its implementation done.

Chapter 7, *Testing APIs with API Fortress*, talks about API Fortress. With an API configured and deployed it needs to be tested. Whilst there are a number of tools available for this task API Fortress has a level of integration with the APIP CS, which makes the process even easier.

Chapter 8, *Implementing OAuth 2.0*, looks at how to set up OAuth 2.0 with the APIP CS and Oracle Identity Cloud, now that OAuth is becoming the defacto norm for authentication and authorization for user-based credentials for web services, particularly REST ones. In this chapter, we look at how to setup OAuth2 with the APIP CS and Oracle Identity Cloud.

Chapter 9, *Implementing Custom Policies*, will walk through the process of building custom API policies using Groovy scripting or the policy Java SDK. APIP CS provides several approaches to develop our own API policies and these will be covered in this chapter.

Chapter 10, *Moving from API Management 12c to APIP CS*, talks about transitioning to APIP CS. APIP CS is not the 1st Oracle API product. API Management 12c represents Oracle's 2nd generation of API Platform, and for those not starting with a clean sheet will need to understand the options for migrating from the older product.

How we have approached this book

The approach we have adopted with this book is worth explaining. If you read the section on the target audience, you'll note we're not aiming only at the developer community but at a wider potential user audience of API Platform Cloud Service. To help us do this, we have set ourselves some parameters that will help you understand why things have been done a particular way.

1. Use tools that the entire target audience can use and understand. So nice integrated developer tools are not used for most of the book. There are a couple of areas where they are relevant, though.
2. Do not force the reader to buy lots of extra products to allow the majority of the examples to be exercised. This does mean that rather than real-end systems, we use tools to allow us to pretend they exist. For example, the use of Apiary to mock up an API.
3. Use a real-world based use case to help illustrate the use of APIs.
4. Rather than explaining every step in each example, we have reduced the amount of explanation provided as certain activities need to be repeated, such as setting up certain API policies.
5. Conveying the ideas and concepts will always take priority over being puritan with best practice.

6. The Oracle APIP CS is fairly new and therefore is a maturing product. Everything in this book will hold largely true for a few years, even if the occasional screen label changes or stylesheets get updated the reader should understand what they are being shown, as well as how.

What you need for this book

Beyond the use of Oracle APIP CS, we have taken the approach of utilizing additional services and tools that are free wherever possible. We will explain in more detail the different tools and services, but let's start by just introducing what is needed:

- Oracle Cloud Account—a trial Oracle APIP CS account will be sufficient for most things (as long as you have tried everything in the book within the trial period obviously)
- Free accounts with Apiary (https://apiary.io/)
- The CURL command-line tool to allow us to make simple calls to some API (https://curl.haxx.se/)
- API Fortress for API testing (http://apifortress.com/)
- Node.js as the core technology to build a microservice (https://nodejs.org/en/)
- The Atom editor for editing a Node.js-based microservice (https://atom.io/)
- Docker community edition for running the microservice in a container (https://www.docker.com/community-edition)

Who is the book for?

This book is mainly intended for architects and developers in general that wish to:

- Understand the architecture and use cases for Oracle APIP CS
- Implement API management enterprise-wide to govern the entire API life cycle
- Implement API-first in the context of microservices architectures
- Understand how to use Oracle APIP CS to manage microservice endpoints
- Implement a developer portal to manage communities of developers

Conventions

The book has two key textual conventions. Identifying specific parts of the user interface are indicated by bold text like this, for example, click on the **OK** button. Where we are directing you to enter specific values into fields or looking for values that are driven by our inputs, then this kind of text is used. For example, complete the description with `this is a description` I have added.

Tips and tricks and additional useful information appear like this.

Reader feedback

Feedback from our readers is always welcome. Let us know what you think about this book—what you liked or may have disliked. Reader feedback is important for us to develop titles that you really get the most out of.

To send us general feedback, simply send an e-mail to `feedback@packtpub.com`, and mention the book title via the subject of your message.

If there is a topic that you have expertise in and you are interested in either writing or contributing to a book, see our author guide on `www.packtpub.com/authors`.

Customer support

Now that you are the proud owner of a Packt book, we have a number of things to help you to get the most from your purchase.

Downloading the example code

The entire code used in all chapters of the book can be downloaded from the book's GitHub account at, `http://apiplatform.cloud`.

To get the files for this book from your Packt account at, `http://www.packtpub.com`. If you purchased this book elsewhere, you can visit `http://www.packtpub.com/support` and register to have the files e-mailed directly to you.

You can download the code files by following these steps:

1. Log in or register to our website using your e-mail address and password.
2. Hover the mouse pointer on the **SUPPORT** tab at the top.
3. Click on **Code Downloads & Errata**.
4. Enter the name of the book in the **Search** box.
5. Select the book for which you're looking to download the code files.
6. Choose from the drop-down menu where you purchased this book from.
7. Click on **Code Download**.

You can also download the code files by clicking on the **Code Files** button on the book's web page at the Packt Publishing website. This page can be accessed by entering the book's name in the Search box. Please note that you need to be logged in to your Packt account.

Once the file is downloaded, please make sure that you unzip or extract the folder using the latest version of:

- WinRAR / 7-Zip for Windows
- Zipeg / iZip / UnRarX for Mac
- 7-Zip / PeaZip for Linux

The code bundle for the book is also hosted on GitHub at, `https://github.com/PacktPublishing/ImplementingOracleAPIPlatformCloudService`.

We also have other code bundles from our rich catalog of books and videos available at, `https://github.com/PacktPublishing/`. Check them out!

Download the color images

We also provide a PDF file that has color images of the screenshots/diagrams used in this book. You can download it here: `https://www.packtpub.com/sites/default/files/downloads/ImplementingOracleAPIPlatformCloudService_ColorImages.pdf`.

Errata

Although we have taken every care to ensure the accuracy of our content, mistakes do happen. If you find a mistake in one of our books—maybe a mistake in the text or the code—we would be grateful if you would report this to us. By doing so, you can save other readers from frustration and help us improve subsequent versions of this book. If you find any errata, please report them by visiting `http://www.packtpub.com/submit-errata`, selecting your book, clicking on the Errata Submission Form link, and entering the details of your errata. Once your errata are verified, your submission will be accepted and the errata will be uploaded on our website, or added to any list of existing errata, under the Errata section of that title.

To view the previously submitted errata, go to `https://www.packtpub.com/books/content/support` and enter the name of the book in the search field. The required information will appear under the Errata section.

Piracy

Piracy of copyright material on the Internet is an ongoing problem across all media. At Packt, we take the protection of our copyright and licenses very seriously. If you come across any illegal copies of our works, in any form, on the Internet, please provide us with the location address or website name immediately so that we can pursue a remedy.

Please contact us at `copyright@packtpub.com` with a link to the suspected pirated material.

We appreciate your help in protecting our authors, and our ability to bring you valuable content.

Questions

You can contact us at `questions@packtpub.com` if you are having a problem with any aspect of the book, and we will do our best to address it.

1
Platform Overview

The focus of this chapter is to provide a comprehensive yet detailed overview of the **Oracle API Platform Cloud Service** (**APIP CS**) architecture. The chapter starts off by providing a high-level view and explanation of the architectural components that build up the platform, continues by describing the different personas and roles that can interact with the platform, and finalizes by providing a sample implementation architecture.

In this chapter, you will find:

- A walk-through platform evolution into 3rd generation
- An overview of the Oracle API Platform
- A look at the platform architecture
- An introduction to Apiary
- The management service APIs
- Introduction to API plans

What is the Oracle API platform?

The Oracle API Platform Cloud Service is a **3rd generation API management** platform (refer to the *Preface* for further context) built almost entirely from the ground up to satisfy modern integration requirements such as real-time access to information via REST APIs.

As its name suggests, the platform is a cloud-based Platform as a Service (PaaS), meaning that it can be purchased in a subscription-based model, metered or non-metered.

The platform supports the full life cycle of API management, from API design (using **Apiary**, which is described later in the chapter) to continuous integration, implementation, promotion, operations, and decommissioning/retirement.

Please refer to the Oracle API Platform Cloud Service home page for further information `https://cloud.oracle.com/en_US/api-platform`.

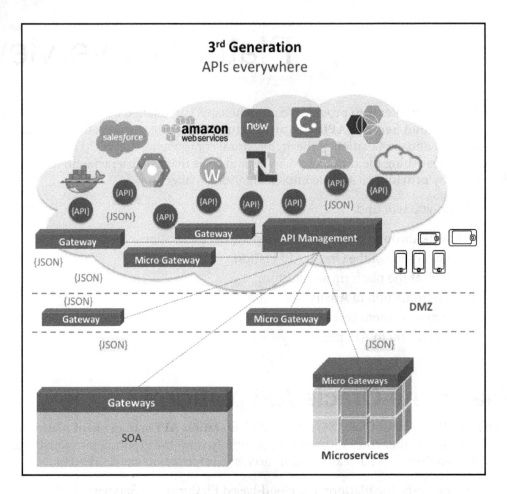

3rd generation API management platforms

The platform is fully hybrid meaning that it can be deployed in cloud computing but also on-premises. It's lightweight and equally well suited for **Microservices Architecture**, in other words, **3rd generation**.

A recommended read would be *3rd Generation API platforms: from proxies to micro gateways* http://www.oracle.com/technetwork/articles/soa/weir-3rd-gen-api-mgmt-3787102.html.

But what exactly is a 3rd generation API Platform in the context of Oracle product offering?

This concept is better understood by understanding the chronological evolution of Oracle's API offering throughout time.

In the following section it is described how Oracle's offering evolved from an Enterprise Service Bus centric architecture, to then becoming a SOA/SCA feature-rich (monolithic) platform, and then evolving into an architecture that is distributed, lighter weight, and therefore, suitable for hybrid and microservices architectures.

The following presentation is recommended as it provides a good overview as to how SOA is related to Microservices, and what Microservices actually are:
https://www.slideshare.net/capgemini/microservices-and-soa

Evolution of Oracle's API offering

As described in the *Preface* of this book, APIs are not really new. What is new is how we refer to them in the context of the web architectures and the standards/technologies/protocols used to deliver them. For this reason, when looking back through time, one must also look at traditional integration platforms such as **Enterprise Service Bus (ESB)**.

For example, Oracle's first ESB offering was part of the very first release of **Oracle SOA Suite (10g)** launched mid/late 2006. This ESB centric architecture, offered support for SOAP/WSDL-based APIs that at the time we referred to as **web services**. It also offered support for emerging standards such as **Business Process Execution Language (BPEL)** with **BPEL Process Manager**, **WS-*** standards such as **WS-Security** with **Web Services Manager (WSM)**, **business rules** with the **Rules Engine** (also known as Rules Author) and real-time **business dashboards** with **Business Activity Monitoring (BAM)**.

This ESB and **open-standards** centric architecture delivered the initial capabilities for XML-based APIs. This is why it is referred to in the diagram as **Generation Zero**. In other words, the starting point:

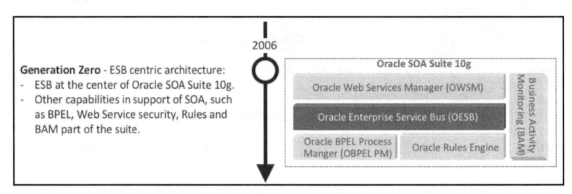

Oracle's Generation Zero API platform

As SOA continued to gain popularity, Oracle's offer also evolved to offer richer capabilities in support of **Service Oriented Architectures** (**SOA**).

It is worth mentioning that some of the reasons SOA had become so popular industry-wide are because it promised to deliver countless business benefits, most notably, it promised to close the gap between business and IT with the adoption of languages such as BPEL that in theory would make it easier for business people to define processes that could later be executed, reduce of IT spending by re-using existing assets exposed as web services, increased business agility by providing an architecture that was easier to change and evolve, and better visibility and insight over how and when business assets were used and reused and how processes were executed.

Oracle SOA Suite 11g, released around 2008, was an important milestone for Oracle and it enjoyed vast community support and wide-spread industry adoption. The product was the result of the merge of SOA Suite 10g with the then recently acquired **BEA Aqualogic** offering. It was (and still is) feature-rich and many used it as a *one-stop-shop* to deliver SOA and requirements around it:

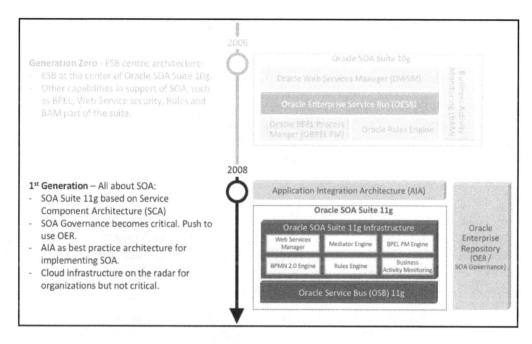

Oracle's 1ˢᵗ generation API platform

An important characteristic of 1st generation is the appearance of what was referred at the time as **XML Gateways**. The main purpose of such Gateways was to act as a **Security Proxy** to **SOAP Web Services** in **Demilitarized Zones** (**DMZ**) so when exposed to untrusted or insecure networks (for example, the internet), the Web Service would have an additional layer of security. Some of the capabilities introduced by such gateways were **SSL termination**, **WS-Security** and protection against major treats such as the ones mentioned in the **Open Web Application Security Project** (**OWASP**) **Top 10**. Although at this time Oracle did not offer a specific solution for this, the industry saw the likes of Vordel (later acquired by Axway), DataPower (later acquired by IBM), and Layer 7 (later acquired by CA) emerging as leaders in this space.

As the adoption of SOA proliferated across organizations of every size, almost in parallel the popularity of smartphones and mobile apps rocketed, to the point of becoming an essential part of everyone's everyday life. From this point forward, mobile apps became a vehicle for organizations to not just more intimately engage customers, but also to introduce mobility to the workforce which would in turn optimize processes and increase productivity.

It's worth noting that the popularity of smartphones really started with the launch of Apple's first iPhone back in 2007. Although the concept of *apps* wasn't really new (specially in *Linux* communities), the iPhone made it a marketing session and mobile apps became the new session.

As communities of mobile developers grew exponentially around the globe, a common trend started to emerged. When it came to delivering access to backend enterprise information assets, majority of mobile developers favored Roy Fielding's **REpresentational State Transfer** (**REST**) architectural style to implement APIs over the technologies and protocols commonly used in traditional SOA architectures (for example, XML/SOAP web services).

By many, web services and standards around it had perhaps become too complicated, both to understand and implement, and therefore, a simpler way of implementing APIs was well received, not just by mobile developers, but eventually also by application developers and SOA practitioners as well. Needless to say, the popularity of SOAP-based web services started to decline, and the use of REST APIs became prevalent.

At this point a new architectural component was introduced in the majority of solutions: the **API Gateway**. The purpose of the API Gateway was (and still is to an extend) to not only provide the security capabilities offered previously by XML Gateways, but also the message routing capabilities offered by ESBs, however in the context of REST APIs, and thus supporting different message notations (like for example the JavaScript Object Notation (JSON) as alternative to XML).

Perhaps because of the obvious similarities of API Gateways to ESBs and also XML Gateways, majority vendors opted to adjust their existing (1st generation) offerings.

2nd generation API platforms are therefore nothing but (1st generation) ESBs and/or XML Gateways that had been extended and/or enhanced in support of rich REST APIs capabilities and the life cycle management of API, disciplined later known as **API management**.

For example, **Oracle's 2nd generation API Management Suite** (launched between 2013 and 2015), consisted of the following components:

- **Oracle API Catalog 12c**, an adaptation (simplification) of Oracle Enterprise Repository (OER) to support the harvesting and cataloging of REST APIs
- **Oracle's API Manager 12c**, an extension to Oracle Service Bus (OSB) to support management capabilities of REST endpoints
- **Oracle API Gateway 11g**, an OEM of Axway's (former Vordel's) XML Gateway which was adapted/extended to support REST and JSON payloads

More on this in `Chapter 10`, *Moving from API Management 12c to APIP CS.*

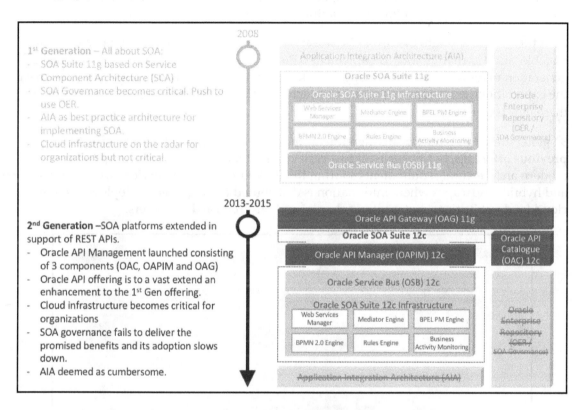

Oracle's 2nd generation API platform

Although 2nd generation API Platforms did provide some of the answers many customers were after, they also had a major pitfall. As they are in effect the result of additional layers of capabilities and extensions added to an existing (perhaps already complicated) stack, instead of delivering the simplicity that made the REST architectural style so popular, the entire process of installing/configuring the platform plus building, deploying and managing APIs on top tended to be very complicated, to say the least.

During this same period, **Cloud Computing** had also become a serious choice for large organizations to run their workloads. This meant that information assets were no longer to be available in on-premise data centers, but also in a vendor's cloud (and not necessarily Oracle's). Because of this, capabilities to being able to also implement APIs in the cloud were also expected of a vendor's API Platform.

As if this wasn't enough, the rise of **Microservices Architectures** as a more flexible, highly scalable, and alternative way to implement APIs and realize SOA meant that traditional 2nd generation platforms seriously struggled to keep up with the pace of change and thus, meet the expectations of customers – many of which had already been exposed to a degree to all these new technology trends.

3rd generation API Platform are therefore born **not as enhancement or extension of previous offerings**, but rather built to a very large extend from the ground up to satisfy modern architectural requirements souring REST/Web APIs, microservices architectures and hybrid landscapes where information is distributed among systems deployed in the cloud (and not just one, but multiple clouds) and on-premise data centers:

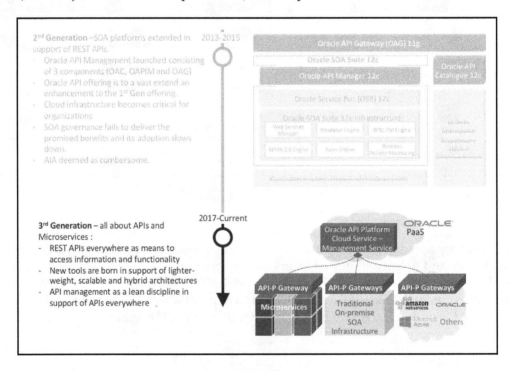

Oracle's 3rd generation API platform

That said, **Oracle API Platform Cloud Service** was launched early 2017 as a strong response to the industry demands and as a **flagship product** for API Management in general. The offering aligns perfectly well with the concept of 3rd generation API Platforms not just because of its hybrid capabilities, but also because of its flexible and scalable architecture which makes it suitable for use not just in traditional SOA landscapes, but also modern Microservices Architectures, both on-premise or cloud.

The platform, built almost entirely from the ground up, does not have any relation with Oracle's previous (2nd generation) API offering as it is much simpler, lighter weight, and scalable. The following chapter describes this in more detail.

Platform architecture

As briefly described earlier, the platform is modular, hybrid, and highly customizable. The following figure shows the core components that build up the platform:

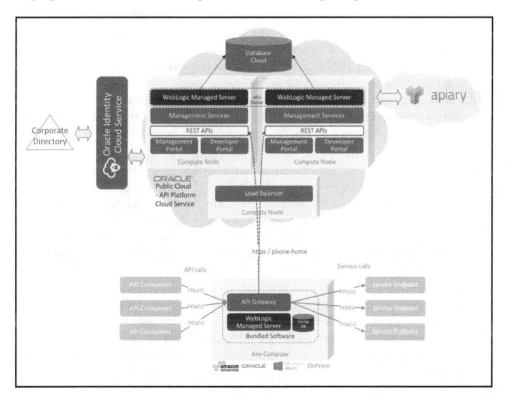

Oracle APIP CS – high-level architecture

As the diagram suggests, the platform consists the following components:

1. **Management Service**: The management service is a cloud-based application that underpins the management console, developer portal, and platform API. It's the engine of the entire platform, in other words, the brains of the platform.

2. **Management Portal**: As the name suggests, this is where APIs, Gateways and User/Roles are managed. It's a role-based application so what a user can do pretty much depends on the role the user belongs to.

3. **Developer Portal**: A web-based application where developers can search and subscribe to APIs. This is where all of the API documentation can be found and also where application keys are provided after a subscription to an API takes place.

4. **REST APIs**: Oracle APIP CS was built following an API-first approach and therefore, all functionality available via the different portals are also accessible via the REST endpoints. In fact, more capabilities are available via the API than available than from the portals–at least in the first release of the product.

5. **Apiary**: This is the component of the platform responsible for delivering **API-first design** capabilities and enables a documentation-driven API design approach. Apiary in itself is feature-rich delivering capabilities such as support for Swagger and API Blueprint specifications, a mockup engine that allows automatic stubs generation based on a API specification, assertions engine for team-based semantic validation, team collaboration, among many others, which will be described in the next section. It is also worth noting that both the management console and the developer portal have already been integrated with Apiary.

6. **API Gateways**: These are the engines that enforce/apply the different API policies to the managed endpoints. They can be deployed virtually in any computing infrastructure, cloud and/or on-premises, so long that the right (certified) operating system is used. Gateways communicate with the management service implementing a featured known as **phone-home**. The way it works is that the gateways are configured to periodically call the Oracle API-CS platform API to download new policies that are to be applied to the specified APIs and also download platform updates that need to be applied to the gateway infrastructure. In this model, it is the gateways responsibility to establish the communication to the management service and not the other way around, therefore making it a lot easier to deploy gateways as no firewall ports or network changes are required-so long that the gateways have outbound internet access.

7. **Identity Cloud Service**: Although this component is not really part of the Oracle APIP CS, but rather a related cloud service, it's important to depict as it enables the platform to integrate with an organization's existing LDAP directory. Given that the majority of organizations may already have an LDAP directory of some sort (that is, MS Active Directory) to manage their users and roles, this capability becomes quite critical when implementing the platform in a landscape that has many users especially developers.

Note that in the very first release of Oracle APIP CS, the use of Identity Cloud Service is not supported. Instead, WebLogic Console is configured to in order to support

8. **Compute nodes, Oracle Traffic Director (OTD)** and **Database Cloud**: All Management Services, including the Management and Developer Portals, run in Oracle cloud infrastructure. When the platform is set-up, these components are provisioned in 4 compute nodes: two for the management service and portals, one for the OTD load balancer and one for the database cloud instance. The creation of this IaaS infrastructure has to have happened prior the provisioning the Oracle APIP CS.

The following section elaborates each component in detail.

Components description

This section elaborates into detail each of the components of the management portal.

Management portal

The management portal is the main console for the Oracle API platform. A web-based application deployed in the Oracle Cloud PaaS, it delivers capabilities to manage an API throughout the entire lifecycle. From API creation, policy implementation, access management, and API documentation to API documentation and analytics. In addition, depending on the user role (described later in the chapter), it is also possible to manage users, API gateways, and platform settings. The management portal comes with several features as illustrated in the following diagram:

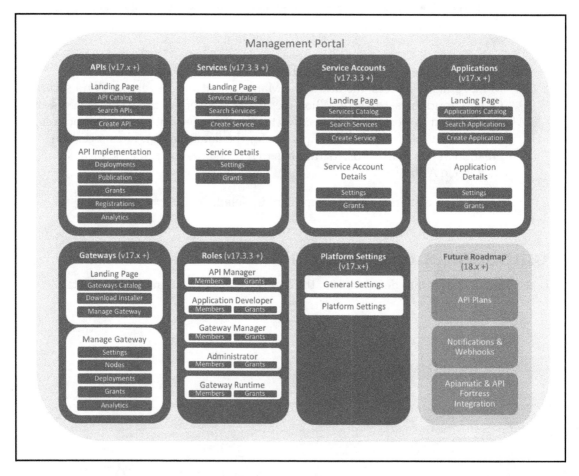

Oracle APIP CS-management portal

The following section describes each of the pages illustrated in the diagram.

Note that the pages available in the management portal, depends on the **version** of the platforms being used. Versions have been appended to the page name to show from which release a given page is available. Nomenclature for versions are simple: **<year>.<quarter>.<release number>**. For example, v17.x + indicates that a page is available from 2017 onwards including any quarter.

This book is based on version **17.3.3**. (3rd quarter 2017). This chapter will be updated yearly to reflect the latest additions and key known features of the roadmap.

APIs page

The APIs page is the landing page after a user has signed in into the management portal. The landing page is also an API catalog as all APIs created in the platform are initially listed here and can also be searched upon based on different criteria:

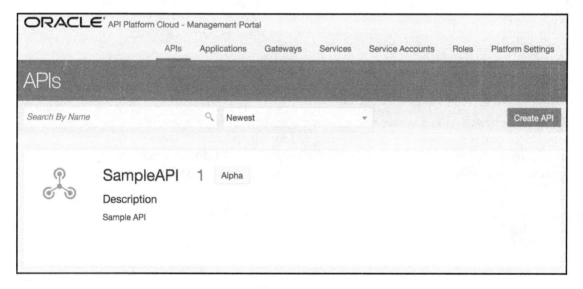

Management portal–APIs page

It is also from this page that a user can either create a new API by clicking on **Create API** or edit an existing by simply clicking on the name of a given API. This action will take the user into the **API implementation** page:

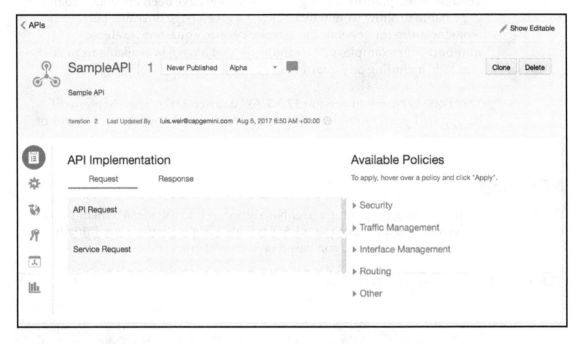

Management portal–API implementation page

When it comes to API life cycle management, this is one of the most (if not the most) important pages as from here it is possible to **implement** an API by assigning and configuring any relevant **policies**, deploy it, create the **API documentation**, manage the **user grants**, **application registrations**, and also retrieve insightful **API analytics**.

Note that the **APIs page** is overall targeted mainly at **API Managers**, which in API Platform is the role responsible for implementing an API. Roles and responsibilities are described in greater detail in section Roles later in the chapter.

The API implementation page

The API implementation page's main purpose is to provide all capabilities needed in order to fully implement an API. For example, policy implementation, deployment, documentation, security, and monitoring are all capabilities provided within this page.

The page is divided into six different sections, each of which can be accessed by clicking on the relevant icons located on the right-hand side of the page.

The implementation section

The landing section allows for **API policies** to be implemented on an API.

An API policy is, in essence, a configurable rule that is enforced at runtime when the API is called. Policies come in many flavors and for different purposes. A mature API management offering should provide a variety of policies to ensure that several needs can be satisfied, such as authentication, authorization, key validation, throttling, and routing, to name a few.

The management portal comes with twenty-one predefined policies (at the time this book was written based on API Platform Cloud Service version 17.3.3), grouped in 5 main categories. Policies can be applied to request and response payloads in **HTTP methods**: **GET, POST, PUT,** and **DELETE**.

Refer to the following link for the latest list of available policies:
`https://docs.oracle.com/en/cloud/paas/api-platform-cloud/apfad/i`
`mplementing-apis.html#GUID-99A486F8-6A5C-4E62-9E20-B641790509EA`.

The policies that can be applied to request payloads are as following:

1. **Security**: policies that focused on enforcing authentication, authorization, key validation, and other thread protection policies such as IP filtering and cross-origin resource sharing (CORS):

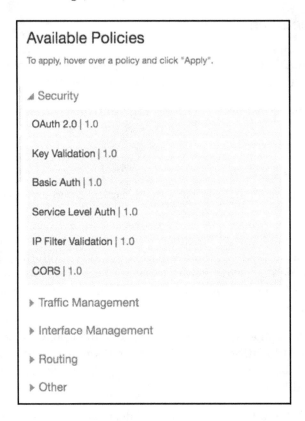

Implementation section–security policies

2. **Traffic management**: this group of policies deliver capabilities to throttle and limit the number of API calls made by consumers based on multiple criteria. In other words, handle the volume of traffic sent to the API. This type of policy can as well be useful to prevent against denial of service attacks (DoS). The following screenshot shows the **Traffic Management** policies as shown in the management portal:

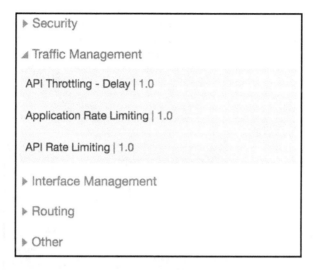

Implementation section–traffic management policies

3. **Interface management**: Policies that deliver capabilities to manage what and how HTTP resources (that is, /<resource>), methods (GET, POST, DELETE, UPDATE) and payloads can be accessed. The following screenshot shows the **Interface Management** policies as shown in the management portal:

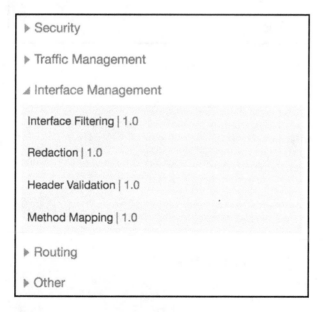

Implementation section–interface management policies

4. **Routing**: Policies focused on routing HTTP calls to service endpoints based on multiple criteria such as HTTP header values, the specific gateway handling the traffic, the application calling the API or based on HTTP resource accessed. The following screenshot shows the **Routing** policies as shown in the management portal:

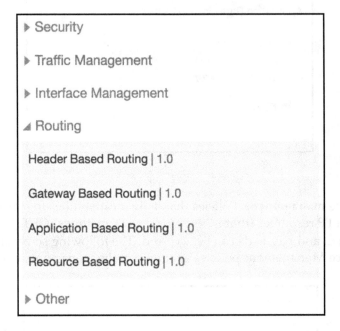

Implementation section–routing policies

5. **Other**: Complementary policies that deliver additional capabilities that don't fall in any of the above categories like for example service callouts, logging, and custom policies based on groovy scripting. The following image shows the **Other** policies as shown in the management portal:

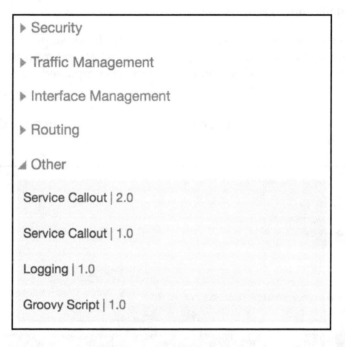

Implementation section–other policies

For an example on how to implement API policies refer to `Chapter 6`, *Defining Policies for APIs*.

For further information on policies available in management portal and how to implement them, please refer to the following link:
`https://docs.oracle.com/en/cloud/paas/api-platform-cloud/apfad/i`
`mplementing-apis.html#GUID-1EE65B88-5050-4AFE-8F53-4B256D4E2AA3`

The deployment section

The **deployment** section of the **API implementation** page allows for the API to be deployed into any registered **logical gateway**. When an API is deployed to a given logical gateway, all gateway nodes will deploy the API. From this same section, it is possible to undeploy APIs and also visualize any rejected or failed API deployments:

In the management portal, all gateways nodes (instance of gateways running on a machine), are grouped into what's referred to as **logical gateways**. A logical gateway, therefore, encompassed all gateway nodes associated to the same logical instance.

The concept of a logical gateway will be explained in more detail later in the chapter.

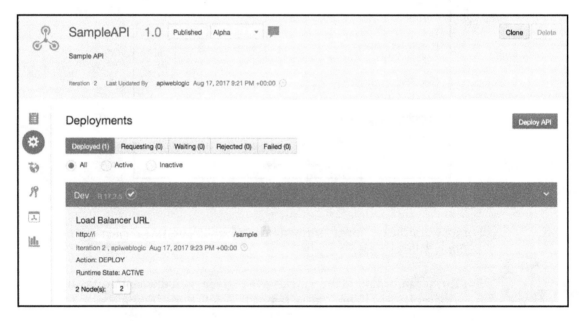

API implementation page–deployments section

The publication section

The **publication section** allows for API documentation to be created and then published in the developer portal. The documentation consists of two main parts:

1. **API overview documentation**: Simply put, free text to help describe the functionality and usage of the API. It can be **HTML** or **Markdown** text.
2. **API specification documentation**: The **API Blueprint** or **Swagger** specification document for the API created in **Apiary**:

API implementation page–publication section

APIs can be specified in a number of ways, as opposed to web services where the main mechanism to define a service is by creating a WSDL (web service description language) document. For APIs, the most popular specifications are **Swagger** and **API Blueprint**. Apiary supports both.

Recommend reading the following article for further information on the topic:
`https://nordicapis.com/top-specification-formats-for-rest-apis`

The grants section

The **Grants** section allows for different grants to be specified and therefore, control which users or groups can manage, deploy, register, and read private/public information for the API. There are six grants available:

- **Manage API**: Allows to modify the definition of and issue grants for the API
- **View all details**: Allows to view all information about the API in the management portal
- **Deploy API**: Allows to deploy or un-deploy the API to a gateway for which they have deploy rights
- **View public details**: Allows to view the publicly available details of this API on the Developer Portal
- **Register**: Allows to users to register their applications to use the API
- **Request registration**: Allows to users to request registration of their applications to use the API

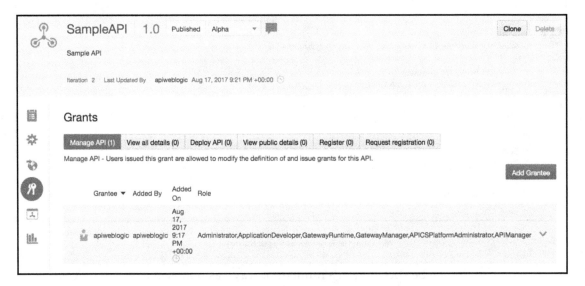

API implementation page–grants section

Registration section

Developers that can access the developer portal can create applications that are then registered to consume any given API they have been granted access to. When an application is registered to a given API, an **application-key** is provided. Presence of the application-key when calling an API can then be enforced by using the **Key Validation policy**.

From this page, registrations to the API can be created, approved, rejected, or suspended:

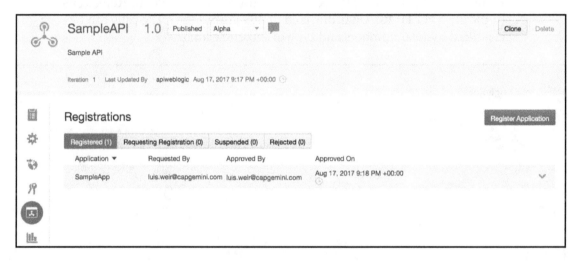

API implementation page–registration section

The analytics section

The **Analytics** section delivers insightful near-real dashboards and stats for the API. Information such as the total number of calls, successful versus failed calls, response times, and payload size can be visualized and filtered as well based on criteria such as gateways that processed the calls, name of the consumer application and timeframes.

In the section there are three main tabs:

- **General**: this tab provides a summary of all API calls in a single dashboard. The calls are can be seen classified by volume and status (All, Successful, Rejected or Failed), payload size, or API resource.
- **Applications**: this tab provides a summary view of API calls broken down by Applications. It provides a total of successful calls, rejections and errors.
- **Errors and Rejections**: this tab provides great insight on API calls that resulted in **Errors** (most likely a **HTTP 5xx Server Error** response code) or **Rejections** (typically a **HTTP 401 Unauthorized** or **403 Forbidden**). The calls can be seen classified by total numbers and type of error/rejection.

API implementation page–analytics section

The APIs page documentation can be accessed from the following URL:
`http://docs.oracle.com/en/cloud/paas/api-platform-cloud/apfad/ma`
`naging-apis.html`

Applications page

As it was briefly described earlier, an application in Oracle APIP CS represents the consumers for one or many APIs. For API-Platform an application is just a logical representation, therefore it does not matter what the application actually is. It can be a mobile application, a web application or even a wearable device.

Applications are uniquely identified with applications keys which can be visualized by clicking on the application itself and accessing the **application details page**:

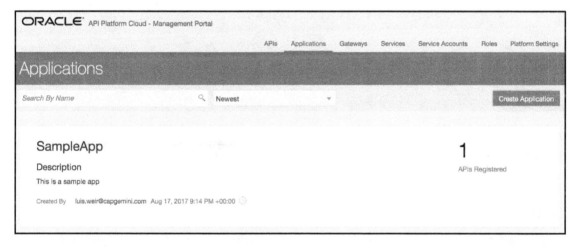

Management portal–applications page

The settings section

Once in the application details page, the **Settings** section is displayed. From here, it is possible not only to visualize the application key or **App Key** for short, but also reissue it. This can be useful for security purposes. Other details such as contact details for the owner of the application and type of application (that is, mobile app, backend system, and so on) can be visualized:

Applications page–application details

Grants section

Applications grants can also be accessed from this page by clicking on the grants icon (icon with shape of a key located on the left-hand side of the screen).

> Application grants work in a similar to API grants (explained in the API section) however in the context of an application.

The applications page documentation can be accessed from the following URL:
`http://docs.oracle.com/en/cloud/paas/api-platform-cloud/apfad/ma naging-applications.html#GUID-F035A756-2934-40EB-8D03-1FC610E8FE5D`

The gateways page

From the **Gateways** page, all registered **logical gateways** and **gateways nodes** can be visualized and managed. Details such as **gateway names** and **description**, **load balancer URLs** and number of APIs deployed are visible. Also, note that next to the gateway name the version of the gateway is visible. This is important to make sure that the version implemented is compatible with the version of the management service (ideally both should be in the same version):

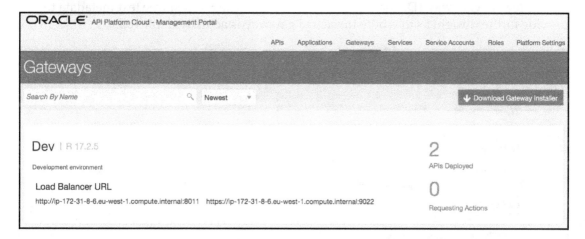

Management portal–gateways page

 A logical gateway as the name suggests, represents a grouping of one or many gateway nodes. A gateway node is an actual physical instance of the gateway that's running on a compute instance (could be in the cloud and/or on-premise) and is capable of handling API requests.

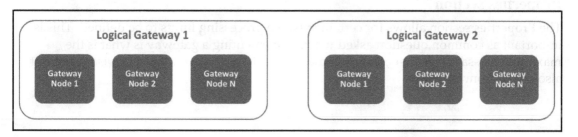

Logical gateways and gateway nodes

By clicking on a given gateway listed, the **Gateway** details page opens, and from there gateway settings, gateway properties, physical gateway nodes belonging to the logical gateway, deployments, grants, and gateway analytics can be visualized and certain properties edited.

Settings section

The settings section (landing section), provides details such as the load balancer URL, the unique logical **Gateway ID**, and the gateway location which is just free text metadata to provide further insight as to where the actual gateway is actually deployed:

Gateways page–settings section

Properties section

The **Properties** section allows for certain message processing limits to be defined. This is important as common question asked when implementing a gateway is what is the maximum message size that can be handled, so such details cannot just be visualized but also edited from this page.

Following is the description as per Oracle documentation:

1. **Maximum Message Size**: Specifies the maximum size, in bytes, of the request, excluding attachments. The default value is set to 1024000. The maximum allowed value is 200 MB.
2. **Maximum Number of Unbounded Items**: Specifies the maximum number of unbounded items that a message can contain. The default value is set to 1024.
3. **Maximum Size of a Single Message Entry**: Specifies the maximum size of a single message entity, such as an element, attribute or comment. The default value is 102400.
4. **Maximum Nested Elements in a Message**: Specifies the maximum number of nested elements allowed in a message. The default value is 1024 nested elements.

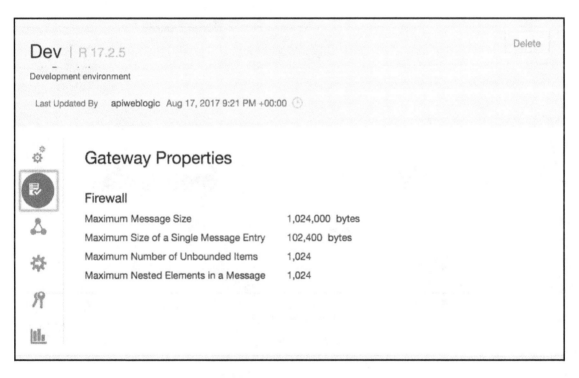

Gateways page–gateway properties section

Nodes section

From the **Nodes** section, details of all physical nodes (in other words running gateway instances) that belong to the logical gateway can be visualized. From this page, details of the physical **host URL** where the gateways are running are visible. If the host URLs are to be accessed via **HTTP proxies**, the proxies' URLs can be specified from this page.

Of special interest, is the **polling intervals** information which is available on the top-right-hand side of the section.

 This information is important as it informs how often gateways are supposed to phone-home and when was the last time it occurred. When troubleshooting, this is an important page to look at.

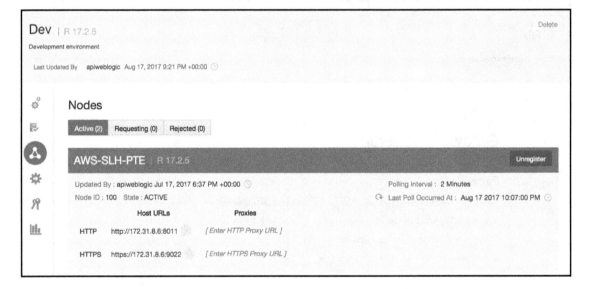

Gateways page–nodes section

Deployments section

The **Deployments** section page lists APIs that have been deployed to the logical gateway. The page is equivalent to the API deployments section; however, all APIs deployed to the logical gateway are listed as opposed to a single API. Therefore, it is a useful page if actions are required in more than one API (that is, undeploying more than one API):

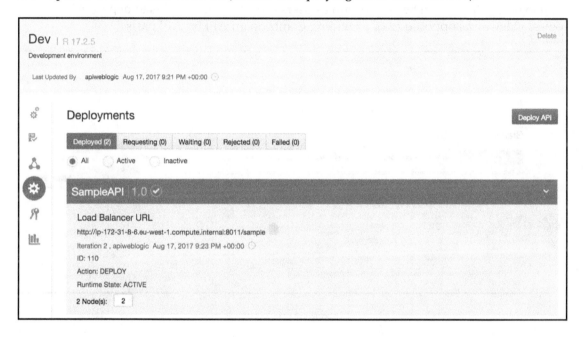

Gateways page–deployments section

Grants section

The **Grants** section works in a similar way to the API grants section but in the context of the logical gateway. Of special interest is that grants specific to system users for the operation of the logical gateway (**node service accounts**) and also deployment grants to the logical gateway, can be managed from this page. Especially the deployment grants management for a logical gateway can be very useful as users can be granted rights to deploy APIs to a logical gateway as opposed to of providing grants on an API by API basis:

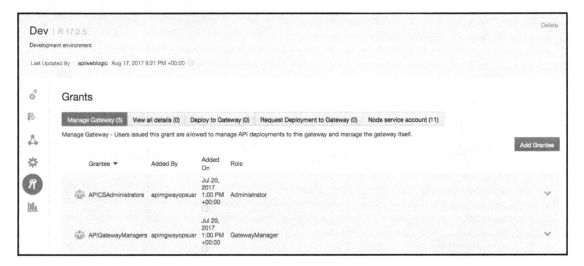

Gateways page–grants section

The analytics section

The **Analytics** pages are similar to the API analytics page in the way stats and dashboards are presented and how it stats be filtered, however in the context of all APIs running in the gateway as opposed to just an individual API. For operators of the platform, this page is especially important to monitor overall performance and health for a logical gateway and all nodes within it. It can also be handy to identify if a specific API is being problematic:

Gateways page–analytics section

 The gateways page documentation can be accessed from the following URL:
`http://docs.oracle.com/en/cloud/paas/api-platform-cloud/apfad/managing-gateway-settings.html#GUID-A4FF2A7E-1CEF-4396-BD50-54D506F711E7`

The services page

From the **Services** page backend services can be registered and managed.

 A backend service is basically an unmanaged REST endpoint fronted by the API Platform's API Gateway.

A service registered in this page can be referenced from the API implementation page that way preventing a backend endpoint URLs to be manually typed every time an API is created.

 This page is only available but from version 17.3.x onwards.

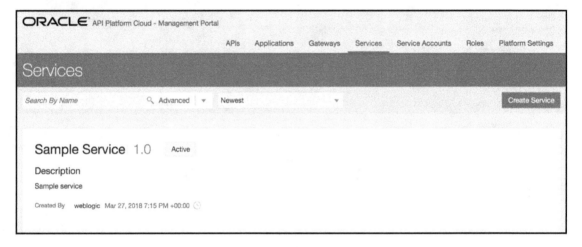

Management portal–services page

Once a service is created, it can be edited just clicking over it. This will take the user to the service settings page described subsequently.

The settings section

From the **Settings** section, it is possible to edit a REST endpoint name and its corresponding URL. Although in version 17.3.x only one endpoint can be entered per service, in future versions it will be possible to assign multiple endpoints, which will be useful as each environment (for example, dev, test) can have its own endpoint.

From this same section it is also possible to assign a **Service Account** which is useful if the backend REST endpoint requires some form of authentication.

> Refer to next section *Service accounts* for further information on authentication types supported.

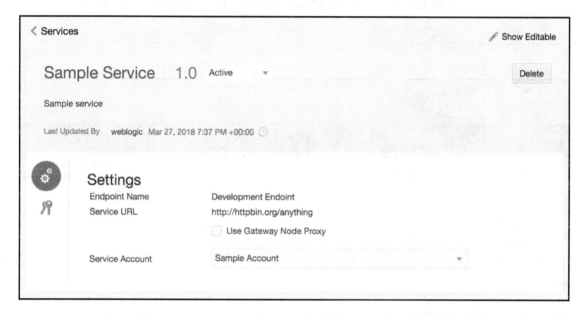

Services page–settings section

The grants section

Services grants can also be accessed from this page by clicking on the grants icon (icon with shape of a key located on the left-hand side of the screen).

> Services grants work in a similar to API grants (explained in the API section) however in the context of an Services.

Service accounts page

The **Service Accounts** page is used to effectively store authentication secrets that can be used by service (registered in the services page) when calling backend endpoint URLs that require some form of authentication and authorization. In version 17.3.x, two authentication types are supported, **HTTP Basic Authentication** and **OAuth 2.0**.

 Note that this page is only available but from version 17.3.x onwards.

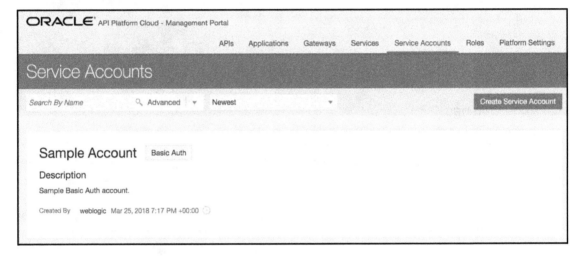

Management portal–services accounts page

Once a service account is created, it can be edited just clicking over it. This will take the user to the service accounts settings page described subsequently.

The settings section

From the settings section it is possible to change the authentication type used in the service accounts, along with its relevant details (for example, username and password in the case of Basic Authentication):

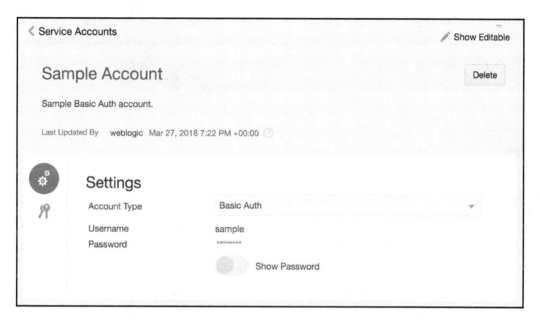

Services page–settings section

The grants section

Service accounts grants can also be accessed from this page by clicking on the grants icon (icon with shape of a key located on the left-hand side of the screen).

Service accounts grants work in a similar to API grants (explained in the API section) however in the context of a services account.

The roles page

The roles page lists all the available user roles to which different users and grants can be assigned to.

This page is only available but from version 17.3.x onwards.

ORACLE® API Platform Cloud - Management Portal

APIs   Applications   Gateways   Services   Service Accounts   Roles   Platform Settings

Roles

Application Developer

API consumers granted self-service access rights to discover and register APIs, view API documentation, and manage applications using the Developer Portal.

3

Gateway Manager

Operations team members responsible for deploying, registering, and managing gateways. May also manage API deployments to their gateways when issued the Deploy API grant by an API Manager.

3

API Manager

People responsible for managing the API lifecycle, which includes designing, implementing, and versioning APIs. Also responsible for managing grants and applications, providing API documentation, and monitoring API performance.

3

Gateway Runtime

This role indicates a service account used to communicate from the gateway to the portal.

2

Service Manager

People responsible for managing resources defining backend services. This includes for example managing service accounts.

3

Administrator

System Administrators responsible for assigning people roles in the system. Administrators possess the rights of all other roles and rights to all objects in the system.

4

6 of 6 items
∧ Top | Bottom ∨

Management portal–roles page

To better understand users and roles of in Oracle APIP CS, the following diagram illustrates some of the main roles available in the platform (including in Apiary) and how they relate to the different components of the platform:

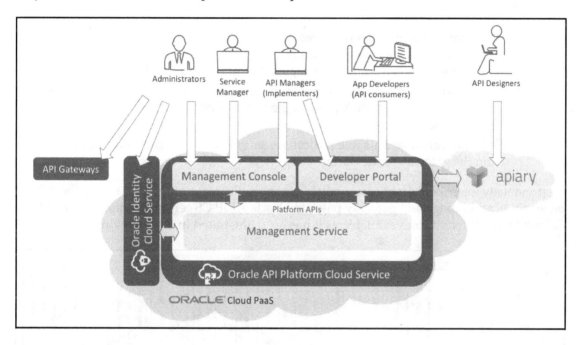

Management portal–roles

1. **API manager**: People responsible for managing the API lifecycle, which includes designing, implementing, and versioning APIs. Also responsible for managing grants and applications, providing API documentation, and monitoring API performance.
2. **Service manager**: People responsible for managing resources defining backend services. This includes for example managing service accounts.
3. **Application developer**: API consumers granted self-service access rights to discover and register APIs, view API documentation, and manage applications using the developer portal.
4. **API Designers:** This role does not exist in the API platform, but rather to represent API managers and/or application developers that have access to Apiary and therefore can either produce API designs, participate in the API design process and/or associate Apiary documentation to a specific API in the APIs page.

That as of version 17.3.x of the platform, users are not integrated with Apiary. Therefore, Apiary has its own user store.

5. **Gateway manager**: Operations team members responsible for deploying, registering, and managing gateways. They may also manage API deployments to their gateways when issued the deploy API grant by an API manager.
6. **Administrator**: System administrators responsible for assigning people roles in the system. Administrators possess the rights of all other roles and rights to all objects in the system.
7. **Gateway runtime**: This role indicates a service account used to communicate from the gateway to the portal.

As previously described, grants are available in multiple pages of the portal, like the APIs page, applications page and gateway page. In Oracle APIP CS certain grants are assign by default to the different roles available as it has been illustrated in the following diagram:

Grants	APIs				Services			Service Accounts			API Gateways					Application		Plans				
	Manage API	View all details	Deploy API	View public details	Manage Service	View Service details	Reference Service	Manage Service Account	View Service Account details	Reference Service Account	Manage Gateway	View all details	Deploy to Gateway	Request Deployment to Gateway	Node Service Account	Manage Application	View all details	Manage the plan	View all details	View public details	Register	Request registration
API Manager	Y	Y	Y	Y	N	Y	Y	N	Y	Y	N	Y	Y	Y	N	Y	Y	Y	Y	Y	Y	Y
Service Manager	N	N	N	N	Y	Y	Y	Y	Y	Y	N	N	N	N	N	N	N	N	N	N	N	N
Application Developer	N	N	N	Y	N	N	N	N	N	N	N	N	N	N	N	Y	Y	N	N	Y	Y	Y
Gateway Manager	N	Y	Y	N	N	Y	N	N	Y	N	Y	Y	Y	N	N	N	Y	N	N	N	N	N
Gateway Runtime	N	N	N	N	N	N	N	N	N	N	N	N	N	N	Y	N	N	N	N	N	N	N
Administrator	Y	Y	Y	Y	Y	Y	Y	Y	Y	Y	Y	Y	Y	Y	Y	Y	Y	Y	Y	Y	Y	Y

Oracle APIP CS-roles to grants mapping

Similarly, the following diagram provides grants centric view, where each grant and the group it belongs to is described and then also mapped to the corresponding user roles for which the grant is available by default:

Grants	Description	API Manager	Service Manager	Application Developer	Gateway Manager	Gateway Runtime	Administrator
API							
Manage API	Users issued this grant are allowed to modify the definition of and issue grants for this API.	Y	N	N	N	N	Y
View all details	Users issued this grant are allowed to view all information about this API in the Management Portal.	Y	N	N	Y	N	Y
Deploy API	Users issued this grant are allowed to deploy or undeploy this API to a gateway for which they have deploy rights. This allows users to deploy this API without first receiving a request from an API Manager.	Y	N	N	Y	N	Y
View public details	Users issued this grant are allowed to view the publicly available details of this API on the Developer Portal.	Y	N	Y	N	N	Y
Services							
Manage Service	Users issued this grant are allowed to modify and delete this service.	N	Y	N	N	N	Y
View Service details	Users issued this grant are allowed to see all details about this service.	Y	Y	N	Y	N	Y
Reference Service	Users issued this grant are allowed to reference this service.	Y	Y	N	N	N	Y
Service Accounts							
Manage Service Account	Users issued this grant are allowed to modify and delete this service account.	N	Y	N	N	N	Y
View Service Account details	Users issued this grant are allowed to see all details about this service account.	Y	Y	N	Y	N	Y
Reference Service Account	Users issued this grant are allowed to reference this service account.	Y	Y	N	N	N	Y
API Gateways							
Manage Gateway	Users issued this grant are allowed to manage API deployments to this gateway and manage the gateway itself.	N	N	N	Y	N	Y
View all details	Users issued this grant are allowed to view all information about this gateway.	Y	N	N	Y	N	Y
Deploy to Gateway	Users issued this grant are allowed to deploy or undeploy APIs to this gateway.	Y	N	N	Y	N	Y
Request Deployment to Gateway	Users issued this grant are allowed to request API deployments to this gateway.	Y	N	N	N	N	Y
Node Service Account	Gateway Runtime service accounts are issued this grant to allow them to download configuration and upload statistics.	N	N	N	N	Y	Y
Application							
Manage Application	Users issued this grant are allowed to modify and delete this application.	Y	N	Y	N	N	Y
View all details	Users issued this grant are allowed to see all details about this application in the Developer Portal.	Y	N	Y	Y	N	Y
Plan							
Manage the plan	Users issued this grant are allowed to modify the definition of and issue users grants for this plan.	Y	N	N	N	N	Y
View all details	Users issued this grant are allowed to view all details of this plan in the Management Portal.	Y	N	N	N	N	Y
View public details	Users issued this grant are allowed to see the public details of this plan in the Developer Portal.	Y	N	Y	N	N	Y
Register	Users issued this grant are allowed to register applications for this plan.	Y	N	Y	N	N	Y
Request registration	Users issued this grant are allowed to request to register applications for this plan.	Y	N	Y	N	N	Y

Oracle APIP CS–grants to roles mapping

The roles page documentation can be accessed from the following URL:
`http://docs.oracle.com/en/cloud/paas/api-platform-cloud/apfad/ma naging-roles.html#GUID-F87B1C66-355F-441C-97B5-34D8C42C96C1`

Users and groups

In versions 17.2.x, 17.3.x, and of the API platform, users and roles are still managed via the **WebLogic Management Console** which is accessible through the same URL as the management console but with the URI `/console` instead.

Therefore, when handling users and groups in Oracle APIP CS, it is critical to understand that each role has a corresponding WebLogic user group. And therefore, when creating users in WebLogic console, they should be assigned to the corresponding WebLogic group that matches the Oracle APIP CS role to which the user is to belong to.

Weblogic Group	Oracle APIP CS Role
APIManagers	API Manager
APPDevelopers	Application Developer
APIGatewayManagers	Gateway Manager
APICSAdministrators	Administrator
APIGatewayRuntimeUsers	Gateway Runtime
ServiceManagers	Service Managers

Details on managing users and group are available in the following URL:
`http://docs.oracle.com/en/cloud/paas/api-platform-cloud/apfad/ma naging-users-and-groups.html#GUID-055CE442-17FB-4CB7-848D- A762540F6DEE`

Platform settings page

From the **Platform Settings** page, general management, and developer portals properties can be set, such as, time zone settings, contact information, base URLs and others.

There are two main sections.

General settings section

In this section, the **Time Zone Settings** for the platform can be set:

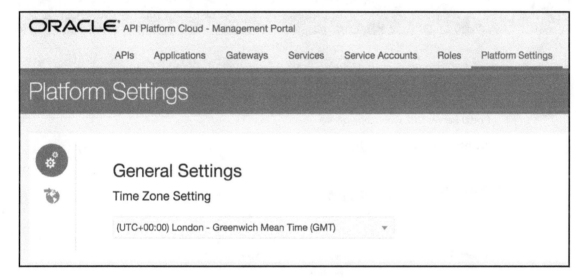

Management portal – platform general settings

Developer portal settings section

As the name suggests, from this section, properties specific to the developer portal can be set. For example, enabling or disabling the portal, defining its base URL, and also enabling or disabling the display of the application keys once in the portal, all can be managed via this section:

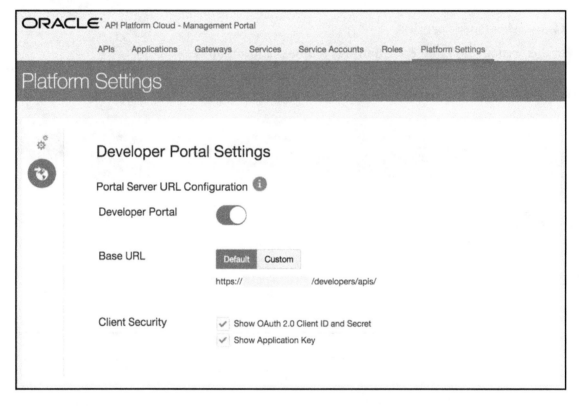

Management Portal – Developer Portal Settings

Development portal

The API **Developer Portal** is a web-based application meant to be used by **application developers** and/or **API implementers** in general (that is, API managers, designers) to discover and subscribe to available APIs. The developer portal can also be used to manage applications:

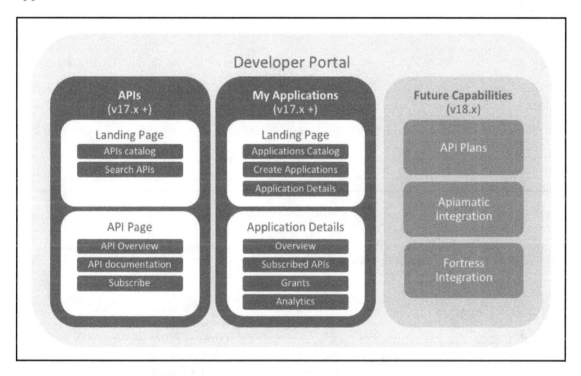

Oracle APIP CS–developer portal

The landing page after a developer has signed in into the developer portal is the API catalog. From here, all APIs a developer has been granted access to, are listed and can be searched upon based on different criteria:

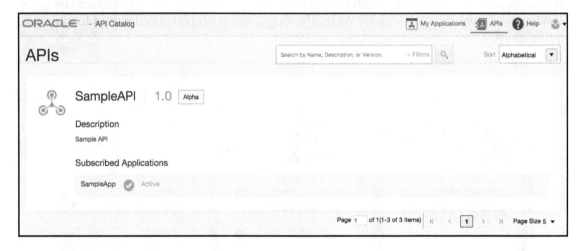

Developer Portal – APIs page

From this page, a developer can access an API's documentation by just clicking on any of the listed APIs. This action will take the user to the API page.

The API page

The **API page** is the one-stop-shop for all API related documentation. It consists of two main sections. The landing section displaying the **API overview** documentation and the **API documentation** section that displays the **API Blueprint** or **Swagger** document created in **Apiary** for the API.

Creating comprehensive API overview and Apiary documentation (API Blueprint or Swagger) is extremely important as this is what application developers will be looking at when consuming an API.

The better the documentation, the more usage the API will receive. If the API is poorly documented, application developers will avoid its use by finding workaround which could even imply creating new APIs.

Developer Portal – API page

From this page, the API documentation can be accessed (icon with shape of a document located on the left-hand side of the section) as well as a subscription for the API can be created.

The API documentation section

The API documentation section displays the Apiary document associated with the API:

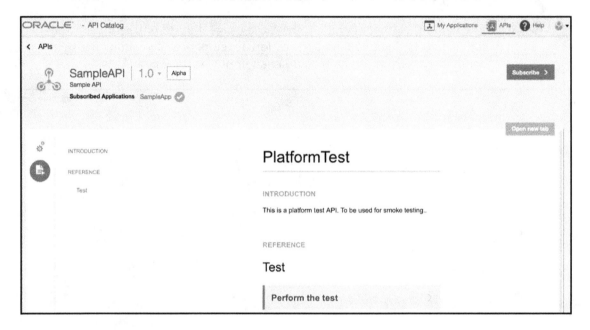

API page – documentation

 An overview of Apiary will be covered later in the chapter.

API subscription

When a developer clicks on the **Subscribe** button, the subscription page opens. From here a developer can select which client application is to be subscribed to use the API. Note that for this to work, an application has to be created by the developer. If the relevant application hasn't already been created, a new application can be created directly from this page or from the **My Applications** page-covered in the next section:

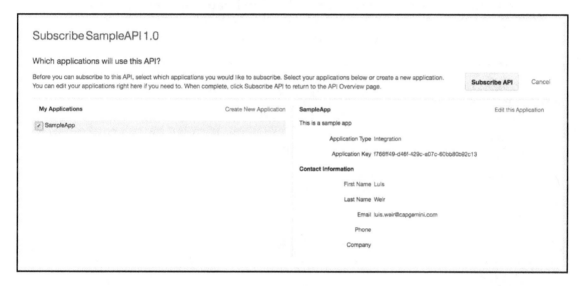

API page–subscription

My applications page

From this page, developers can create and manage applications that consume APIs. Properties such as application keys, API subscriptions and grants can be managed from this page. Also, analytics information related to the application can be visualized.

As briefly described earlier, In Oracle APIP CS an application represents the consumer of one or more APIs. Applications are uniquely identified with application keys which in turn can be used by policies such as key validation and application rate limiting to restrict access to the API.

My Applications page

The overview section

When a developer clicks in any of the listed applications, the **Overview** section opens. From this section metadata details associated with the application can be detailed, but most importantly the application key can be visualized and also re-issued:

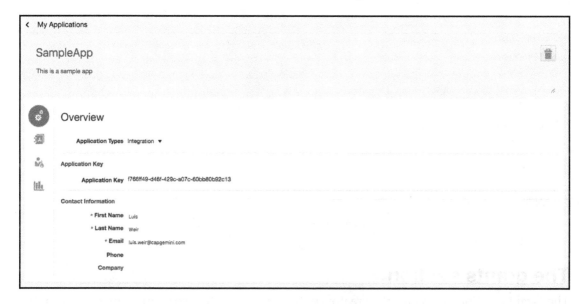

My Applications page–overview section

Subscribed APIs section

The subscription section lists all of the APIs that the application is subscribed to. From here it is also possible to unsubscribe any of the APIs:

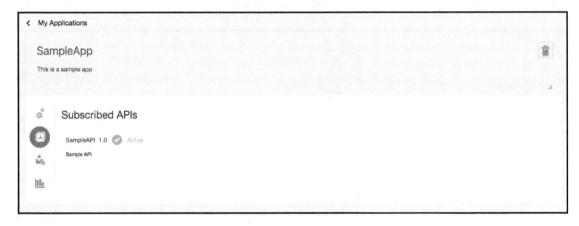

My Applications page–subscriptions section

The grants section

The **Grants** section allows for the creator of the application to also share management rights to other users and roles:

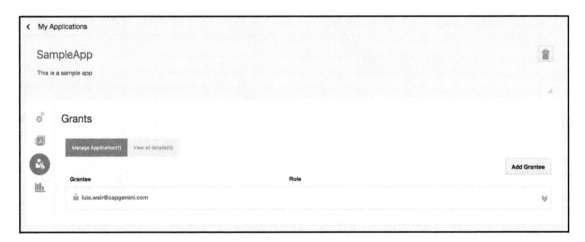

My Applications page–the Grants section

The analytics section

Lastly, the **Analytics** section provides an application-centric view of the usage of those APIs the application is subscribed to. This view can be very useful for developers looking to analyze API usage by any given application:

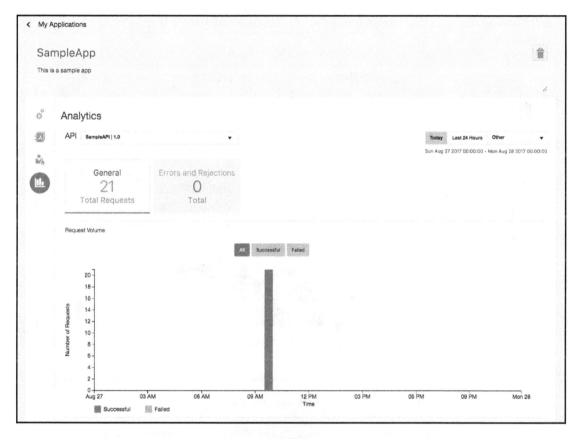

My Applications page-analytics section

Management service REST APIs

Oracle APIP CS was created following an API-first approach. What this means in practice is that all of the functionality available via the portals, in fact more, is also available via the **management service REST APIs**.

The following diagram illustrates the different resources available through the Oracle APIP CS management service APIs:

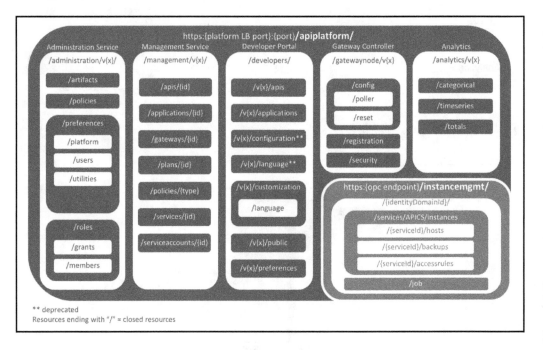

Oracle APIP CS–management REST APIs

 In order to consume the management REST APIs, a user must belong to the administration role.

Oracle classifies the following management REST APIs:

- **Administration service**: Accessed through the `/apiplatform/administration` endpoint, this resource delivers platform administration capabilities, such as configuration of platform preferences and management of users and roles.

Further information available from the following URL:
`http://docs.oracle.com/en/cloud/paas/api-platform-cloud/apfrp/index.html`

- **Management service**: Accessed through the `/apiplatform/management` endpoint, this resource delivers equivalent and additional capabilities to those available via the management portal.

Further information available from the following URL:
`http://docs.oracle.com/en/cloud/paas/api-platform-cloud/apfrm/index.html`

- **Developer portal**: Accessed through the `/apiplatform/developers` endpoint, this resource delivers equivalent and additional capabilities to those available via the developer portal.

Further information available from the following URL:
`http://docs.oracle.com/en/cloud/paas/api-platform-cloud/apfrd/index.html`

- **Gateway controller**: Accessed through the `/apiplatform/gatewaynode` endpoint, this resource delivers gateway administration and monitoring capabilities. This resource is used by the gateway nodes during the registration and join process when installing a gateway.

Further information available from the following URL:
`http://docs.oracle.com/en/cloud/paas/api-platform-cloud/apfrg/index.html`

- **Analytics**: Accessed through the `/apiplatform/analytics` endpoint, this resource can be used to retrieve analytics metrics for APIs, applications and gateways.

Further information available from the following URL:
`http://docs.oracle.com/en/cloud/paas/api-platform-cloud/apfra/index.html`

- **Life cycle management**: accessed through the `/instancemgmt/` endpoint, delivers Oracle APIP CS instance provisioning and management capabilities.

 Further information available from the following URL:
`http://docs.oracle.com/en/cloud/paas/api-platform-cloud/apfrl/index.html`

Now that the management APIs have been described, it is equally important to understand in what use cases they could be use.

For example, the management APIs `/apiplatform/` and `/instancemgmt/` could be used in any of the following use cases:

1. **Configuration management**: Using the `/management/` resource to version control APIs (that is, in a GIT) and manage releases (that is, in Nexus).
2. **Continuous integration/continuous delivery (CICD)**: Although related to the previous point, this use case is about using `/management/` resources along with CI tool (that is, Jenkins, Hudson, Circle CI) to automate the software development lifecycle (that is, promotion of APIs across environments, regression testing, API contract validations with Dredd).
3. **Infrastructure as code**: A relatively new discipline, infrastructure as code is all about taking infrastructure provisioning automation and management by adopting practices originated in software engineering. By using **Oracle Public Cloud (OPC) PaaS APIs** (`/instancemgmt`) it is possible to also automate the actual provisioning of Oracle APIP CS instances. Then combined with the use of other resources in `/apiplatform/` robust automation solutions can be achieved.
4. **Developer portal extensions**: In some scenarios, it might be required to either extend the developer portal, embedded some developer portal functionality within other corporate intranet portals or simply create custom portal front-ends (that is, for individual APIs). All of this is available by using the `/developers/` resources.

API plans

Starting from the **release 18.1.5** a new feature is introduced to the API Platform called **Plans**.

As illustrated in the following diagram, plans are used to handle entitlements to one or many APIs such as client applications can subscribe to a given plan and through it, gain access to all APIs associated with it:

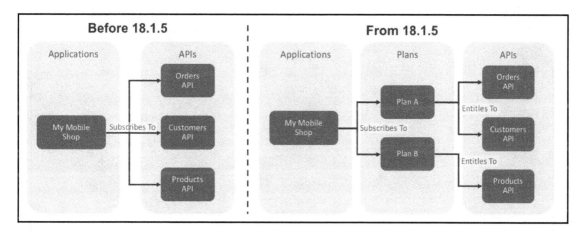

Oracle APIP CS–API plans

In releases prior 18.1.5, API managers have to first publish each API to the developer portal before developers can discover and subscribe them to client applications.

From release 18.1.5 onwards, a plan can be created in the management portal that entitles (grants access) to any given API. Once this is done, an API manager can publish the plan to the developer portal (as opposed to just the individual API) so sub-sequentially, developers can discover and subscribe to the plan via the developer portal.

Because plans effectively act as a **unit-of-visibility** to all APIs associated with it, they provide a great mechanism to apply common **quality-of-service** controls, like for example, limit the total number of calls that can, within a given timeframe, be collectively made to APIs within the plan:

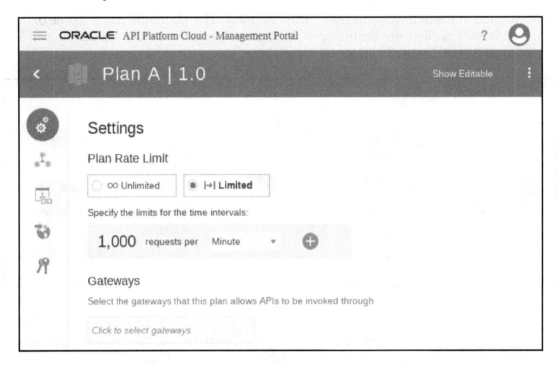

Plans also play an important role in enabling the so-called **API economy.** If properly implemented, a plan can act as act as an **accounting log** of who/when/which/how many times any given API within the plan was consumed. With such information at hand, monetizing on APIs (term known as **API monetization**) becomes more a business strategy question as the core technology building blocks would be in placed to enable such business capability.

This section was courtesy of **Ricardo Ferreira** from the **Oracle A-Team** and **Black Belt** instructor for the Oracle API Platform.

Apiary

Apiary is a cloud-based platform specialized in the delivery robust API-design first, API documentation, API mocking and API unit testing capabilities. Apiary is also a great tool for team collaboration as it offers the ability to create feedback loops between API designers and API consumers very early in the development life cycle.

The following diagram illustrates the capabilities available in Apiary:

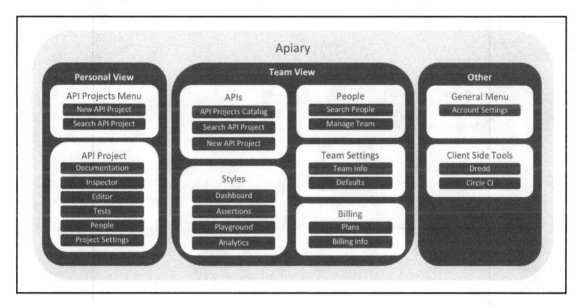

Apiary overview

It is worth noting that although Oracle acquired Apiary in January 2017, the partnership between both companies started way before that. For this reason, the integration of both products was already in place prior acquisition and launch of Oracle APIP CS.

This integration is explained in far more detail in Chapter 3, *Designing the API* as it shows from design to publication how Apiary and the Oracle API Platform are used together seamlessly.

The Apiary account

The first step to access Apiary is by opening an account. There are 3 different options to select from. **Free**, **Standard**, or **Pro**:

	Free	Standard	Pro
Core Toolset • API Description Editor • Mock Server • Interactive Documentation • Testing Debugger • Automated Implementation Testing (using Dredd) • RSS feeds for API changes	✓	✓	✓
API Projects Create as many API Projects as you want — Apiary supports API Blueprint and OpenAPI (Swagger) formats.	Unlimited	Unlimited	Unlimited
Collaborators Number of participants in an API Project or team.	5 per API Project No team	10 per API Project Unlimited team members	Custom
Basic GitHub Sync Connect Apiary with your GitHub repository to instantly sync changes you've made between the online editor and GitHub.	✓	✓	✓
Team Management Create a team to manage multiple API Projects or Microservices.	✕	✓	✓
Private API Projects Control access to your API designs, documentation, and associated tools across your team.	✕	✓	✓
Embeddable Documentation Embed interactive API documentation in your website or internal portal.	✕	✓	✓
Customizable Documentation Ensure embedded documentation adheres to your corporate identity standards.	✕	✓	✓
Advanced GitHub Integration • Multiple branches • Multiple API descriptions per repository • Support for integration with GitHub Enterprise	✕	✕	✓
Style Guide Rules Establish rules to ensure API design patterns are maintained across API Projects.	✕	✕	✓
Read Only API Projects and Branches	✕	✕	✓
Multiple Blueprints	✕	✕	✓
Priority Support Guaranteed 24x7 response times from our dedicated support team.	✕	✕	✓
Pricing Please see Oracle Apiary Cloud Service pricing.	Free	Per user in team	Per team member

Comparison of Apiary plans

For teams that are just getting started with API-first design and Apiary, the recommendation is to sign up for a free account to start with. As the skills of the team mature and more product features are needed, at this point upgrading to a paid plan is probably a good idea.

Apiary views

Apiary offers two views: **personal view** and **team view**. Each view provides a different set of navigation options. Personal view focuses on API projects whereas team view in the management of team assets and people.

Apiary personal view

When an API designer selects to be in personal view mode, navigation options relevant for creating, editing, and managing API projects become visible. Following a description of the options available in this view.

Apiary editor

The landing page after an API designer signs in, from this page an API Blueprint or Swagger file for an API project can be edited. There are a few features available in the editor that are worth highlighting.

As a designer works on the API design, the right-hand side of the screen dynamically renders to show the specification in styled HTML 5. Just as regular API consumers (that is, app developers) would look at it. From this same page, it is possible to test API resources again just like API consumers would-**Apiary comes with a mock-up engine that automatically generates API mockups on the fly**. Moreover, as the API design takes place, **inline conventions and pattern validation** also occurs thus ensuring that the design is consistent with the team-specified **styles** (described later in the chapter). This and more features will be covered in Chapter 3, *Designing the API* in greater detail.

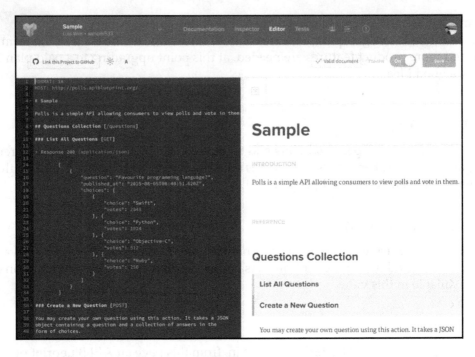

Personal view–editor

From this same page, on the top-right hand side, it is possible to **search** existing **API projects**, open a project, or **create** a new one either in API Blueprint or Swagger:

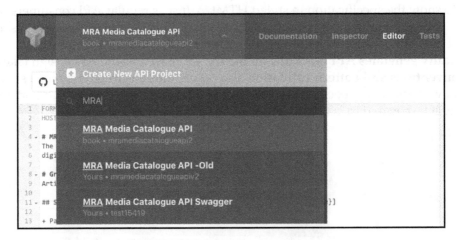

Personal view-create/search API project

When a user clicks on **Create New API Project**, then the **New API** window appears. From here the user can decide to create an API only accessible by its creator, a **Personal API**, or an API that can be viewed and edited by the entire team, a **Team API**:

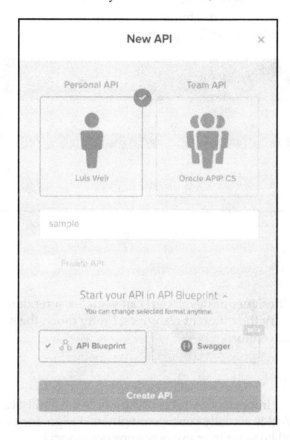

Personal view–create/search API project

A concept worth understanding up-front when creating a new API project is the notion that an API belongs to either a person or a team. When an API belongs to the person, only the user that created the API can see it and edit it. However, when a project belongs to the team, the entire team can see it and those with designated rights can also edit it.

Inspector

As the design of the API progresses and developers start trying the API and start to provide feedback, from the Inspector section it is possible to also see what tests are being executed and what resources are being called. This is very useful as if issues occur it is also possible to drill down into each call and check requests and response payloads and HTTP headers:

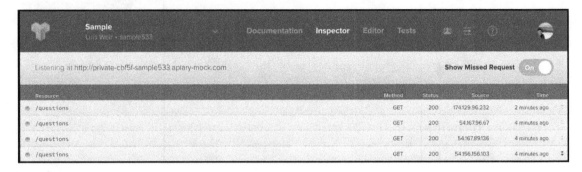

Personal view–inspector

Documentation

From this page, a user (designer or developer) can visualize a rendered API design in styled HTML5 and also try the different resources. Pretty much the same is page shown on the right-hand side of the editor.

Testing with Apiary

One of the best and most important features of Apiary is the ability to verify that the implementation of an API is actually consistent with its design, for example, an API blueprint. This is critical because in many occasions developers might deviate from the actual design and without the ability to test this, issues could occur later in the lifecycle whereby API consumers don't get the API they expected.

To prevent this issue from materializing, the Test your API feature of Apiary allows for a utility call **Dredd** to be download and installed. Dredd can then be used to automatically verify that a service endpoint matches a given API definition:

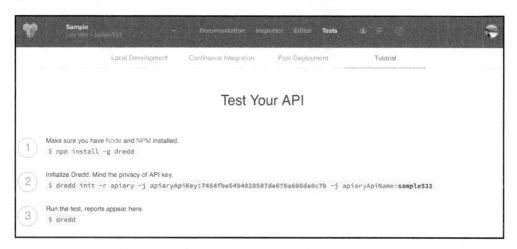

Personal view–tests

 Note that the use of Dredd for API unit testing is covered extensively in Chapter 3, *Designing the API.*

Apiary settings

The project settings page is where properties specific to the API project are defined. There are different options available from this page, worth highlighting:

1. Define **API Domain**–used to uniquely determine an URL to access the API documentation.
2. Enable/disable cross-origin requests headers (**CORS**).
3. Enable/disable a **Proxy** so instead of using the mock-up engine of Apiary, route the calls to the implemented API endpoints.
4. Remove the API project.

5. Transfer ownership of the API to the team.
6. Make the project private or public.
7. Link the project to a GitHub account. If one doesn't exist, it can be configured.

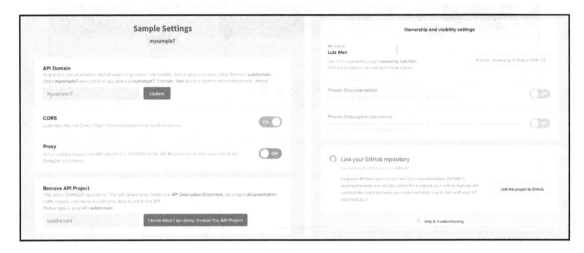

Personal view–project settings

People

The main purpose of this page is to enable API designers to define who can edit and view the API:

Personal view–people

Apiary team view

As the name suggests, when the team view is selected, navigation options related to the management of the team become available. From here it is possible to manage users, APIs that belong to the team and most importantly the **styles** that apply to all API projects within the team.

APIs

From this page, APIs that belong to the team can be searched upon and accessed. This page is very useful as members of the team can discover API designs that already exist, which can help avoid duplication, but also ensures that members of the team can learn from each other:

Team view–APIs

Styles

Styles in Apiary are a set of pre-defined modeling patterns and conventions that are used to validate that API designs within the entire team are consistent.

 The styles feature is only available in the **Pro** plan.

This page can only be accessed by admin users and is broken down into 3 sections.

The **Dashboard** section provides a summary of the validation outcomes for all APIs within the team. This is extremely useful especially in large teams so admin users can get quick feedback on the status of API designs being created.

Styles–dashboards

From the **Assertions** section, assertions can be enabled, disabled, modified or created (for the last two options a user needs to switch to **Advanced Mode**). Assertions are the actual rules tested against the API designs in real time from the editor:

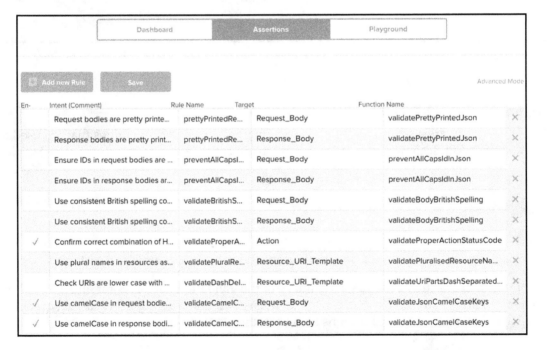

Styles – assertions

And the **Playground** section, as the name suggests, can be used to test assertions. Either existing ones that are being modified, or new ones:

Styles–assertions

People

From the people page of the team view, admin users can manage the team. For example, new users can be invited to join the team and/or existing users can be made admins or regular users.

Note that in terms of user roles, Apiary is quite straightforward. There are only two types of users:

1. **Regular**: Non-admin users that have access to personal view and limited access to team view pages.

2. **Admin**: Administrative users that have access to all full views. Only admin users have access to the people, style and billing pages of the team view:

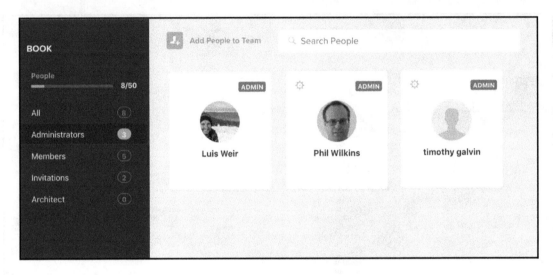

Team view - people

Settings

From this page, some basic default settings can be specified by admin users. The **Team Project Template** property is worth highlighting as it allows to specify an API design to use as a template when creating a new project:

Team view—settings

Billing

The main purpose of this page is to allow admin users to manage the account billing information and the Apiary plan the team is subscribed to. From here it is possible to cancel the existing plan or upgrade to a new one.

Account settings

The account settings page can be accessed from any of the views and allows for personal account settings to be managed as well as linking the user account to a GitHub account. From here the user can also choose to leave a team:

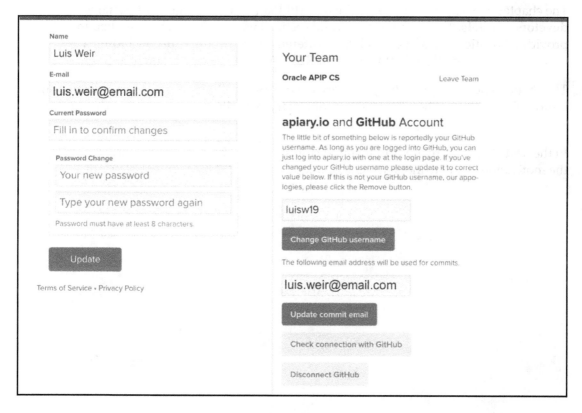

Account settings

Summary

The chapter started by providing a comprehensive walk through of how Oracle's API offering evolved from being a traditional SOA stack, into a **3rd generation API Platform**, capable of satisfying numerous use cases and scenarios, both on-premise and cloud.

The chapter continued by providing a detailed overview of the **Oracle API Platform Cloud Service (APIP CS)** architecture and **Apiary**. Comprehensive diagrams were introduced to illustrate the different features available in the product, all of which were described throughout the chapter.

The chapter then carried on to describe the API Platform's **management portal** and **developer portals**. The different pages and sections within each were described in order to provide a holistic view of the capabilities offered by the product, also including a description of the platform's management REST APIs, its resources and use cases.

The chapter ended by providing an overview of Apiary although not in great detail as more information regarding how to make use of Apiary is available in `Chapter 3`, *Designing the API*.

In the next chapter, a real-world inspired case study will be described where it is explained the motivations and business drivers for adopting an API Management platform.

2
Use Case

In Chapter 1, *Platform Overview*, we looked at the key building blocks that make up the API Platform Cloud Service (APIP CS). In this chapter, we will look at a use case that will be used to illustrate the rest of the book. Each of the subsequent chapters will look at different aspects of the APIP CS and illustrate how they can be applied to address the needs of this use case. The use case itself is fictional, however it is inspired by those real-world problems, which the authors have been involved in helping clients overcome them.

In addition to looking at the use case, we will introduce you to some architectural and design ideas, particularly a reference model, which the authors of this book have contributed, called **Open Modern Enterprise Software Architecture Project** (or **OMESA** for short).

Scenario

The record company Monster Records & Associates (referred to as **MRA**) has struggled to cope with the changes in the music industry. With new leadership at MRA, the way the company is perceived is changing. Record companies, including MRA are no longer in the business of running recording studios, CDs and vinyl presses, or helping artists become media friendly. They are digital companies and their assets are largely data. Today, the majority of MRA's revenue comes directly through downloads and streaming, both directly from MRA and via Amazon, Spotify, and other services. Significant revenue also comes in from other means such as licensing music to television, films, podcasts, radio, and advertising.

Modern recording deals with artists look more like agreements to lease the right to use a recording or composition. This at least in part has come from the fact an artist or composer doesn't necessarily need big budgets for expensive studios such as Abbey Road. In fact, if an artist wanted, they could do everything themselves. More innovative record companies are starting to offer services to artists in an à la carte model—from just building and maintaining an artist's website, or provision of physical media production and distribution, to supplying streaming services with media, through to the traditional full end picture covering finance, marketing, distribution and touring.

Manufacturing of physical media, even with the resurgence of vinyl, is done by 3rd party presses because the volumes are often too small to make it cost effective for MRA to own their own traditional high-volume manufacturing plant. MRA see their role as having the expertise to manage all the different processes in the distribution of the artist's media. Managing all the legal agreements from recording copyright, licensing agreements for commercial use, to touring and merchandising processes in what have become known as 360° agreements.

Artists can sign deals with record companies that may be global or restricted to regions or countries. This makes the data and the management of it rather complex. This complexity can be further compounded by the fact that a record company like MRA can effectively subcontract or sell their rights onto another company (or buy the rights) for to handle part or all of an artist's requirements.

MRA have elected to take cautious approach to the transition to a new digital business model. As such an approach represents a perceived significant risk to the business and the cost to transform their IT landscape is significant. The risks are seen from a number of perspectives-how the change may be received by the recording artists. The risk in the possibility of disrupting current revenue streams-while contracting are well understood, through making a large capital investment in the IT transformation draining financial reserves which may be needed to sustain the company until the next major success in terms of an artist recording creating a surge in revenue. As a result, MRA have determined that they should develop a high-level strategy, roadmap and a target state that means that they can gain the most revenue from their assets (that is, data) while providing the relationship and engagement of artists that have kept MRA's reputation as a company that cares about the art.

The first steps in the process has been to understand their data assets, where they exist in the current landscape and determine how to best leverage the data. MRA believes its data assets are:

- Digital audio recordings (and older physical media)
- Sales data, particularly over time as it provides insights into which trends and styles best sell and where
- Buyer insight-through the capture of information through artists websites, MRA have not only a list of potential direct sales opportunities, but also sufficient means to build profiles of their customer base to both understand the kind of music to offer but also the most effective channels to reach the consumers
- Contracts, particularly with artists which allow MRA to understand how they should relate to their artists, and how and where they can sell their works

Given that MRA want to start cautiously, it was determined that they should choose a couple of use cases that had core value to the business and a broad range of internal, partner and pure digital opportunities. The internal and partner opportunities particularly need to either reduce costs or directly improve revenue. As part of this the company have identified a couple of pilot projects that would meet these criteria.

Use case opportunities

The first of these would be to provide up to date and accurate information about artists, and their recordings. Reflecting the contractual right to sell the recordings, depending on the consumer access to digital media as a stream or download.

When it comes to physical media whether there was stock available, and if the recording was *in print*. If there was no physical stock, then would or could MRA manufacture (contract out the manufacturing) on demand the physical CD, vinyl and so on.

To create such an offering means that the data and algorithms need to be exposed between systems either within MRA, between MRA and its suppliers and partners, and even to 3rd party service providers who could ultimately build new capabilities based on the data MRA has, such as websites like AllMusic (`https://allmusic.com`) or Discogs (`https://www.discogs.com`). As a result, MRA realizing new sales. To expose this data in a controlled manner MRA need to provide APIs that can be both understood and used by the appropriate organization(s). These API(s) would need to be designed to support the following features:

- See what products are available (licensed) and shippable (stock available to be used in each country).
- Provide a means for a customer to discover where they could buy a recording from. (this in turn will need different areas of MRA's systems to expose APIs to allow this capability to be provided).
- Provide controlled access to content for the benefit of journalists, services that license music for the use of advertising and so on.
- Ability to reflect back to artists the status of their catalogue with MRA on demand-today this takes time for administrative staff to pull data from different systems and pull it together to provide to artists.
- Create conditions in which master data management can be better provided around recording data. For example, rather than duplicating or rekeying information across internal IT systems in MRA, those systems could use the APIs to obtain *ground truth* data from a single master source.
- To allow MRA to better understand the data, a logical model of the relevant data has been put together.
- Create conditions in which MRA can offer its own streaming service or provide the media streams for other services, giving the label more control of the media and visibility into media use.

IT landscape

The existing landscape is an aging set of on-premises solutions and makes heavy use of human processes. To establish some direction, it is obviously necessary to both understand the existing and desired IT Landscapes.

The core components of the existing landscape are made up as follows:

Financial processes

All the financial processes are realized by an on-premises ERP fronted by services deployed on top of Oracle SOA Suite. The data to be consumed by ERP comes through several approaches:

- Keying or rekeying of data
- Manually imported from spreadsheets and CSV files, driven through the UI
- A number of Oracle SOA Suite services receiving SOAP/WSDL calls from other systems within the organization or exposed by VPN tunnels with a few service providers and protected and exposed through the use of the previous version of Oracle API Gateway
- Data extraction through reports driven by manual processes or scheduled jobs

The financial processes cover activities including:

- Artist management-this covers the payment of royalties, managing artist advances (calculated as loans with no interest and repayment is deducted from royalties), and payments to organizations such as recording studies on behalf of the artists
- Payments to other labels and royalties' organizations where material has been licensed, or when an artist records material with rights held by others
- Manufacturing processes, such as the printing of CDs, albums, artwork and so on
- General business accounting operations and legal financial reporting

Recorded material and related assets

The handling of recordings, artwork, and other media assets is done through the use of a basic document management system. This includes manual backup and remote storage of the contents as this is the label's crown jewels.

Older content is still on physical media, and it is represented by a library system that catalogues all the relevant media such as tapes. The data in the library system is considered as inaccurate as often, the tapes are taken and not always correctly returned (if at all returned).

The library also currently gets used to manage the available recordings. It is the human process of managing the library that allows the organization to publish updated catalogues of material to partners.

Contracts

Contracts are a pivotal document for managing agreements with artists, sublicensed material, along with the artist by artist agreements with online services. These are handled in their own discrete document repository. Handling the coordination of agreements with catalogue generation is essentially a manual process.

Identities

As mentioned previously, data is becoming the critical asset of businesses upon which the business can succeed or fail. Given the importance of the data, accessing and utilizing data are highly sensitive issues. Also, there is value in tracking data use as it gets exposed in the future. Today, user information including identity and authorization are managed by **Microsoft Active Directory** (and associated services), and this includes the foundation of master data management of not just staff but also artists, composers, and other third parties with respect to unique identification and contact details.

Existing systems currently authenticate directly against Active Directory. Consumer-based services, such as artist websites, are presently managed through completely decoupled registration and authentication solutions. This combined with the possibility of establishing user trust relationships with partners is leading to the idea of adopting a federated authentication solution. Though not currently implemented, the preference is to use **Microsoft Active Directory Federation Service (ADFS)** as an easy and natural evolution from the current use of Active Directory. With this comes the recognition that authentication should move away from a **Lightweight Directory Access Protocol (LDAP)** basis to at least **Security Assertion Markup Language (SAML)** if not **Open Authorization (OAuth)**, which are more sustainable contemporary standards. ADFS' ability to support OAuth2 makes it a preferred option for MRA as the API Platform can support this easily. Federation then allows the API Platform to do user authentication against multiple sources.

More information on OAuth can be found at `https://oauth.net/`.

The SAML standard is described at `http://saml.xml.org/`.

LDAP is described at `https://tools.ietf.org/html/rfc4511`.

Audit trail

Currently, each system records its own audit and logging information. It has been very difficult to trace events between systems. So, having the ability to record data coming in and out of a boundary point such as gateway can be of great value. Not only for audit but also to understand what is being requested and the data being sent back—the key to understanding if a system has been compromised by some form of attack resulting in data leakage.

The considerations around how we demonstrate not leaking data and at the same time being compliant in terms of the data that should be available have become increasingly important as data security and compliance is continuing to become more demanding. Demands such as with challenges of new legislation such as **General Data Protection Regulation (GDPR)** and **Payment Services Directive 2 (PSD2)**.

More information on General Data Protection Regulation (GDPR) in the UK can be found at `https://ico.org.uk/for-organisations/data-protection-reform/overview-of-the-gdpr/` and the European Union information on the legislation is at `https://gdpr-info.eu/`.

Payment Services Directive 2 can be read about at `https://www.paymentsuk.org.uk/policy/european-and-uk-developments/second-payment-services-directive-psd2`.

As a result, as part of MRA's initiative a **Security Information and Event Management (SEIM)** solution which captures logs and other activity information to provide analytics on the use or misuse of systems, and ideally tie information from disparate systems to provide end-to-end visibility of what is happening. Going forward, APIs will need to provide logging capabilities and calls between systems and in the future, they need to be traceable from end to end when possible.

Logical data view

The following diagram shows the functional entity relationships within MRA:

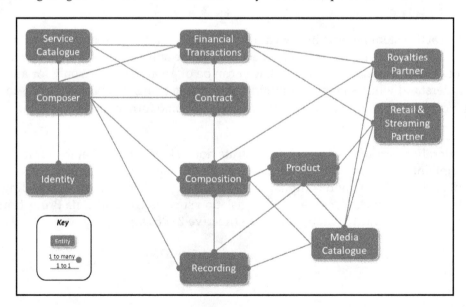

Logical data view of MRA

The following table provides further elaboration on the meaning of the entities in the preceding diagram:

Entity	Description
Service Catalogue	This describes all the services that MRA can legally offer and is available for the artists or composer to request use of. Elements of this data become incorporated into a contract.
Composer	The idea of Composer and Artist can be blurred. The composer is deemed to be the individual who wrote a piece of music or song lyric. The composer may also be the artist, namely the individual or group who recorded the composition. The difference is important when handling compilation albums or when an artist records a cover or samples another artist's work. The business tends to use the term composer, as in contemporary music, the composer and artist are the same.
Identity	This is the identity used by the artist(s) or composer(s) to access information. The information is distinguished because an artist or composer may work under different pseudonyms, or a composer may comprise a group, but individual members may wish to access information.
Financial Transactions	These cover the normal financial activities of any business from covering costs and payroll, profit, and loss. This also accounts for the transaction agreements with different partners including the receipt and payment of royalties, plus, transactions performed as an organizing agent for the artists, such as the hire of recording studios.
Contract	This is the legal agreement primarily with artists, and also with partners.
Composition	This represents the music composition and/or lyrics and so on. In a contemporary scenario, a composition would represent a single song.
Recording	This represents the physical performance of a song. Recordings are then compiled into a product.
Product	This represents how MRA will sell a composition or collection of compositions. For example, a CD typically will be made up of a number of compositions. But with downloading and streaming services, an artist may agree for individual tracks to be purchased, in which case, the product is that single song. With the associated recording is the artwork, producer information and so on.

Media Catalogue	This links the recording to a composition and identifies the physical or data media used for the composition. This in turn is linked to the products, as this is how we sell the works.
Royalties Partner	These are partner organizations that will be paid by MRA (when licensing another record labels material, for example, for a compilation or cover recording), and they will as well make payments to MRA for the broadcast of a recording by a Radio station, for example.
Retail & Streaming Partner	Where music is sold in a transaction, the royalty payment is incorporated into the media purchase, therefore we have a different set of arrangements. For example, we can discount the sale of an MP3 or CD to a partner. However, the royalties rate will remain unchanged.

API requirements in detail

With the IT landscape outlined, the goals wanted in broad terms is that it would be normal to drill into identifying the value propositions of APIs on the different areas, qualifying success criteria, and so on. With this, the domain partitions would be further analyzed to ensure that they're well understood.

 For a fuller understanding of Domain Driven Design, the best source of information is *Eric J. Evans'* book or this website
`http://www.methodsandtools.com/archive/archive.php?id=97`.

However, this book isn't aiming to be a benchmark on analysis and design, but it aims to draw out the issues relating to APIs and the adoption of a suitable platform.

To meet these identified goals several APIs have been identified. The next section works through what these APIs are.

Product

To make product data more usable both internally and externally, it is clear that APIs to expose master data for product (along with recording and composition) are needed. The API is going to provide the ability to serve multiple scenarios. This means that we will need to provide what **OMESA** describes as a **Multi-Purpose API** (we will look more closely at OMESA later in this chapter).

In addition to the Multi-Purpose API, the product data will need to have several **Single Purpose APIs** (another OMESA concept we will explain later in the chapter) to help fulfill several different use cases. These are listed as follows.

Product for partners

This API will only be available to partner organizations that have been approved, such as retailers, licensing and royalties' organizations such as Performing Rights Society, ASCAP (American Society of Composers, Authors and Publishers), and would reflect system to system.

Both partners and retailers will need to have a contractual agreement in place before they can use the partner services being offered. In this case, the provisioning of the API need to include the ability to have the following:

- Partner identifying token as part of access control
- Usage metrics and possibly monetization (fees for API calls)
- Explicit audit trail of each call, as the service utilization could become key to any contractual dispute, either with an artist or a partner trying to misuse the service

To support product marketing initiatives such as allowing journalists to hear recording previews and notification of press information, an API will be needed to support requests to certain product-related information. Such a capability would require these:

- Self-registration
- Log of interactions
- Rate limiting-ensure that if a retailer's credentials are stolen, they can't be over used in an attempt to harvest data

Control through applying geographical awareness to IPs and preventing traffic originating from countries where the label was not supplying retailers or had contracts where artists would allow MRA to trade.

Product for composers and artists

As previously mentioned, it is necessary to allow the artists to examine the information relating to the contract, which the artists have with MRA, including the ability to instruct the label to retract the media from different channels. For example, consider retracting, or allowing the ability to stream music through a partner services, such as Spotify, as has been the case with a number of artists such as Taylor Swift. This scenario needs the following:

- An easy-to-use authentication at an individual level rather than for an organization such as OAuth-based authentication; as a specific composer would need to be authenticated and authorized, and the data shared would be dependent upon that composer's identity
- Rate limiting to prevent overuse/exploitation of account credentials, if the permissions where hijacked
- Simple auditing of traffic was desired to understand the service usage

Product availability

One of the first steps to get closer to the consumer is to provide the means for them to determine what formats the artist is making their music available in. Then depending on the consumer's preferred format (physical media or streaming, for example), which partners can sell/stream the music to them, taking into account the consumer's location and the agreements that MRA has with the artist.

It is envisaged that this API will allow MRA to offer a lookup website to the customer without any login, and additional composer information, if the user was to register and log in into MRA's site. In doing so, more detailed analytics could be gained to understand market dynamics (knowing who is doing the look up against artists, when aggregated with user information, and derived information such as location will mean that marketing profiles could be built—what lookups come from what locations and so on.).

Where MRA provide the service of hosting an artists' website, there this API would be used to provide the appropriate links for buying that artist's catalogue.

In this case, the API would need policies to protect the MRA in the following form:

- Rate limiting, to mitigate denial of service attacks
- Control through applying geographical awareness to IPs (more information on how IP addresses can indicate a location is described at `http://whatismyipaddress.com/geolocation`) and preventing traffic originating from countries where the label was not supplying retailers or had contracts where artists would allow MRA to trade

Structuring the design approach

To move forward, MRA determined that they need to adopt some strategic approaches and design models. In doing this, MRA are trying to ensure that industry good practices get incorporated into the future IT landscape.

To this end, MRA looked at several different reference architectures such as **IT Strategies from Oracle** and **Open Modern Software Architecture Project** (`http://OMESA.io`). As OMESA reflects the current thinking and is relatively lightweight, it recognizes the fact that there is an existing IT environment that needs to be accommodated. OMESA is also vendor agnostic.

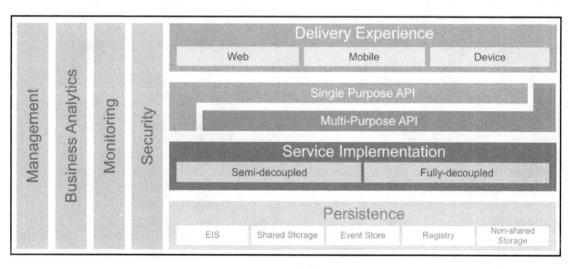

Top level OMESA architectural view (OMESA.io)

Exploring OMESA

Open Modern Software Architecture Project (`http://OMESA.io`) is a contemporary vendor neutral reference architecture which while recognizing and supporting more traditional solution models, such as large **Enterprise Resource Planning (ERP)** and the use of **Enterprise Service Buses (ESBs)**, embraces and supports a strong API-based philosophy. This approach provides a means to drive decoupling and to easily and naturally segment the IT environment to meet different needs. With decoupling and segmentation, we can engage effectively with the ideas expressed by the concept of shear layering or pace layering (`https://en.wikipedia.org/wiki/Shearing_layers`) and the bimodal delivery approach (`https://martinfowler.com/bliki/BimodalIT.html`).

Importantly, APIs are a key ingredient to the effective realization of the microservice design paradigm. It is through the use of APIs that define and publish HTTP-based end points as well as provide structure for service **choreography**. It is this relationship between the APIs and microservices which often brings people to describing microservices as SOA 2.0.

The preceding diagram identifies the high level of capabilities that any architecture will need. We aren't going to describe every OMESA capability here, as this is a book about Oracle API platform not OMESA, and of course, all the information is available on the OMESA website. We will however examine a couple of the basic concepts that OMESA describes, as they impact our use case solutions as well as provide us with some terminology to make it easy to communicate some ideas.

 If you would like to know more about pure API Architecture, then we would recommend the *Enterprise API Management* (`https://www.packtpub.com/virtualization-and-cloud/enterprise-api-management`) book, also by *Packt Publishing*.

We should clarify a couple of terms here as they will be regularly used.

Firstly, let's look at the difference between service orchestration and choreography. Orchestration requires something like an ESB to guide and instruct each component on when to perform their part of a solution. Choreography on the other hand only provides the means for each actor to emit signals that other components can listen for or ignore allowing them to decide when they need to perform an action.

The analogy is best understood if you think of a conductor in an orchestra, compared to a choreographer of a dance or ballet. In the former, the conductor is very much a part of the performance. In a ballet, the choreographer will not be present in the performance, but will ensure that each dancer recognizes the cues for them to perform their piece during the development of the performance.

Microservices is a heavily used term within IT and is used to mean different things by different people. Microservices are the realization of an architectural paradigm that embodies a number of characteristics including small services that can be independently deployable, focused on a single business capability, minimal or no dependencies or knowledge of other components. Microservices will be typically deployable and can managed in an automated or semi-automated means. These characteristics allow solutions to be easily and quickly scaled up and down—often referred to as having elasticity, `http:/ /microservices.io/patterns/microservices.html`.

As we don't want to misuse the term microservice, we have started to use the expression, **Micro Application**. The idea of a micro application is that we adopt the principles of microservices, but as often happens in the real world, we are constrained by business and organizational decisions such as not abandoning investment in technologies that don't align well to the paradigm. This does not mean that we should not seek to adopt the design ideals, but we have to adapt or compensate for not having the ideal technologies.

The expression, API Application is also used, this relates to the idea of an application or microservice that exists to meet the needs of an API.

Single purpose versus multipurpose APIs

OMESA creates this differentiation of APIs for significant reasons. Firstly, a multipurpose API is designed to be a general-purpose API that can be consumed by many different systems. As a consequence, it should not be designed to favor any one system. These kinds of APIs should be *information rich,* that is to say, offer a wealth of information of which any one consumer may only need a limited set of attributes.

When these APIs support system-to-system communication, and our user is immediately affected, then OMESA refers to such integrations, as horizontal (because you often see in diagrams the linkages as being horizontal). While you can use the APIs in horizontal integrations it is common to also see batch/bulk data processes happen. As a result, thought should be given as to whether the APIs are necessarily the right vehicle.

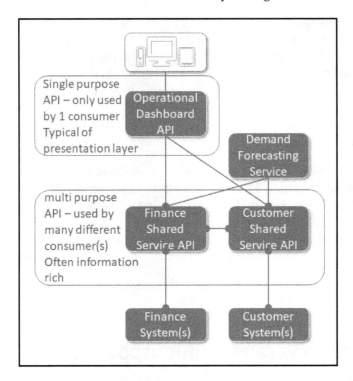

Single purpose versus multipurpose APIs

A single purpose API is designed for a specific requirement such as servicing a mobile application, where you want the API to only provide the data needed and optimized to minimize the number of calls, so may not make use of **Hypermedia as the Engine of Application State**, commonly referred to as the **HATEOAS** (`https://spring.io/understanding/HATEOAS`) design ethos. A single purpose API is typically going to be built on top of a multipurpose API, maybe even several different multipurpose APIs.

OMESA also has the concept of Vertical integrations (and therefore APIs), Horizontal integration, and APIs. The terminology is linked to how the APIs are shown to interact with other components. When we represent communication that typically is aligned to passing events between the different layers, for example, data store to business logic layer(s) to data publication or presentation layers and ultimately users, we often see this flowing vertically through the stack-hence Vertical. Horizontal APIs reflect system to system (particularly in a monolith world) and often data store to data store. As a consequence, Horizontal APIs may actually be realized through bulk data transfers. In the case of a bulk data connection, we can only talk about the interfaces as the APIs in the most general terms. In the microservices world, we can also talk about a choreography component, such as Kafka, as being horizontal in nature.

Semi-decoupled and fully decoupled

This reflects the level of autonomy and independence that any service may have. A semi-decoupled solution reflects service thinking, but will reuse common building blocks and often run on a shared platform such as an ESB. It is not unusual for different components to have a degree of awareness of the existence and characteristics of other components. As a result, these components will be managed by orchestrations (or will be subject to orchestration). This orchestration will often embody business knowledge (the business process) and understanding of how another component plays a role in an end-to-end activity. Most traditional SOA solutions will reflect this state of affairs, where services will be deployed together onto a shared platform.

This contrasts with a fully decoupled solution that works on an isolated model, with a share nothing mentality (within the context of the microservice or application itself) meaning that there is very little or no dependence on anything. Dependencies, when they do exist, will be most probably down to an API gateway, a service registry (to go from a known contract to an instantiation of a contract), and a pub-sub framework for choreography—although this is more likely to be a more contemporary form such as Kafka rather than a traditional JMS (as most JMS implementations lean toward a centralist model). In this framework, each decoupled component then simply subscribes to the events it is interested in. As a result, the event framework has no comprehension of any consumer. This approach reflects the microservice or self-contained system models.

Note that neither model is necessarily wrong, as both have advantages and disadvantages (elasticity versus overhead of greater coordination and extra compute cost of running the containerization; risk data duplication and the need to protect data integrity).

Bounded context

When designing data models, a common approach was to develop global (organization wide) definitions and representations of the data. To achieve consistency across such a large model can consume a lot of time and result in complex data models and slow progress in the design and development of solutions. The data models could also risk leading to tighter coupling between subsystems. Perhaps the easiest way to illustrate the challenges of an enterprise-wide unified model is to take an example. In the eyes of the legal department, a customer could be just as easily a recording artist, music composer, streaming service, or fan purchasing music. In the eyes of the retail side of the business (that is the team selling CDs, and so on.), the customer is clearly the fan or the retail store. This issue can be overcome with the concept of bounded contexts.

A bounded context looks at the domain and breaks it into manageable segments or contexts, where data use and semantics will be consistent and have shared relationships. This reduces potential impacts without sacrificing practical levels of consistency and integrity. Taking our example again, with legal and retail in different contexts, we can continue to use the customer language in each *context* with the remaining and data structure aligned to that context.

Not only does it simplify modelling, it also makes it easier for the IT business to relate to the real business people, as you can use the terminology and semantics of that business area without translation.

 For more information about the idea of bounded context, refer to the following link:
`https://martinfowler.com/bliki/BoundedContext.html`

We can take our high-level entities and identify some contexts to help manage the APIs and data semantics. The following diagram builds upon our previous logical view and adds the dashed red line to show the context boundaries:

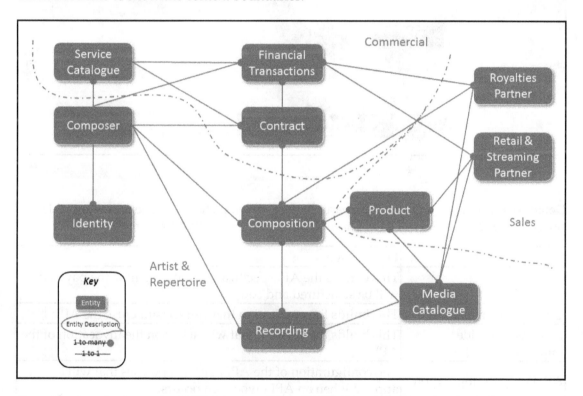

MRA contexts

Next steps

With an understanding of the existing landscape and where we need to get to go, working with an approach of a minimal viable product and API 1st in terms of solution for MRA, we can sketch out a roadmap which the following chapters will follow, as shown in the following diagram:

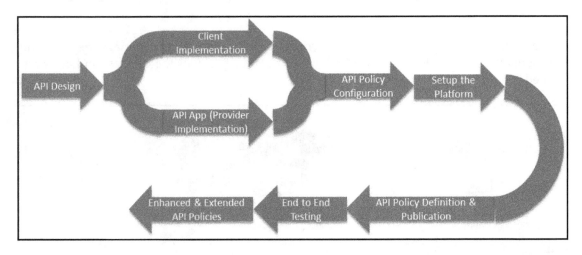

Solution lifecycle general

Details of this *lifecycle* will become clearer in the following chapters. The following table provides a brief summary of each phase shown in the preceding diagram:

Phase	Description
API Design	This defines the API specification showing how the payload will be structured and communicated.
Client Implementation	This builds the application that can consume/use the API.
API App (provide implementation)	This builds the solution that will act upon the invocation of the API.
API Policy Configuration	The configuration of the API Platform policies that will be applied when an API invocation occurs.
Setup the platform	Policies and routing of calls are achieved through the use of a gateway. The gateway needs to be deployed and configured.
API Policy Definition & Publication	With the policies defined, the API definitions that completed the information needs to be published so that the right communities can see and access the information.

| End to end Testing | With both the consumer and provider built, policies configured and deployed along with all the necessary documentation the solution need to undergo some testing from end to end to ensure the right experience is achieved. |
| Enhanced & Extended API Policies | Overtime, we may wish to extend and enhance the APIs, but providing finer controls, expose APIs to other users, and so on. |

Summary

In this chapter, we described the situation our fictitious company MRA sees itself in, which isn't too different from that of many real businesses. We described where MRA wishes to get to, including the capabilities the APIs will need to help deliver. We also took a good look at OMESA as an architectural framework and some of the design concepts techniques that lend themselves to the approaches we will adopt. We also introduced you to certain terminology and ideas that we will explore later in the book. In addition to this, we looked at a roadmap for developing capabilities to take MRA forward. We then ended the chapter with certain high-level API requirements and some steps of progress that need to be taken.

In the next chapter, we will explore the API 1st approach in depth along with the means by which we can design and communicate the API definitions. The value of API 1st will also be addressed (the previous diagram has also indicated this).

Designing the API 3

As it was described in the previous chapter, Monster Records and Associates (MRA)—a fictional music records company—having realized that its biggest asset is, in fact, its data, embarked on a digital transformation with the aim to offer its product and offerings completely online and via APIs.

The chapter starts by walking through the process and steps performed by MRA to adopt an **API design first** approach for building its APIs. Given the approach, the chapter will start by explaining how **Apiary** is used to quickly design and mock an API.

The chapter continues by illustrating how the API mock is made discoverable and accessible by making use of the **Oracle API Platform** and how this same approach initiates a **feedback-loop** between API consumer and API designer early in the life cycle.

The chapter then concludes by elaborating on how Apiary's GitHub integration can be used along with Apiary's Dredd testing tool to ensure that a subsequent service implementation matches the API Apiary design.

Scenario

As it was thoroughly described in Chapter 2, *Use Case*, MRA had embarked on a digital transformation journey with the objective to truly become a digital organization capable of offering tailored (à la carte) offerings to artists, such as handling of an artist's online presence to on-demand distribution of an artist's digital media to music streaming services such as Spotify, Apple Music, Google Play Music, Amazon Prime Music, Pandora, and Deezer, to name a few.

Having fully acknowledged that their most valuable asset is, in fact, their media data, MRA wanted to materialize in such assets and determine that the quickest and most effective way to achieve this was by exposing a **public API** capable of providing access, on-demand, to MRA's **Media Catalogue** assets such as artists, songs, and albums:

MRA's Media Catalogue API

The idea being that once such assets became accessible via an API, streaming services could, on-demand and 24x7, explore MRA's repertoire, purchase rights-to-use, and start streaming. In addition, the API could also open the door to a brand new global audience: millions of app developers constantly innovating. If only a fraction of such a huge audience leveraged MRA's Media Catalogue API, it would still represent a considerable success for MRA.

However, as with everything, there is a challenge to realize such vision.

MRA like many other organizations had a level of experience with systems integrations and Service Oriented Architectures (SOA). One of the lessons learned from SOA, however, was that the cycles for designing, building, prototyping, and testing SOAP-based web services could be quite lengthy and expensive.

An API differs from a service. This means that the former represents the RESTful interface a consumer application interacts with, whereas the latter is the actual implementation (the code) behind an API. An HTTP endpoint exposed by a service is defined as an unmanaged API.

 When a service endpoint is accessed via an API Gateway where policies such as app-key validation, authentication/authorization, and other policies are enforced, then it becomes a managed API.

This book refers to managed APIs as simply APIs and unmanaged APIs as simply service endpoints.

Refer to the *Exploring OMESA* section in `Chapter 2`, *Use Case*, for a more detailed description on how OMESA defines APIs and services.

Especially when it came to capturing and accommodating the feedback from client application developers (API consumers building applications that consume APIs), MRA has had very bad experiences, as in the majority of occasions they came to realize very late in the software life cycle that the web service developed did not meet the expectations of its consumers:

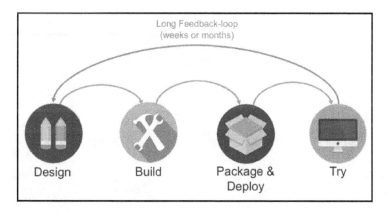

Feedback loops in traditional web service design

Refactoring web services in this approach wasn't just time-consuming but also an expensive exercise as both the service design (WSDL) and code had to be refactored and retested in order to accommodate the feedback received and before application developers could try a service again.

Naturally, service designers and developers avoided making changes as much as possible, thus challenging feedback received from application developers, which in turn created friction among both teams. However, sometimes it meant application developers found alternative routes to solve their needs rather than using the web service. This was the worst possible scenario as it meant that the investments made in implementing a web service could've been wasted.

The API design-first process

Learning from previous experiences and acknowledging the challenges that such waterfall-like process imposed to a digital transformation initiative, MRA were quite keen to adopt a more agile, interactive, but also quicker way to deliver modern RESTful-based APIs.

The idea was clear. By engaging application developers (API consumers) in the initial stages of the design process, feedback would be captured and reflected back in the interface design (API) early as well. Not only would this shorten feedback loops, but also enable application and service implementation to occur in parallel. Likewise, it ensures that once the underlying services are implemented, it would expose an interface already endorsed and tested by its consumers, as opposed to risk building a service that won't satisfy the client expectations and needs late in the process:

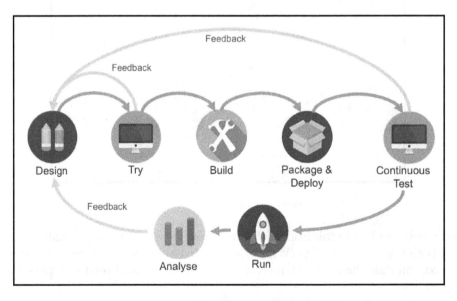

The API design-first approach versus traditional service design

The implication of this approach, though, is that the tooling and notation to define the API had to be both simple, yet rich in capability such that the task of designing and mocking API endpoints is quick and easy, given that if the process becomes cumbersome it would defeat its purpose.

The following section elaborates on the different steps undertaken by MRA when designing its Media Catalogue API using Apiary and related tools.

Step 1 – defining the API type

A fundamental step when designing any API is to first define what the type is. This is important as it will determine the guiding principles to consider when working on the design.

As described earlier in Chapter 2, *Use Case*, MRA decided to adopt the **Open Modern Software Architecture Project** (OMESA.io) as its reference architecture. OMESA, as illustrated in the following diagram, defines two main types of APIs:

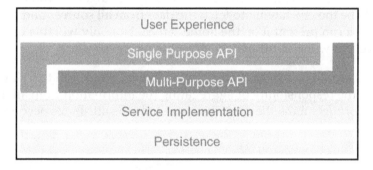

Types of API in OMESA.io

The following sections will cover a detailed description of each type.

Single-purpose APIs

As its name suggests, these are APIs that serve a unique and specific purpose, typically derived from an unambiguous need associated with a user journey or use case. Because of this, they aren't suitable for reuse outside the context which they are built for.

In terms of guiding principles, apart from the ones prescribed in the RESTful definition, there is a fair degree of flexibility as to how a single-purpose API is defined. The key and main requirement for this type of APIs is ensuring that it satisfies the explicit needs of its consumers in the best possible manner.

Let's take, for example, the landing page of the MRA's customer mobile app.

Being the first screen displayed when the app opens, it usually shows summary information around a customer's account details, latest orders, account usage, and so on.

As this information would typically come from multiple sources, it would be inefficient for the mobile app to be the one having to fetch the data from all sources and then transform it and combine it so it can present it on the home screen. Not only will this have a hit on the app performance, but will also ultimately affect the user experience.

A better approach would be for the mobile app to make a single call to a single-purpose API that takes on the responsibility of aggregating the information from all the relevant targets and transform/combine the data objects so only the attributes needed for the home screen are returned:

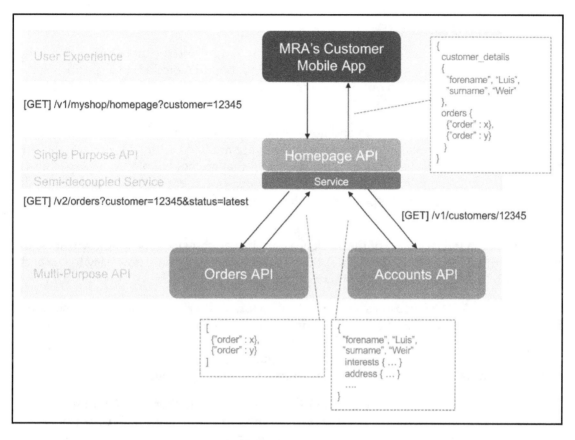

A single-purpose versus multi-purpose API example

The immediate benefit of this approach is that the client application (in our example, MRA's customer mobile app) won't have to deal with the complexities involved in having to orchestrate/aggregate data from multiple sources and transform it so it can be presented to the user. Rather, this becomes the problem of the single-purpose API and its underlying service implementation.

Whereas this approach has many benefits, an obvious counterargument is the fact that these APIs are not really suitable to be reused outside the context for which they were built-in our example, the retailer's mobile app. Doing so means having a hard dependency on the retailer's mobile app release cycle and code changes.

Multi-purpose APIs

As the name suggests, these APIs are more generic in nature and meant to satisfy not just one but multiple use cases and scenarios. They are not bound (coupled) to a specific user journey or system of engagement (for example, a mobile app), and are therefore ideal to be reused enterprise-wide.

Because of this, guiding principles and governance for designing such APIs tend to be more rigorous. One obvious example is how data objects are modeled with JSON objects should be defined in such APIs. Normalized data structures that are not coupled to any specific backend or frontend application should be used. Otherwise, there is a risk that the API will have to change along with changes made in backend and frontend systems, which isn't ideal at all.

As most likely a large portion of the audience (and its use cases) will be unknown, at least when designing the API, design assumptions will determine not only how easy to use and feature-rich the API will be but also how future-compatible it will be.

Versioning the API also becomes a more critical factor, and serious considerations should be made as to how versions, handled as a single change in the API, could have a serious impact on several consumers at once. Remember, this type of APIs are meant to satisfy multiple use cases, meaning several consumer applications might be binding to it. Thus, a breaking (non-backward compatible) change could impact all consumers at once.

Note that when it comes to REST API versioning, there is no right way of doing it. Whereas some experts promote versioning through URIs (for example, `/api/v1.1/resource`), others do so by using HTTP headers (for example, `version=1.1`) or GET parameters (for example, `resource?version=1.1`). Some even argue that REST resources should not be versioned at all and changes should always be backwards compatible.

This book does not favor any particular versioning approach, rather it is recommended that the reader conducts hers/his own research on the topic and that an approach is chosen based on fitness, not just to the requirements but based on organizational and IT landscape suitability.

MRA's Media Catalogue API – public and multi-purpose

As previously mentioned, MRA's Media Catalogue API was specifically targeted at two main audiences: music streaming services and application developers in general. Therefore, the API had to be both **public** and **multi-purpose**:

- Public because the API had to be accessible via the public internet and without having to be inside MRA's corporate network or a virtual private network (VPN).

A public API is only as good as its documentation. Therefore, public APIs should also have public facing developer portals for external audiences (for example, developers) to register and find useful information on the functionality offered and code samples.

NASA's API developer portal is a good example of what should look like: `https://api.nasa.gov/.`

Not only comprehensive information is provided on how to register, but also useful and working code samples are provided so developers can get started quickly.

Note that an API developer portal should not disclose the ins and outs of an API. Rather, it should focus on the usability of the API, or in other words, the API developer experience. Therefore, the documentation should always be kept up to date, the process of which can be automated or delegated to a librarian type.

- **Multi-purpose** because both audiences were unknown to MRA and could ultimately end up using MRA's API in a variety of use cases without MRA's understanding of it. Because of this and as described in the previous section, the API had to be designed more rigorously.

Step 2 – defining the API's domain semantics

The next step in the process was to elaborate proper understanding of the API's **bounded context**, Media Catalogue. To do so, based on the domain model described in Chapter 2, *Use Case*, entities, key attributes, and relationships within the bounded context itself were identified and also defined using semantics appropriate for the purpose of the API.

A **bounded context** represents an area of the domain that has a specific responsibility that can and should be independently developed. The responsibility is bounded because it has clear and explicit boundaries, hence the term.

The following article explains this concept and others quite well:

`https://codeburst.io/ddd-strategic-patterns-how-to-define-bounde`
`d-contexts-2dc70927976e`

Because the audience of the API is public-facing, and to a vast extent, unknown, the semantics adopted were fairly common hoping that this would make it easier to use the API:

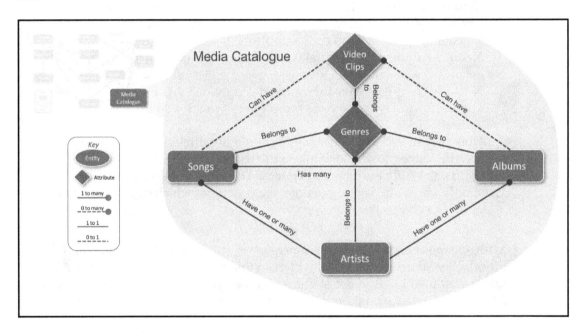

The MRA's Media Catalogue API bounded context

As the model illustrates, the entities and its relationships would be as following:

- An artist can have many albums and songs
- An album can have many songs and belongs to an artist
- Songs belong to an album and artist
- All artists, albums, and songs can belong to a genre
- A song and can have video clip, which can also be part of an Album

The following section walks through the API design-first steps, followed by MRA when defining the Media Catalogue API.

Step 3 – creating the API definition with its main resources

The subsequent instructions describe the steps followed by MRA when creating the Media Catalogue API definition and its associated API mock:

1. Log in to Apiary using a previously created account. Then on the upper left-hand side menu, click on **Create New API** (**1**). Then select **Team API** (**2**) so other members of the team can access and edit API, select **API Blueprint** (**5**) as the API definition language, leave the **Private API** (**4**) option unchecked (so, read-only access to the API documentation is accessible to external users outside the team), and finally click on **Create API** (**6**). Notice that a boilerplate API definition is loaded into the **API Editor** (**3**). Modify as described in the subsequent steps:

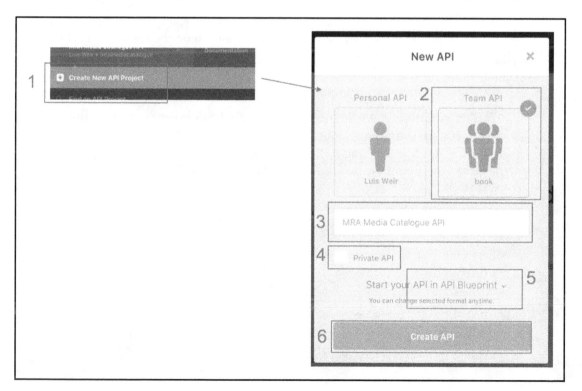

Note that Apiary supports both **API Blueprint** and **Swagger** (also known as, **Open API Project**). Both API definition languages are popular and even though Swagger/OpenAPI has more extensive support industry wide, MRA found API blueprint more intuitive and simple to use because of its Markdown-based notation (as opposed to YAML used in Swagger), and also because it's much richer support when it comes to modeling data, where several options are supported, such as plain **JSON, JSON Schemas**, and Apiary's own **Markdown Systems for Object Notation** (**MSON**).

For further information on Markdown notation refer to the following link: `https://github.com/adam-p/markdown-here/wiki/Markdown-Cheatsheet`

2. Modify the metadata section as following:
   - Leave the **FORMAT** variable to the defaulted value

   - Change the **HOST** for the either a temporal value or if known to the URL of the actual server that will host the API

Refer to the following link for more information on the metadata section: `https://apiblueprint.org/documentation/specification.html#def-metadata-section`

3. The API name is always defined with a **single hash** (#) at the start of the document, for example, `# MRA Media Catalogue API`. The name is defaulted to the one specified during API creation. In addition, a description of the API can be added by typing the desired text in the in the next line (see the screenshot in next step).

Refer to the following link for more information on the API name and overview section:
`https://apiblueprint.org/documentation/specification.html#def-api-name-section`

4. Create **resource groups** similarly by using a **single hash** (#) followed by the name of the group. Create three resource groups, for Artists, Albums, and Songs accordingly. Resource groups help with the visualization of the rendered API definition, which is shown on-the-fly in the right-hand side of the screen.

```
1    FORMAT: 1A
2    HOST: https://api.mra.com/
3
4 ▾  # MRA Media Catalogue API|
5    The Music Catalogue API is provides access to MRA's
6    digital media assets such as artits, albums and songs.
7
8 ▾  # Group Artists Resources
9    Artists related digital media resources.
10
11 ▾  # Group Albums Resources
12   Artists-related digital media resources.
13
14 ▾  # Group Songs Media
15   Songs and Video digital media resources.
```

 Refer to the following link for more information on how to define resource groups in API blueprint:
`https://apiblueprint.org/documentation/specification.html#def-resourcegroup-section`

5. **Named resources** for the API are defined with a **double hash** (##), followed by a name and the actual **Uniform Resource Identifier (URI)** in brackets. URI parameters can also be included by appending curly brackets followed by a question mark and parameters separated by a comma. For example, ## name [/resource?{param1,param2}]. Define Artists, Albums, and Songs named resources accordingly:

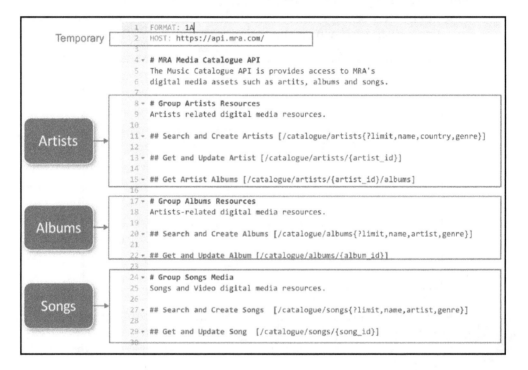

Note that named URIs define API resources, not the specific actions that can be performed against each resource. Therefore, a single URI can support more than one action, and for this reason it is recommended to name resources according to the actions they can support and not specific ones. That is, Search and Create resources describe URIs that support search and create actions.

The following link provides an excellent guide on how to define resource URIs:

`https://restfulapi.net/resource-naming/`

Note that if resource groups are not included in the API blueprint, named resources are defined with a single hash (#) instead.

Refer to the following link for more information on how to define resources in API blueprint:

`https://apiblueprint.org/documentation/specification.html#def-resource-section`

6. Named **actions** are defined for each resource with a **triple hash** (###) followed by the name of the action and its corresponding **HTTP verb** in brackets. For example, `### Search Artist [GET]` is an action that allows searching artists by making use of the HTTP verb **GET** against the URI `/catalogue/artists`. Actions against each of the previously defined URIs can be defined as following:

```
 8 ▾ # Group Artists Resources
 9    Artists related digital media resources.
10
11 ▾ ## Search and Create Artists [/catalogue/artists{?limit,name,country,genre}]
12
13 ▾ ### Search Artists [GET]
14    Returns all MRA Artists that match the specified criteria.
15
16 ▾ ### Create Artist [POST]
17    Creates an Artist
18
19 ▾ ## Get and Update Artist [/catalogue/artists/{artist_id}]
20
21 ▾ ### Get Artist [GET]
22    Returns the details for a specific Artist such as bio and Albums.
23
24 ▾ ### Update Artist [PUT]
25    Updates an existing Artist.
26
27 ▾ ## Get Artist Albums [/catalogue/artists/{artist_id}/albums]
28
29 ▾ ### Get Artist Albums [GET]
30    Returns all the Albums for the specified Artist.
```

1

2

3

One of the main characteristics of RESTful APIs is the explicit use of HTTP verbs as specified in the HTTP protocol (**RFC 2616**). The following link provides an excellent guideline on adequately using HTTP verbs for different actions:
`https://restfulapi.net/http-methods/`

Note that if resource groups are not included in the API blueprint, named actions are defined with a double hash (##) instead.

Refer to the following link for more information on how to define actions in API Blueprint:
`https://apiblueprint.org/documentation/specification.html#def-action-section`

7. Now that all resources and actions have been defined, **URI parameters** and **HTTP Request/Response** payloads can also be specified against each resource as follows:

- Parameters are defined against each resource as following:

```
## <resource name> [/<uri>?{parameter 1, parameter 2}]
+ Parameter

    + <parameter name>: `<optional example value>` (<type>, required
| optional) - <optional short description>

    <optional description>

    + Default: `<optional default value>`
```

- Follow the indicated steps for defining the parameters on the
  resources Search and Create Artist (**1**), Get and Update
  Artist (**2**) and Get Artist Albums (**3**) resource:

Note that **indentation** and **markdown list syntax** play an important role in API blueprint. Indentation is used to defined hierarchical elements (for example, list of parameters supported), and the list syntax to list the different options available. Also note that although in the example the plus (+) sign was used, any markdown list syntax such as minus sign (–) and/or asterisk (*) can be used interchangeably.

Refer to the following link for more information on how to define URI parameters in API blueprint:
https://apiblueprint.org/documentation/specification.html#def-uriparameters-section

- HTTP request/response payloads are defined against each action as follows:

```
## <Action Name> [<HTTP verb>]

+ Request (<media type>)

        <sample JSON object, optional>

    + Attributes <optional>

        <MSON reference>

    + Body <optional>

        <sample JSON object>

    + Schema <optional>

        <JSON schema>
```

```
+ Response <HTTP response status code> (<media type>)

        <sample JSON object, optional>

    + Attributes <optional>

        <MSON reference>

    + Body <optional>

        <sample JSON object>

    + Schema <optional>

        <JSON Schema>
```

Note the following when defining request/response payloads:
It is not required to use all keywords when defining a payload. The
simplest way to define a payload is by simply including a sample JSON
object after a request/response keyword. This payload would also be used
in the Apiary mock that is autogenerated.

The keyword **Attributes** can be used when defining payloads with the
MSON—this will be described later in the chapter. If Attributes are used,
then the **Body** and **Schema** keywords may not be used, and although
possible, it would be redundant. Body may be used together with
Attributes if it is desired to specify a specific JSON object and override the
default one derived from the MSON definition.

Body and Schema can be used together to define a sample JSON object
along with its corresponding **JSON schema**.

Refer to the following link for more information on how to define
request/response payloads in API blueprint:
https://apiblueprint.org/documentation/specification.html#def-
request-section

- Follow the indicated steps for a simple **1. request** and **2. response** payload definition for the resource action **Search Artists**:

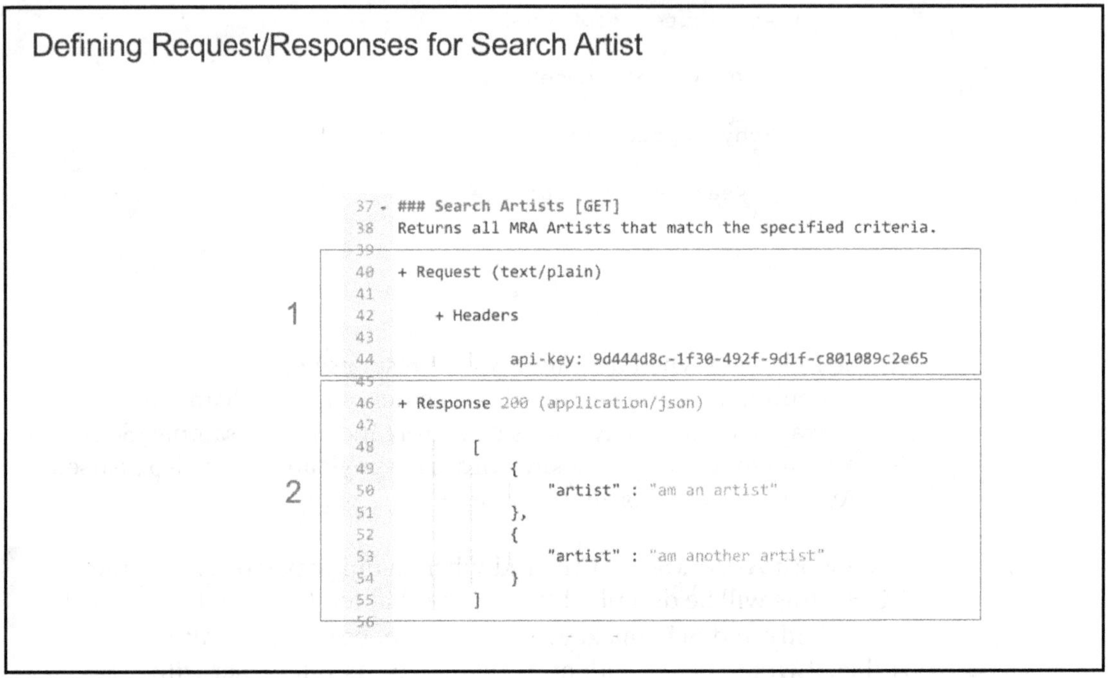

Defining Request/Responses for Search Artist

```
37 ### Search Artists [GET]
38 Returns all MRA Artists that match the specified criteria.
39
40 + Request (text/plain)
41
42     + Headers
43
44             api-key: 9d444d8c-1f30-492f-9d1f-c801089c2e65
45
46 + Response 200 (application/json)
47
48         [
49             {
50                 "artist" : "am an artist"
51             },
52             {
53                 "artist" : "am another artist"
54             }
55         ]
56
```

1 (marks lines 40–44)
2 (marks lines 46–55)

---

8. On the left-hand side of the page, notice that there is an exclamation mark icon indicating **4 semantic issues** (**1**). Click on the icon for a description of the issues. Notice that all issues are because resource actions are either missing Request and/or Response payloads. Ignore these issues for now and just click on **Save** (**3**).

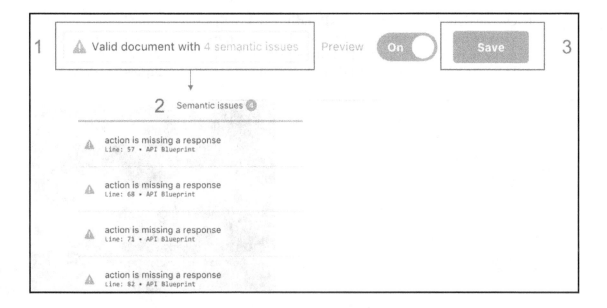

Step 4 – trying the API mock

In the previous steps it was described how to create an API, define its main resources, parameters, and sample payloads. In the subsequent steps it will be described how Apiary's automatically generated API mocks can be used to satisfy one of the most important steps in API design-first: try an API early in the life cycle, before the API is actually implemented. This is a critical step as collecting feedback from API consumers early can potentially save numerous hours in code refactoring later in the project. Do this as follows:

1. On the right-hand side of the **API Editor**, notice that there is an HTML rendered view of the API definition. This view is rendered dynamically as changes are made to the definition and its purpose is to help visualize the API definition. Look for **Search Artists** and then click on it to open the **Examples** window:

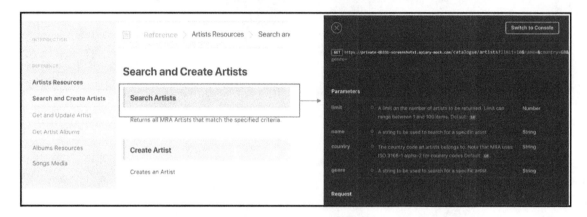

2. From the **Examples** window, client code can be generated for several programming languages. For example, if you select **cURL** from the dropdown, **cURL** code is generated, which can be used straight away. Alternatively, click on **Try** to call the API from the **Console**:

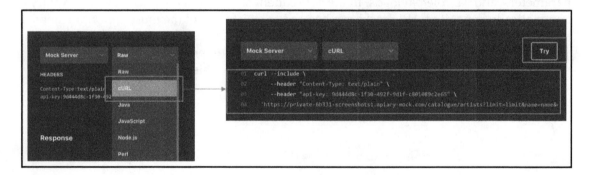

3. Once the **Console** opens, type some sample parameters values (**1**), select **Mock Server** (**2**), and click on **Call Resource** (**3**):

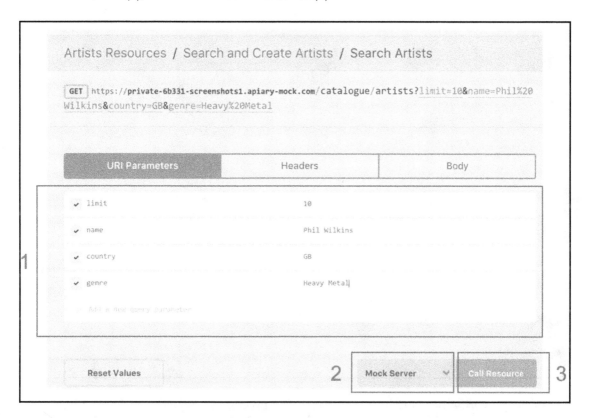

Notice that the **Mock Server** was selected from the dropdown. If the value **Production** is selected instead, then the hostname URL specified in the **HOST metadata** variable definition will be used instead.
Also, note that the mock endpoint URL can be accessed with any other tool such as Postman or Curl.

4. Scroll down and notice that the **Request** and **Response** payloads corresponds to actual definitions in the action `Search Artists`:

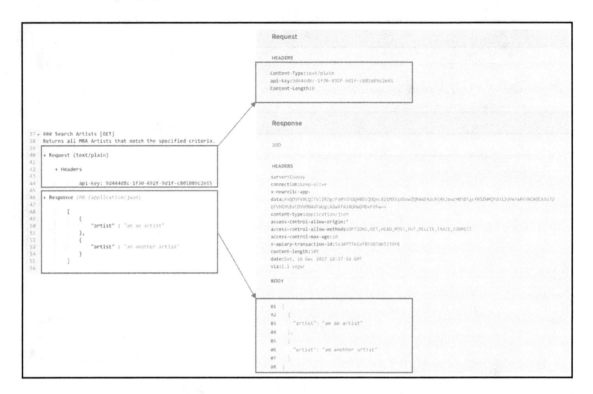

5. To verify that the Mock Server is in fact processing requests, click on the menu option, **Inspector**. See that the API call made appears in the table and that it is green. Click on it to see details of the Request and Response:

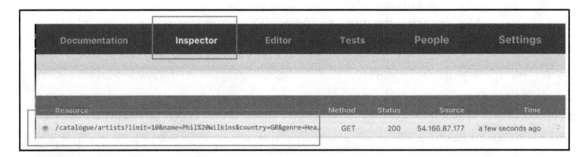

Note that if an invalid call is made to the API mock, a red dot will appear in the list instead of the green one shown on the image.

Step 5 – defining MSON data structures

The **Markdown Syntax for Object Notation** (**MSON**) is a plain-text syntax for the description and validation of data structures in API Blueprint. It provides a way to represent objects (for example, an artist) in a human-readable plain text form.

It is recommended to use MSON data structures over plain JSON objects when defining Request/Response payloads. Using MSON provides consistency and reusability across the entire API blueprint definition. This is the case because data structures can be defined just once and then referenced from all resource actions, as opposed to having to define plain JSON objects multiple times, which is prompt to human error and data structure inconsistencies.

The full MSON specification is available at the following link: https://apiblueprint.org/documentation/mson/specification.html

Follow these steps to define the **Artist**, **Album**, and **Song** objects using the MSON notation:

1. First of all, add a `# Data Structures` section at the bottom most of an API definition. Within this section, MSON objects are subsequently defined with double hashes (`##`).

2. Define MSON objects `Artist`, `Album`, and `Song` as indicated. Notice that an additional object, `Search Metadata`, has also been defined. This object is to be used as metadata in resource action responses that conduct searches.

```
 96 ▾ # Data Structures
 97
 98 ▾ ## Search Metadata (object)
 99    - total_count: 1 (number, required)
100    - result_count: 1 (number, required)
101    - offset: 1 (number, required)
102
103 ▾ ## Artist (object)        ◄─────────────────          Artists
104    - artist_name: Oasis (string, required)
105
106 ▸ ## Album (object)
107    - album_name: `(What's the Story) Morning Glory?` (string, required)
108
109 ▾ ## Song (object)      ◄─────────────
110    - song_name: Wonder wall (string, required)                  Songs
```

Albums

Note that the syntax for defining object properties is similar URI parameters are defined, with the difference that in this case, the minus (−) symbol is used instead of a plus (+) to specify object properties. In practice, MSON doesn't distinguish between these two symbols so either could be used.

The following link is recommended for a simple tutorial on MSON and its syntax:
`https://apiblueprint.org/documentation/mson/specification.html`

3. Now that a simple MSON data structure has been defined, the `Response` payload for the `Search Artists` resource action can be modified to use the keyword `Attributes` instead of a plain JSON object. MSON objects can then be referenced by their name with the syntax `<JSON property>` `(<MSON Object Name>)` as indicated in step (**2**) of the image. If a given object has to be referenced as a collection (for example, a search response may contain many artists), then the syntax `<JSON property>` `(array[<MSON Object Name>])` can be used:

```
37 - ### Search Artists [GET]
38   Returns all MRA Artists that match the specified criteria.
39
40   + Request (text/plain)
41
42       + Headers
43
44             api-key: 9d444d8c-1f30-492f-9d1f-c801089c2e65
45
46   + Response 200 (application/json)
47
48       + Attributes
49
50    2   + metadata (Search Metadata)
51
52        + artists (array[Artist])

96 - # Data Structures
97
98 - ## Search Metadata (object)
99   - total_count: 1 (number, required)
100  - result_count: 1 (number, required)
101  - offset: 1 (number, required)
102
103 - ## Artist (object)
104  - artist_name: Oasis (string, required)
105
106 - ## Album (object)
107  - album_name: `(What's the Story) Morning Glory?` (string, required)
108
109 - ## Song (object)
110  - song_name: Wonder wall (string, required)
```

4. As previously done, from the rendered view of the **API Editor** on the right-hand side, look for **Search Artists** and then click on it to open the **Examples** window. Scroll down and notice that the sample **Body** is consistent with the response definition:

5. Notice that even though the JSON object was defined with an MSON object, it is also possible to get the equivalent JSON Schema from the **Examples** window by clicking on **SHOW JSON SCHEMA**:

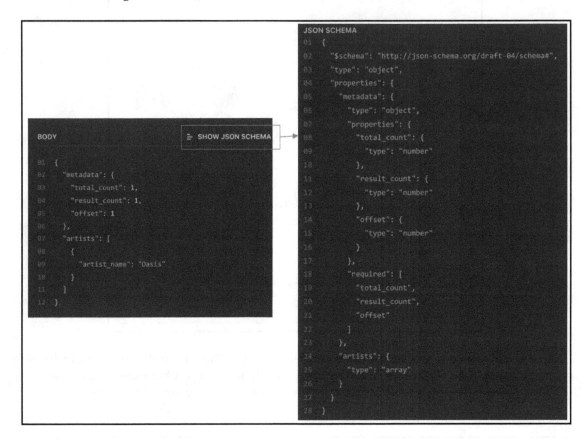

6. MSON supports the use of nested objects. This is very useful in the case of MRA Media Catalogue API, as **Artists**, **Albums**, and **Songs** have many-to-many relationships among them which can be modeled by leveraging this feature. See how such relationships can be appended in the previously created MSON objects. The syntax to establish such relationships is similar to the one used when referring an MSON object from within a response payload:

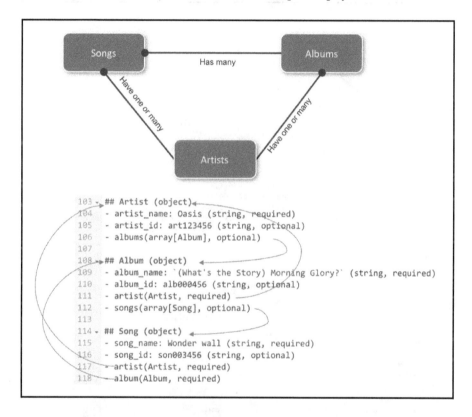

Note that once a change is made in any of the MSON objects, it is immediately reflected in any request/response payload referencing the changed object. It is therefore important to be cautious when making changes, especially once an API has been implemented.

Also note that although there is a cyclical reference between Artist and Album, Apiary's mock engine detects such cyclical references and breaks them when using the mock so no endless loops occur. However, it is important to highlight that when a developer is implementing the API, this have to handle this in the code.

7. Now that all objects have been defined, additional properties can be added to each object. For example, an Artist will have a name, an identifier, and other metadata such as country of origin and even a biography. The following diagram provides an illustration on how each object could look like once all details are added and how the objects map to the domain model described earlier:

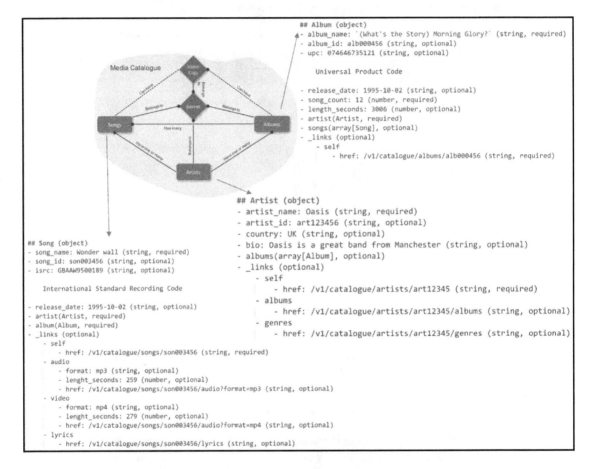

8. Once all MSON objects are defined, the remaining resource actions and their associated request/response payloads can be created by following similar steps to the ones describe so far.

An API blueprint for the MRA Media Catalogue API is available for reference in GitHub under the following URL:
`https://github.com/luisw19/MRAMediaCatalogueAPI/blob/master/apia ry.apib`

Step 6 – pushing the API blueprint to GitHub

GitHub is, without doubt, one of the most (if not the most) popular web-based version control systems in existence today. Not only is it feature-rich when it comes to **source code management** (**SCM**), but it also supports features such as `bug tracking, feature requests, task management,` and `wikis` for every project.

 For further information GitHub and how to use please refer to the following URL:
`https://guides.github.com/activities/hello-world/`

API blueprints can be pushed into GitHub repositories so they can be version controlled but most importantly, it can follow a similar GitHub cycle as any other code asset. This step is also required in order to configure **Dredd** to validate API endpoints against API blueprint definitions (described in *Step 8* section later in the chapter). Following the steps to set up GitHub for the MRA Media Catalogue API:

1. From the Apiary main menu **Settings** (up right-hand side), select **Account Settings**:

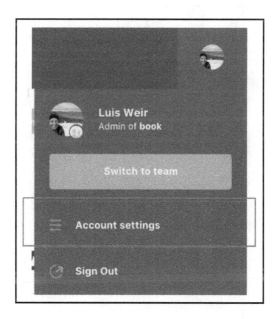

2. Scroll down and select **Connect** under **apiary.io and GitHub Account**:

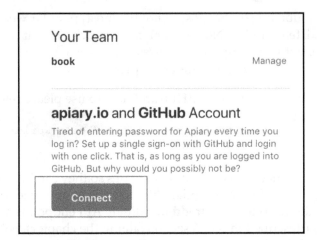

3. Type the GitHub account credentials and click on **Sign In**. If an account is not available, one can be created by clicking on **Create an account**:

4. Once the new page loads, click on **Check connection with GitHub** to verify that the account has all privileges. A message similar to the one displayed should be shown:

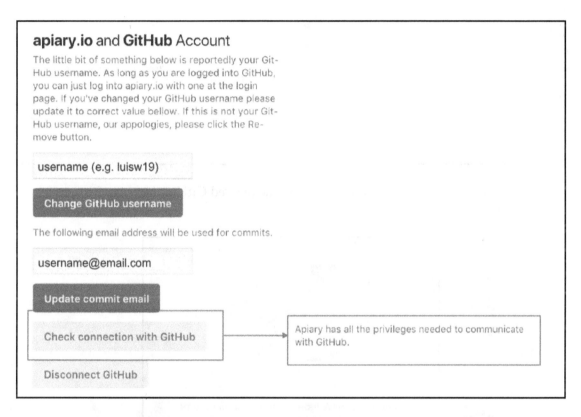

5. Click on **API Settings** and scroll down to section **Link your GitHub account**:

6. Click on **Link your GitHub account**:

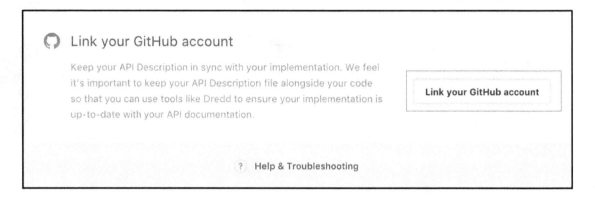

7. Click on **List all repositories** to select the desired GitHub repository to connect to:

8. Click on **Link this project to GitHub**:

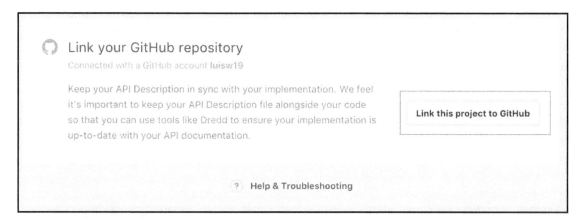

9. Select a GitHub user and type a text to find the desired GitHub repository, and then click on **Search**. When found, click on **Connect**:

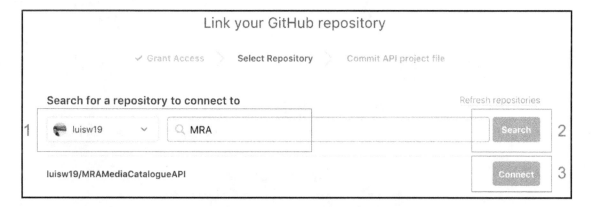

10. Modify the default **Commit message**, if desired, and then click on **Commit and start sync**:

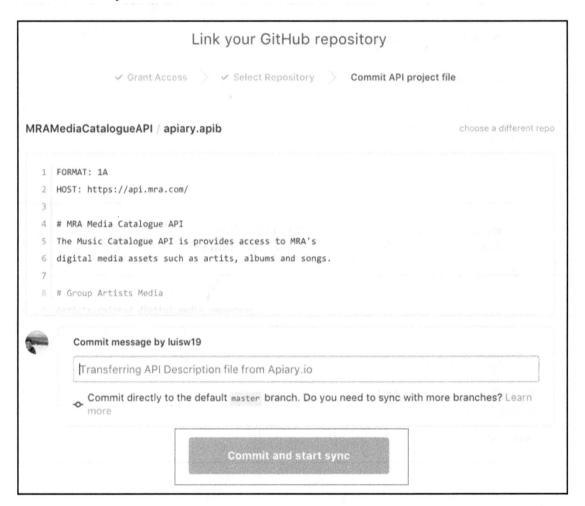

11. If the synchronization is successful, a message similar to the one highlighted in the following screenshot should appear almost instantly:

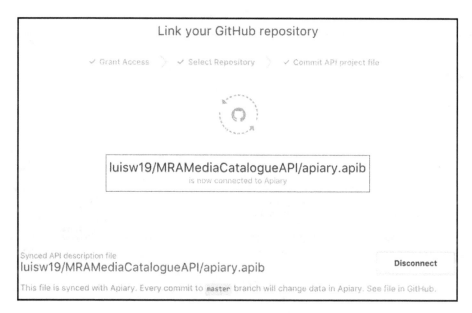

12. Go back to the **API Editor**:

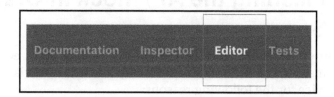

13. On the upper right-hand side of the editor click on **Push** (**1**). Modify the commit message if desired, then click on **Save and Push** (**2**), and verify that the push was successful (**3**):

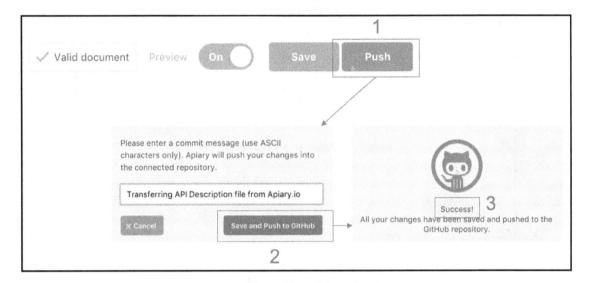

Step 7 – publishing the API mock in Oracle API platform CS

Although Apiary provides an API mock URL that can be can be accessed directly, it is recommended that instead, the API mock is published and accessed via the **Oracle API Platform Cloud Service** for the following reasons:

- It provides visibility over the usage of the API mock.
- Developers are able to easily discover and subscribe to the API mock via the **Developer Portal**.
- If desired, controls can be applied so only registered Client Applications with an **Application Key** (also known as, API key) can call the API mock.
- Most importantly, it **abstracts** the client's application code from the implementation of the API. Once the **Service** is implemented the **Service Request** policy can be modified to point to the actual service endpoint. No changes required on the client's side.

Note that in order to ensure that such abstraction works, **Dredd** should be implemented in order verify that a backend service, once built, is consistent with its corresponding API blueprint definition, thus won't break the client application code. The steps to do this will be covered in more detail in the *Step 8* section.

Follow these steps to create and publish the MRA Media Catalogue API through the Oracle API Platform CS:

1. Open the Management Portal URL and login with an API Manager account through the URL
   `https://<Oralce Public Cloud Host >:<Port>/apiplatform:`

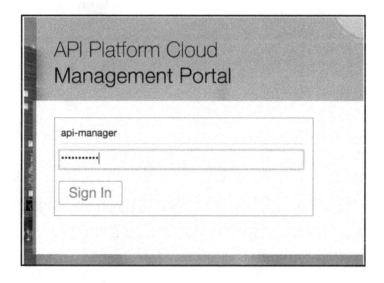

2. On the landing page, click on **Create API**:

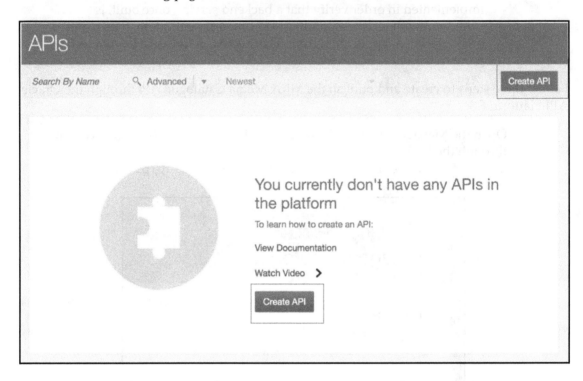

3. Type the **Name**, **Version**, and a brief **Description** for the API and click on **Create**.

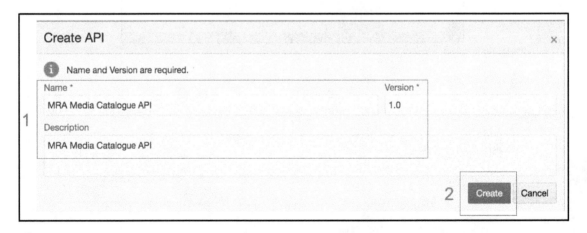

4. Once the page refreshes, the API should now be listed. Click on it (anywhere):

5. Click on **Edit** on the **API Request** policy to define the API endpoint URL:

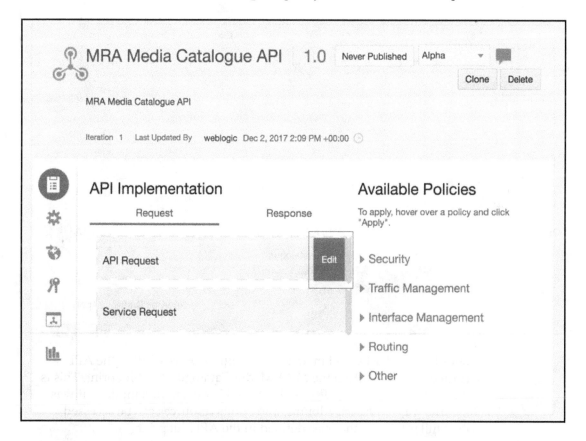

6. Modify the **Policy Name** and type in comments if desired. Select the **Protocols** to be supported, type an **API Endpoint URI (1)** and click on **Apply (2)**:

Notice that the URI typed matches the main resource of all of the API resources defined within the MRA Media Catalogue API blueprint. This is not mandatory, and any URI can be used. However, for simplicity it was done this way, so Artist, Albums, and Songs resources can be accessed with similar URIs to the ones defined in the API blueprint.

7. Click on the **Service Request** to define the backend service URL. In this case, the Apiary mock service URL:

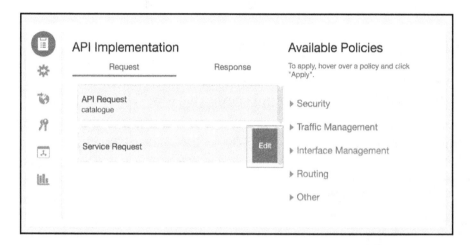

8. Select **Enter a URL** to manually type the Apiary mock endpoint URL and click on **Apply**:

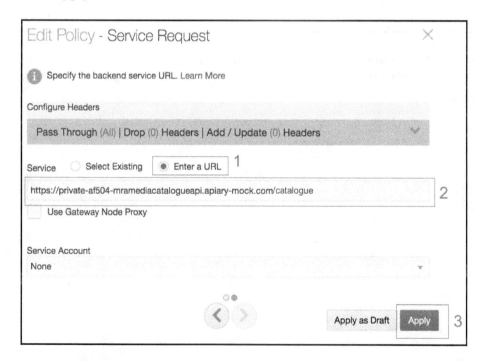

Notice that the URL entered also includes /catalogue URI. As mentioned, this was done so Artist, Albums, and Songs resources can be accessed with similar URLs to the ones defined in the API blueprint.

9. MRA also wanted to add an additional control in this API by ensuring that only registered developers and client applications could use the API mock. To this end, a **Key Validation** policy can be applied by expanding the security policies menu and then clicking on **Apply** next to the **Key Validation** policy:

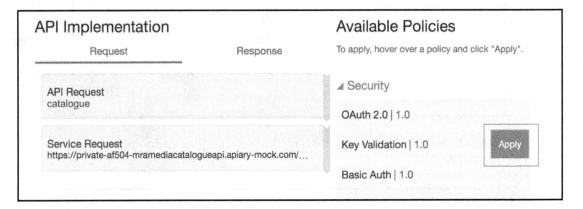

Note that API policies and how they can be applied are described in more detail in Chapter 6, *Defining Policies for APIs*.

10. Change the **Policy Name**, add comments if desired, and click on **Next**:

11. To expect the key in the HTTP header, click on **Header** (**1**), and then type a name for the header property as it should be expected in the actual HTTP call, for example, **api-key**. Then click on **Apply** (**2**):

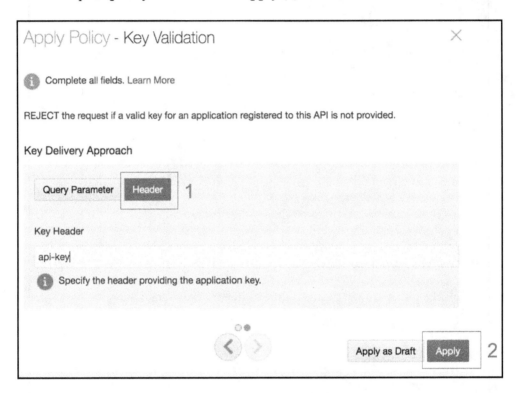

12. When the **Save Changes** bar appears, click on it to ensure all changes are saved:

Note that changes to the API are not autosaved, so it's important to always click on **Save Changes** whenever changes are made.

13. The **API implementation** page should now look like this.

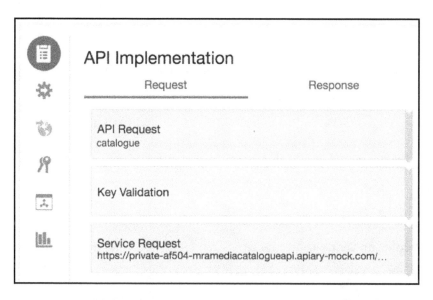

14. To deploy the API to an already available **API Gateway**, switch to the **Deployments** (1) window and then click on **Deploy API** (2):

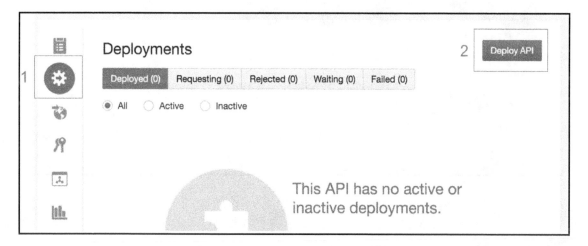

Note that installing and configuring API gateways in Oracle API Platform CS will be covered in Chapter 5, *Platform Setup and Gateway Configuration*.

15. Select any of the listed **API Gateways** and click on **Deploy**:

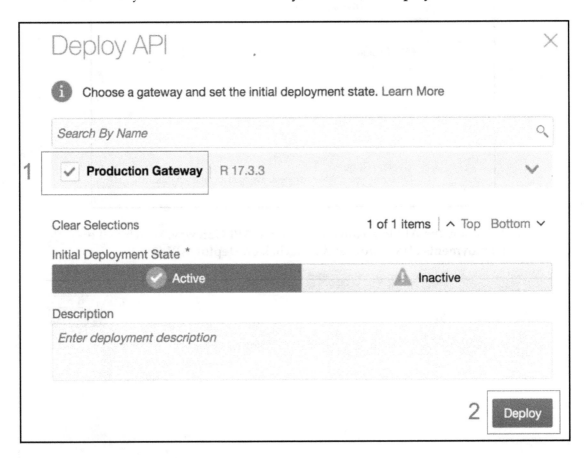

16. Wait for a couple of minutes for the deployment to take place (the exact time will depend on the Gateway configuration—see `Chapter 5`, *Platform Setup and Gateway Configuration* for details). Once the API is deployed, it should appear in the **Deployed** tab with **Runtime State** as **Active**. Also take note of the HTTP Load Balancer URL as it will be required later in the chapter when configuring Dredd:

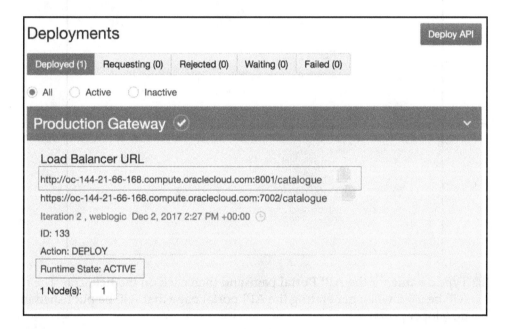

Note that if an API Manager user does not have Gateway Manager grants, deployment will go into a requesting state until a Gateway Manager approves the deployment.

Also note that if the deployment is unsuccessful, the deployment will appear as a failed deployment in the **Failed** tab. At this point it is recommended to undeploy the API and try to redeploy. Should the problem persist, it is recommended to open a service request in `https://support.oracle.com` for further investigation by Oracle as it may refer to a product bug.

Further information on Deploying APIs in the following URL:
`https://docs.oracle.com/en/cloud/paas/api-platform-cloud/apfad/deploying-endpoints.html#GUID-91D6C3B1-7357-43F6-813E-2BD67FE4E251`

17. For the API to be available and discoverable in the developer portal, its documentation must first be created and/or published. To do this, switch to the **Publications** (1) window, and from here follow the steps as indicated. Note that each of the steps illustrated are described subsequently:

18. Type a **name** for the **API Portal** page and then click on the **tick** icon. The name will be used when generating the API portal page that will be published in the developer portal:

Note that although any text may be added as a name, it is recommended that the text used is self-descriptive, meaning it is easy to the tell what the **API Portal URL** is for. It is also recommended to use lowercase and use hyphen to separate a word from another.

19. Under the **Developer Portal API Overview** section, click either on **HTML** or **Markdown** to add an overview description for the API:

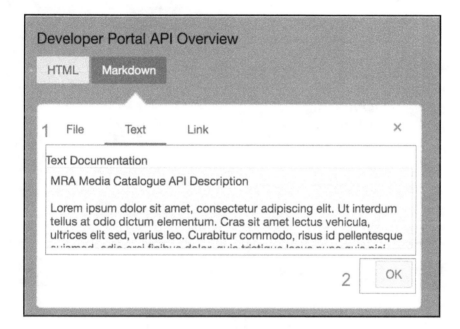

Note that to in our example a random Markdown text was used. In practice, you may use a tool like `dillinger.io` or similar in order to create a nicely styled Markdown or HTML document, which can later on be imported or referenced.

Furthermore, ensure that the API description has clear definition of what the API does, methods it supports, and examples that are not available or obvious in the API blueprint. Also refer to `https://www.programmableweb.com` as a source of inspiration from thousands of already available public API portals.

20. Under the **Documentation** section, click on **Apiary** to associate the previously created API blueprint definition with the API portal page. Once clicked, a pop window will be open. From this, log on to Apiary and find the desired API definition and click on **Connect**:

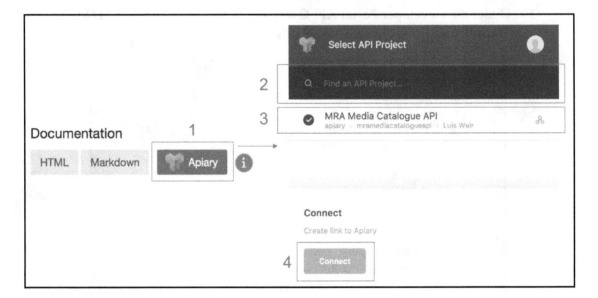

21. When the **Save Changes** button appears, click on it:

22. And finally publish the API portal page into the developer portal by clicking on
Publish to Portal:

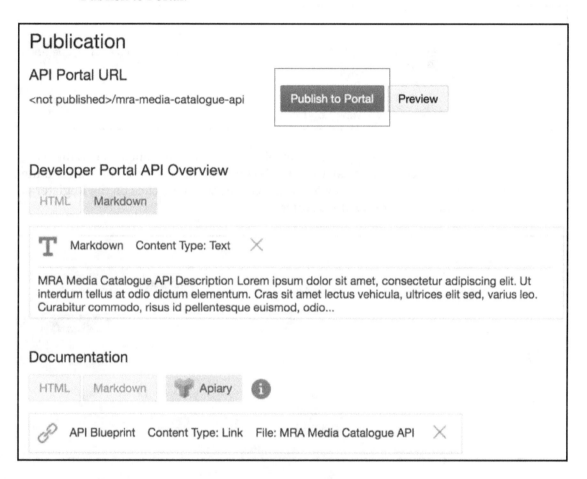

23. The full URL should now appear under **API Portal URL**:

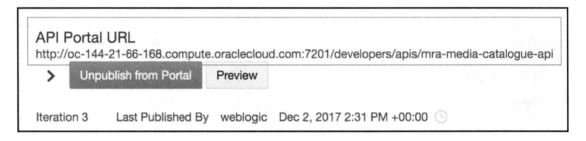

24. In order to ensure that application developers can find and subscribe to the API through the developer portal, the **APPDevelopers** role must first be assigned the **Register Grant**. To do this, switch to the **Grants** window, click on the **Register** tab, and finally, click on **Add Grantee**:

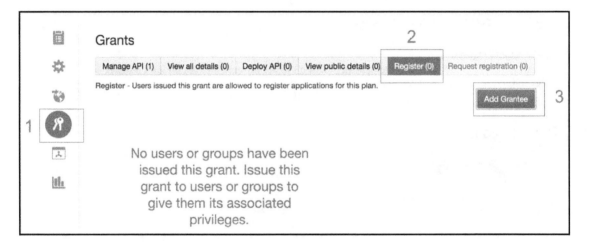

25. Once the **Add Grantee** window opens, Select the **APPDevelopers** group and click on **Add**:

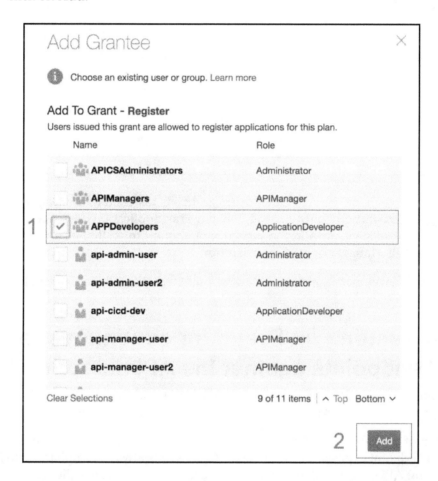

Note that the difference between roles in groups was briefly described in Chapter 1, *Platform Overview* but will be further explained in Chapter 5, *Platform Setup and Gateway Configuration*.

26. The **APPDevelopers** group should now appear as a **Grantee** on the **Register** tab:

> Note that if the **APPDevelopers** groups is assigned to the **Request Registration Grant** instead, whenever an application developer desires to subscribe to an API, the subscription request must first be approved by an **API Manager** or an **Administrator**.

27. Now developers can discover and subscribe to the API via the developer portal.

Step 8 – setting up Dredd for continuous testing of API endpoints against the API blueprint

Dredd is language-agnostic and open source command-line tool, created by Apiary for validating API definitions (API blueprint or Swagger) against API endpoints.

The last step of the API design-first process is to configure Dredd to continuously validate that an API endpoint exposed through the API gateway is always compliant with its corresponding API blueprint definition. The idea is to ensure that the client application code is not broken once an API policy is changed to point to a backend service once it has been built and deployed.

> Further information on Dredd is available from the following URL:
> `https://github.com/apiaryio/dredd`

Follow these steps to configure Dredd to continuously validate MRA's Media Catalogue API compliance against its corresponding API blueprint definition previously created in Apiary:

1. Open the developer portal URL and login with an application developer user account through the URL `https://<Oralce Public Cloud Host >:<Port>/Developers`:

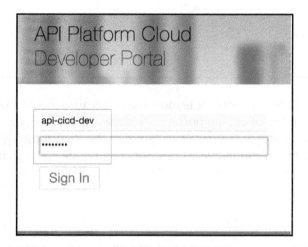

Note that a system account named **api-cicd-dev** was created with the application developer role. The account will be used to create client applications that subscribe to APIs in the context of Continuous Integration/Continuous Delivery; in this example, Dredd. In practice, any application developer account can be used. However, following this approach removes the dependency on individual accounts.

Further information on how to create user accounts is covered in `Chapter 5`, *Platform Setup and Gateway Configuration*.

2. The published **MRA Media Catalogue API** should be visible in the landing **API**s page. Click on it:

If the API is not visible it is most likely because the API wasn't either properly deployed, the portal URL wasn't published, or the APPDevelopers role wasn't assigned to the Register grant. Therefore, it would be recommended to carefully re-execute all steps in section *Step 7 – Publishing the API mock in Oracle API Platform CS Section*.

3. The **API Overview** page is presented by default, as shown in the following screenshot:

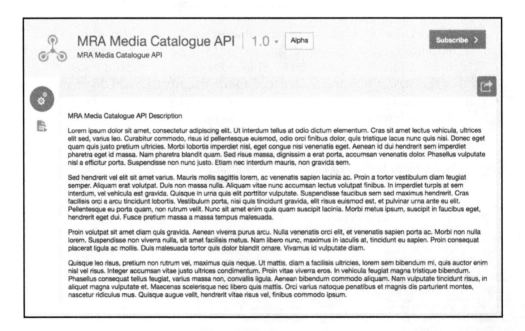

4. The API definition (the API blueprint document) can be accessed by clicking on the **Documentation** icon (**1**). To subscribe to the API, click on the **Subscribe** button (**2**) located at the upper-right hand side of the page:

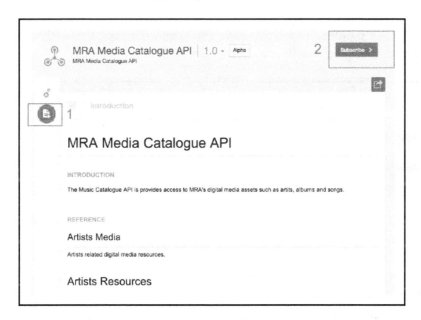

5. Note that subscriptions are made against client applications. As a client application hasn't yet been created, click on **Create New Application**:

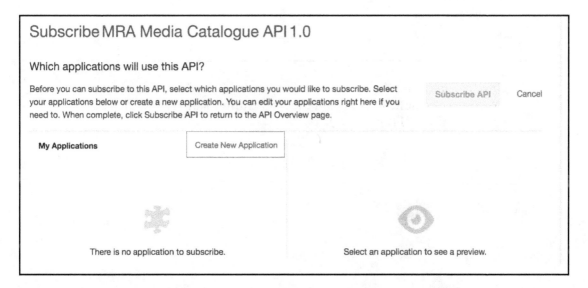

As described earlier in the chapter, a client application can be any application such as a mobile app, a web application, or even devices that consume APIs.

6. Type the details of the client application. In our example, the client application is Dredd. Once the details are typed, click on **Save**:

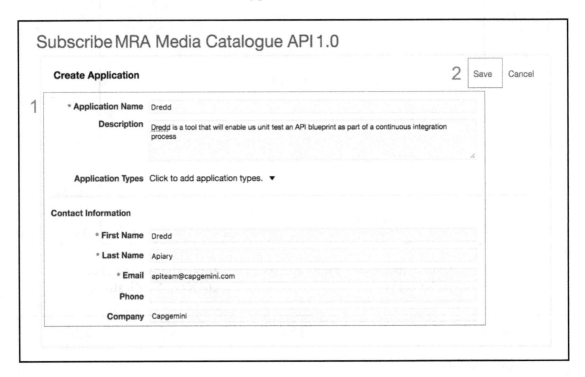

7. Once created, the subscriptions page opens and **Dredd** as a client application is selected by default. Take note of the **Application Key** (1) and then click on **Subscribe API** (2):

8. If the subscription is successful a similar page should appear:

If the subscription is unsuccessful, an error message will appear describing the cause and failure. However, this should not be the case if all steps described in this section were properly followed. In any case, should an error occur, take note of it and open a service request in `support.oracle.com` for further investigation by Oracle as it may refer to a product bug.

9. Install the Git command-line client in the machine that will be running Dredd.

The Git installer can be downloaded for any supported operating system from the site:
`https://git-scm.com/book/en/v2/Getting-Started-Installing-Git`

10. Set up a local working copy of the GitHub repository used by Apiary to push the API blueprint definition. This can be done with the following command:

git clone git@github.com:<username>/<repository name>.git

```
$git clone git@github.com:luisw19/MRAMediaCatalogueAPI.git
Cloning into 'MRAMediaCatalogueAPI'...
remote: Counting objects: 50, done.
remote: Compressing objects: 100% (47/47), done.
remote: Total 50 (delta 17), reused 3 (delta 0), pack-reused 0
Receiving objects: 100% (50/50), 7.52 KiB | 1.25 MiB/s, done.
Resolving deltas: 100% (17/17), done.
$ls MRAMediaCatalogueAPI/
README.md       apiary.apib
```

The following link provides an excellent guide on how to set up and use Git commands:
`http://rogerdudler.github.io/git-guide/`

11. Install **Node Package Manager** (**NPM**) in the same machine.

NPM installer can be downloaded for any supported operating system from the site:
`https://nodejs.org/en/download/`

12. Then install Dredd by running `npm install -g dredd`:

```
$npm install -g dredd
/usr/local/bin/dredd -> /usr/local/lib/node_modules/dredd/bin/dredd
+ dredd@4.9.1
added 6 packages and updated 15 packages in 34.85s
$
```

13. Go back to Apiary and open the MRA Media Catalogue API. Click on the **Tests** menu option, and then click on the **Tutorial** tab. Copy the entire command string displayed in the second bullet:

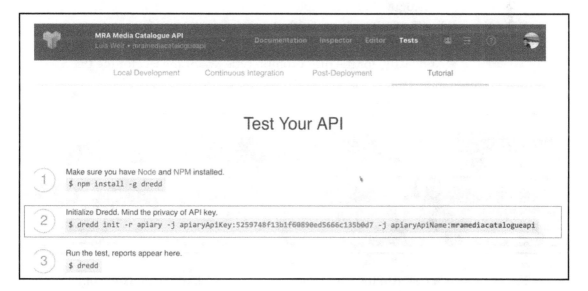

14. Paste the command string and run it in the same folder where the file `apiary.apib` resides (Git working copy created in previous steps) and hit *Enter*.

    As prompted, input the values as following:

    - In the first prompt, leave the default value for the `API description document` (as the command is being executed from the same folder where the file `apiary.apib` is available) and hit *Enter*
    - For the second prompt, enter no value for `Command to start API backend` and hit *Enter*
    - For the third prompt, `URL of tested API endpoint`, type the HTTP URL of the API gateway server where the MRA Media Catalogue API was deployed to
    - For the fourth prompt, select `nodejs` as the `Programming Language` and hit *Enter*
    - And lastly, for the fifth prompt, type `No` for the last for the `CircleCI Continuous Integration` option:

```
$dredd init -r apiary -j apiaryApiKey:5259748f13b1f60890ed5666c135b0d7 -j apiaryApiName:mramediacatalogueapi
? Location of the API description document apiary.apib
? Command to start API backend server e.g. (bundle exec rails server)
? URL of tested API endpoint http://oc-144-21-66-168.compute.oraclecloud.com:8001
? Programming language of hooks nodejs
? Dredd is best served with Continuous Integration. Create CircleCI config for Dredd? No

Configuration saved to dredd.yml

Run test now, with:

  $ dredd
```

15. To execute a test, run the command `dredd`. Notice that the outcome of the execution results in failures with no success. To find out why the test failed and to fix the problem, open a browser and enter the URL that appears immediately after the text `See results in Apiary at`:

```
complete: 0 passing, 6 failing, 0 errors, 0 skipped, 6 total
complete: Tests took 1680ms
complete: See results in Apiary at: https://app.apiary.io/mramediacatalogueapi/tests/run/1bc75c6e-cb20-43d9-b396-7
a28b666cb7e
```

16. Once the page is loaded, click on any of the failed tests (left-hand side of the page) and see the details. Notice that all tests failed with an **HTTP 401** status code, meaning **Unauthorized Access**. This is because Dredd is using the api-key value exactly as typed in the API definition. This value doesn't match the api-key generated in the API platform for the Dredd client application:

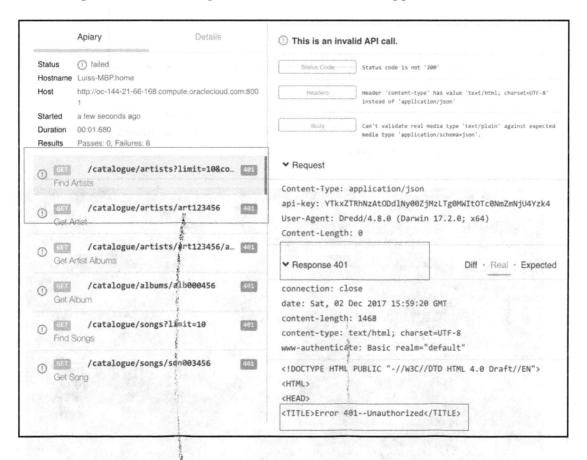

17. To fix this, go back to the Apiary **API Editor** and replace the value for all **api-key** properties with the key obtained in through the developer portal for the Dredd client application:

```
+ Headers

    api-key: ac108161-d3a5-427d-b814-ff977728395b
```

18. Now save the changes and push them to GitHub.
19. Pull the latest changes with the `git pull` command and verify all api-key values were in fact updated. This can be done with the command `git diff HEAD^ HEAD apiary.apib`:

```
$git pull
remote: Counting objects: 3, done.
remote: Compressing objects: 100% (3/3), done.
remote: Total 3 (delta 1), reused 0 (delta 0), pack-reused 0
Unpacking objects: 100% (3/3), done.
From https://github.com/luisw19/MRAMediaCatalogueAPI
   1db0be9..4844bca  master      -> origin/master
Updating 1db0be9..4844bca
Fast-forward
 apiary.apib | 30 ++++++++++++++++---------------
 1 file changed, 15 insertions(+), 15 deletions(-)
$git diff HEAD^ HEAD apiary.apib
diff --git a/apiary.apib b/apiary.apib
index 240ec7c..6523b3a 100644
--- a/apiary.apib
+++ b/apiary.apib
@@ -40,7 +40,7 @@ Returns all MRA Artists that match the specified criteria.

    + Headers

            api-key: 9d444d8c-1f30-492f-9d1f-c801089c2e65
+           api-key: ac108161-d3a5-427d-b814-ff977728395b

   + Response 200 (application/json)

@@ -57,7 +57,7 @@ Creates an Artist.

    + Headers

            api-key: 9d444d8c-1f30-492f-9d1f-c801089c2e65
+           api-key: ac108161-d3a5-427d-b814-ff977728395b
```

20. Run the command `dredd` again and notice that this time around all tests are passed with no errors:

```
$dredd
info: Configuration './dredd.yml' found, ignoring other arguments.
info: Beginning Dredd testing...
pass: GET (200) /catalogue/artists?limit=10&name=Oasis&country=GB duration: 2783ms
pass: POST (201) /catalogue/artists?limit=10&name=Oasis&country=GB duration: 587ms
pass: GET (200) /catalogue/artists/art123456 duration: 770ms
pass: PUT (200) /catalogue/artists/art123456 duration: 545ms
pass: GET (200) /catalogue/artists/art123456/albums duration: 661ms
pass: GET (200) /catalogue/albums?limit=10 duration: 540ms
pass: POST (201) /catalogue/albums?limit=10 duration: 873ms
pass: GET (200) /catalogue/albums/alb000456 duration: 504ms
pass: POST (200) /catalogue/albums/alb000456 duration: 572ms
pass: GET (200) /catalogue/songs?limit=10 duration: 549ms
pass: POST (201) /catalogue/songs?limit=10 duration: 556ms
pass: GET (200) /catalogue/songs/son003456 duration: 531ms
pass: POST (200) /catalogue/songs/son003456 duration: 551ms
complete: 13 passing, 0 failing, 0 errors, 0 skipped, 13 total
complete: Tests took 11339ms
complete: See results in Apiary at: https://app.apiary.io/mramediacatalogueapi/tests/run/384aa4ed-2b91-4e2c-b4a9
-ab608f930997
```

21. Now that Dredd has been properly configured, the command can be continuously executed from any Continuous Integration tool of choice such as Jenkins, Hudson, or something similar.

Summary

In this chapter, a comprehensive API design-first process was covered from beginning to end. The chapter started by describing MRA's business scenario driving the need for more efficient and leaner process for implementing APIs. It was therefore explained why and how an API design-first process could effectively help organizations, such as MRA, gain greater speed, agility, and efficiencies.

The chapter continued by describing all of the steps required to realize such process—from how to make use of conceptual concepts such as OMESA's single-purpose and multi-purpose APIs to decide on what type of API to adopt and how to define an API's domain model, to the creation of an API definition and an API mock in Apiary based on API blueprints and the **Markdown Syntax for Object Notation** (**MSON**), creation and publication of an API using the Oracle API Platform Cloud Service, and finally, the configuration of Dredd to verify API endpoints compliance with the API definition.

The next chapter will focus on explaining how the API blueprint definition created on this chapter can be used to build a fully decoupled service (also known as a Microservice).

4
Building and Running the Microservice

This chapter will build on the previous chapter with the next steps of the API design-first approach to build, package, deploy, and test the backend service. The backend service is built according to the principles of a **microservice** architectural style to allow single or multi-purpose APIs to be routed to an independent service that can be deployed and managed in isolation within the required context or function expected by the API. This means that the microservice can be hosted elsewhere than the API without the need to compromise on security, integrity, and re-usability, making it an ideal match to be used with APIP CS.

The chapter starts with explaining what a microservice is and what technology options there are to build a microservice. The chapter continues explaining how to build the Media Catalogue Microservice and how to package and deploy the microservice in a Docker container.

The chapter concludes with running **Dredd** to ensure the interface definition is aligned with the API design in Apiary.

What is a microservice?

Microservice is an architectural style of implementing independent services that can be deployed and managed in isolation. Microservices can be classified into three areas:

- Technical
- Architectural
- Organizational

Each classification is explained in the following table:

Technical	Architectural	Organizational
Runs in its own process	Bounded context	Teams organized around business capabilities
Faults are isolated into one location	Ideal match with API Management, that is, SOA 2.0	Products not projects
Is stateless	Polyglot, any preferred program language can be used	Culture of automation
Deploys independently	Single responsibility	Smaller teams and works well using Agile like Scrum
Scales independently	Choreographed	The responsibility is with the developer to build and run
Owns its data.	Smart end and dump pipes. This means that the client application doesn't need to worry about any complex transformations, just call it.	Decentralized governance with the goal to increase the overall quality and efficiency of the system due to clearer responsibilities.

The design principles of microservices are not that different from the traditional SOA architecture. The main differences are:

- SOA resources are typical shared across the same application service. The drawback of this monolith thinking is that high volumes of data for one SOA service impacts other SOA services with the risk of slowing or in some situation breaking the system.
- The deployment of SOA is dependent on a single platform and often other SOA components.
- The SOA interface (WSDL) and implementation code are strictly coupled. This means that an SOA interface could not be exposed other than in the environment it is running.

SOA is still very much a proven architecture and does not replace microservices. In fact, SOA can enhance microservices to act as the orchestration layer in the communication between microservices. However, in some scenarios, SOA is still a better fit than microservices. This is true for so-called **horizon integration** use cases. This is where SOA is used as the integration layer to integrate between SaaS Application or SaaS to on-premise applications. These type of integration components are built for a single purpose and can't be re-used between other applications. SOA products, like the Oracle SOA Suite or Oracle Integration Services (OIC), have out-of-the-box functionality like pre-built adapters to quickly integrate between applications either using SOA, REST, Files, B2B, or database type of integrations:

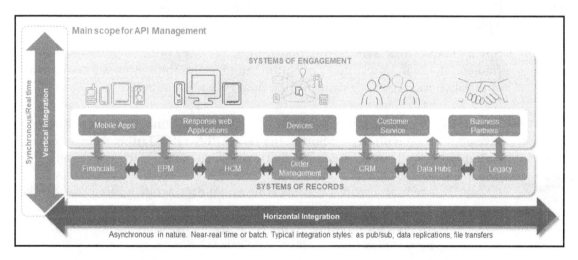

Microservices, at the other hand, are better suited for **vertical integration** use cases that contain re-usable business functions that are often consumed by more than one application like a mobile app or a web application as illustrated in the preceding figure.

For more information about microservices, see:
`http://www.oracle.com/technetwork/middleware/soasuite/learnmore/`
`oow2016-con7364-3237786.pdf`
`https://martinfowler.com/articles/microservices.html`

Understanding the technical requirements

MRA is keen to build the backend microservice to support the Media Catalogue API designed in Chapter 3, *Designing the API*. However, they struggle to determine what technology and storage to use that underpin the Media Catalogue Microservice. The reason is that microservices are **polymorph**, meaning that there are no strict rules of what programming language to use or what database to retrieve or store the data. MRA feels a bit like a kid in a candy shop and can't make up their mind. MRA have invested in researching the best options available and discovered that some programming languages are more established than others due to the level of support of frameworks and tooling available. Please see below some of the most popular languages, frameworks, and toolkits available, while writing this chapter:

- **Spring Framework with Spring Boot**: Spring is a very popular Java-based framework (including support of **Kotlin**) and has the ability to run a Java-based application in a container using Spring Boot with minimum effort (https://spring.io/).

- **Jakarta EE** (re-branded from Java EE): This is the traditional way of developing a Java application with the support of the **Java API for RESTful web services** and **Enterprise Java Bean** (**EJB**) to provide transactions, remove procedure calls, concurrency control, dependency injection, and access control for business objects. This re-branding has been recently announced while writing the chapter, so watch out for more information!

- **Akka**: It is a toolkit for building highly concurrent, distributed, and resilient message-driven applications for Java and Scala (https://akka.io/).

- **Node.js**: This is a more structured programming language than its ancestor, JavaScript, and has many supporting frameworks. ExpressJS is one of the most popular frameworks in building microservices (http://nodeframework.com/).

- **Python**: It has gained a lot of popularity in recent years and has some good web frameworks like Django (https://www.djangoproject.com/) and Flask (http://flask.pocoo.org/), which makes Python a good choice for building microservices.

- **Ruby on Rails:** Ruby is not as established as Java, but its main characteristic is the emphasis on RESTful applications. This means that it can easily be exposed as an API (http://rubyonrails.org/.

MRA decided to look at the experience of their current development team and concluded that most have strong JavaScript experience and some members of the team have built REST services using Node.js. This will save time and money, because there is less investment required in recruiting new people or training existing people. This means that there are no radical changes needed to the dynamics of the team to ensure people are kept motivated.

MRA also found that Node.js is asynchronous as such ensuring that the code is non-blocking and thread safe and an ideal match for building a microservice that can scale easier without threads, which means that more load can be injected into a single instance of a microservice.

MongoDB is selected as the database, because Node.js has excellent support in connecting with MongoDB with the help of the **Mongoose** plugin that supports the Node.js asynchronous pattern philosophy. This is with the fact that a NoSQL paradigm is better equipped in isolating the data than a traditional relational database where data is dependent with the use of foreign keys.

This chapter continues explaining the build of the Media Catalogue Microservice using Node.js, and MongoDB and NoSQL, as the database.

Building the Microservice

The next step in the API design-first approach is to build the Media Catalogue Microservice. This follows from the **Design** and **Try** phases as explained in Chapter 3, *Designing the API*. The aim of the **Design** and **Try** phases is to design and test the API, using Apiary, repeatedly until the API Blueprint is approved between the client and API designer. The API Blueprint is then used as a starting point to build the microservice:

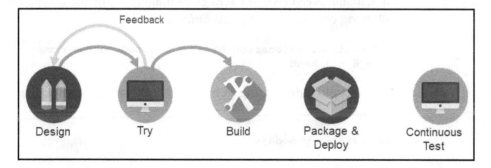

The built, test, and validation of the Media Catalogue Microservice is explained in the following steps:

1. Install Node.js and MongoDB
2. Create the skeleton of the Media Catalogue Microservice
3. Define the structure of the Media Catalogue Microservice
4. Configure the Media Catalogue Microservice
5. Define the data entity
6. Code the interaction with the database
7. Define the controller function
8. Route the incoming request to the new controller function
9. Test the Microservice
10. Package and deploy the Microservice
11. Update the API endpoint and re-test using Dredd

Step 1 – install Node.js and MongoDB

Red Hat Linux 7 is used as the operating system to install Node.js and MongoDB. The working environment assumes that yum is installed. For more information on how to install yum, look at the Red Hat documentation at `https://access.redhat.com/documentation/en-us/red_hat_enterprise_linux/7/html/system_administrators_guide/ch-yum`.

Refer to the steps below to install the required software components:

1. Open a Terminal and install Node.js:

    1. First, install **NPM (Node Package Manager)** using `curl`; type the following command and press *Enter*:

    ```
    curl --silent --location https://rpm.nodesource.com/
    setup_6.x | bash
    ```

    2. Next, install Node.js using yum; type the following command and press *Enter*:

    ```
    yum install -y nodejs
    ```

3. Next, install the development tool, **gcc-c++**. This will install software from other sources using the required function, toolset to compile, and debug code. To install gcc-c++, type the following command and press *Enter*:

```
yum install -y gcc-c++ make
```

4. Verify that both Node.js and NPM are installed correctly:

```
node -version [Enter]
npm -version [Enter]
```

2. Next, install MongoDB:

1. First create a file in the directory /etc/yum.repos.d/mongodb-org-3.6.repo to ensure MongoDB can be installed using yum. The file should contain the following:

```
[mongodb-org-3.6]
name=MongoDB Repository
baseurl=https://repo.mongodb.org/yum/
redhat/$releasever/mongodb-org/3.6/x86_64/
gpgcheck=0
enabled=1
```

2. After the file has been created type the following command to install MongoDB:

```
sudo yum install -y mongodb-org
```

3. After the installation is finished start MongoDB, type the following command:

```
sudo service mongod start
```

4. Check whenever the database has been successfully started by verifying the logs:

```
/var/log/mongodb/mongod.log
```

5. Next, create the Catalogue database, type the following command:

```
use catalogue_db
```

6. Check that the catalogue database is created by typing the following command:

```
show dbs
```

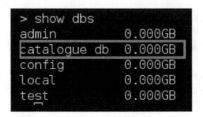

Step 2 – create the skeleton of the Media Catalogue Microservice

The next step is to create the Media Catalogue Microservice Node.js and related libraries:

1. Create a new folder with name media_catalogue_service and within the folder run:

```
npm init
```

This will prompt the user to provide the following information:

- **Name**: Leave the default media_catalogue_service and press *Enter*.
- **Version**: Leave the default 1.0.0 and press *Enter*.
- **Description**: Type The Media Catalogue Service is created for the MRA example use case that supports chapter 4 Building and running the Microservice of the book Implementing Oracle API Platform Cloud Service.
- **Entry point**: Type server.js, which includes the main logic that is called to run the Node.js microservice.
- **Test command**: This field can be populated with the command line to run a test program, like **Mocha**, **Ava**, or **Jest** that is executed when the command npm test is run. This can be left empty and press *Enter*. This will populate the field with a default placeholder that prints an error message.

- **Git repository**: Type `https://github.com/APIPlatform-Book/APIPlatform.git` to reference where the code can be found in Git and press *Enter*.
- **Keywords**: This helps people to discover the package as it's listed in npm search. This can be left empty as such press *Enter*.
- **Author**: In this example `Sander Rensen` and press *Enter*.
- **License**: Leave the default ISC and press *Enter*. ISC is a permissive free software license as such people have permission to use, copy, modify, and/or distribute the microservice for any purpose or without fee is hereby granted, provided that the copyright notice (year and owner) and the ISC permission notice appear in all copies.

The last prompt asks the user to confirm that the values are OK with either a `Yes` or `No`. Confirm with `Yes` as illustrated in the following screenshot. The `package.json` file has been created successfully:

2. Next, install the libraries the code is dependent on. These need to be installed in the same folder location as the `package.json` file.

    1. Install the web framework, Express, to create RESTful applications (`https://www.npmjs.com/package/express`):

    ```
    npm install --save express
    ```

2. Install Mongoose to interact with MongoDB (`http://mongoosejs.com/`):

```
npm install --save mongoose
```

3. Install `body-parser` for parsing incoming request bodies as JSON (`https://www.npmjs.com/package/body-parser`):

```
npm install --save body-parser
```

4. Install halson to support HATEOAS (`https://www.npmjs.com/package/halson`):

```
npm install --save halson
```

The installed libraries will show as dependencies in the `package.json` file.

Step 3 – define the structure of the Media Catalogue Microservice

The Media Catalogue Microservice is structured as illustrated in the following diagram:

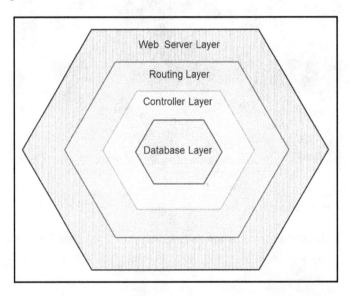

- **Web Server Layer**: This is the layer that pieces the Microservice together to ensure it runs as expected
- **Routing Layer**: This is responsible for routing the incoming request that is called on a specific URI to the correct controller class
- **Controller Layer**: This is responsible for translating the incoming request, controlling the invocation, and ensuring that the correct result is returned
- **Database Layer**: This is the tier that communicates with the database-in our case MongoDB

Step 4 – configure the Media Catalogue Microservice

Before coding the main functionality, let's create a simple *hello world* message to structure the Media Catalogue Microservice as per the four layers explained in the previous step. The first step is to create the folders and files required, as shown in the following diagram:

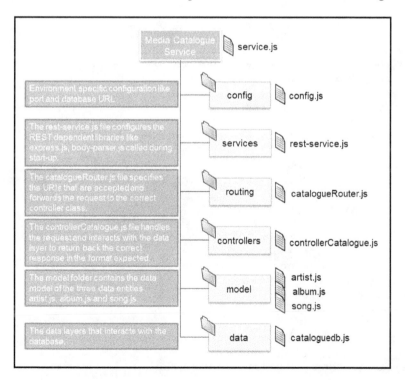

1. Open the `config.js` file and update to include the port number and database URL as an environment property, as shown in the following code block:

```
module.exports = {
  server: {
    port: process.env.PORT || 3000
  }, db: {
    connectString: process.env.MONGODB_URI ||
    "mongodb://localhost:27017/catalogue_db"
  }
};
```

The port is inherited from the environment variable `process.env.PORT` that is set, otherwise the default port `3000` is used.

2. The next step is to set the context of the Media Catalogue Microservice in the `rest-server.js`. The purpose is to configure the foundations on which the Media Catalogue Microservice will be built, that is, REST. The code is shown in the following code block including comments:

```
var express = require('express');
var bodyParser = require('body-parser');
function start(config, router) {
  //declare a variable app that inherit the ....functions
  //available in express.
  var app = express();
  //the app is specified to accept JSON as the ....payload
  app.use(bodyParser.json());
  //each request is forwarded to the router class ....when
  //called on http(s)//[Host]:[Port]/
  app.use("/", router);
  //the application listens on the server with port ....specified
  //in the config file
  var server = app.listen(config.server.port);
}
//connect to the Mongo DB
mongoose.Promise = global.Promise;
var promise = mongoose.connect(config.db.connectString, {
  useMongoClient: true,
}).catch(function(error) {
  console.log(error);
});
module.exports.start = start;
```

The start function will be loaded during startup.

3. Next, is to configure the `server.js` file. This file is initiated during startup and loads the context, that is, the files created considering the four layers. The code is shown as follows:

```
var server = require("./services/rest-server.js");
var config = require("./config/config.js");
var data = require("./data/cataloguedb.js");
var controller = require("./controllers/catalogueController.js");
var router = require("./routing/catalogueRouter.js");

var catalogueController = controller(data);
var catalogueRouter = router(catalogueController);

server.start(config, catalogueRouter);
```

Notice that the files related to each layer are defined in a variable. The `catalogueController` variable contains the value of the `controller` variable, that defines the controller layer, that has an input parameter of value data. This binds the controller and the data layer, with the purpose that both layers can communicate with one and the other.

The `catalogueController` variable is then passed in as an input parameter for the router layer defined as the variable, `catalogueRouter`. This binds the routing layer with the controller layer.

The server is then started with the config file and the `catalogueRouter` as the input parameters.

4. Next, define a `controller` function in the `CatalogueController.js` file that will return the *hello world* message as shown in the following code snippet:

```
module.exports = function (data) {
  var controller = {};
  controller.getArtist = function (request, response) {
    message = {"message": "hello world"};
    response.send(message);
  };
  return controller;
}
```

5. The last step is to define the URI to route the request to the correct controller function in the `controllerRouter.js` file, like shown as follows:

```
const express = require('express');
module.exports = function (catalogueController) {
  var router = express.Router();
  router.route('/catalogue/artists/:artistId')
  .get(catalogueController.getArtist)
  return router;
};
```

6. The configuration is completed. To test run the Media Catalogue Microservice, open a browser and type in the following URL: `http://localhost:3000/catalogue/artists/{artist id}`. The result is the message **hello world** as illustrated:

The Media Catalogue Microservice is configured and ready to start coding the main functionality, starting with the database layer.

Step 5 – define the data entity

The build of the Media Catalogue Microservice is explained with defining the data model of what data needs to be stored in the database. There are three entities: Artists, Albums, and Songs with attributes Genres and Video Clips, as explained in `Chapter 3`, *Designing the API*.

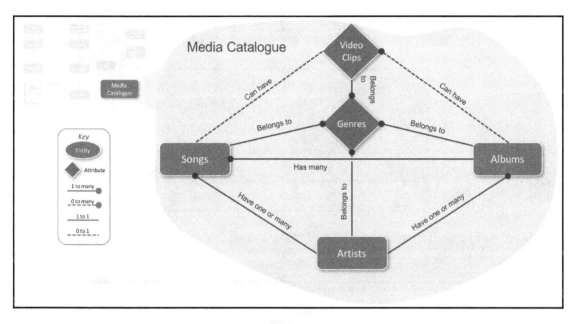

MRA's Media Catalogue Microservice Bounded Context

The combination of Artists, Albums, and Songs (data model) is used by the REST API to map incoming request and response messages. The API design is used as a starting point to define the data model. The creation of the data model is explained by modelling the **Get Artist URI**.

The API design is not a direct representation of the data model, as in many situations there are additional data items that need to be stored, which are not provided by the API, like the creation and updated date or any additional transformation that has an impact on how the data is being processed.

The **Get Artist** in Apiary can be found below. There is no request body as the artist ID is passed in the URI. The response returned is the `Artist` object:

```
### Get Artist [GET]
Returns the details for a specific Artist such as bio and Albums.

+ Request (text/plain)

    + Headers

            api-key: ac108161-d3a5-427d-b814-ff977728395b

+ Response 200 (application/json)

    + Attributes (Artist)
```

The `Artist` object is defined using MSON in Apiary with a reference to `Album` and the `Album` to `Song` object:

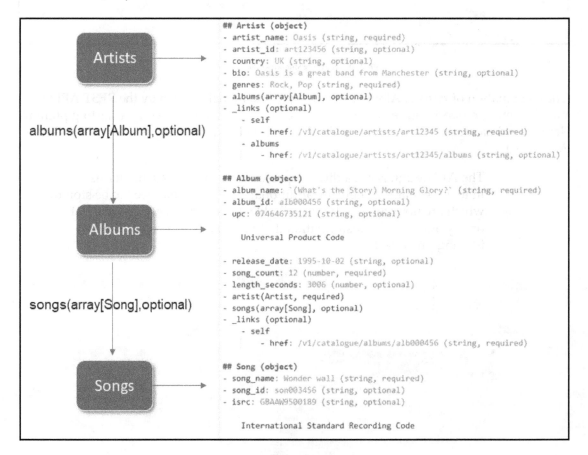

Artist (object)
- artist_name: Oasis (string, required)
- artist_id: art123456 (string, optional)
- country: UK (string, optional)
- bio: Oasis is a great band from Manchester (string, optional)
- genres: Rock, Pop (string, required)
- albums(array[Album], optional)
- _links (optional)
    - self
        - href: /v1/catalogue/artists/art12345 (string, required)
    - albums
        - href: /v1/catalogue/artists/art12345/albums (string, optional)

Album (object)
- album_name: `(What's the Story) Morning Glory?` (string, required)
- album_id: alb000456 (string, optional)
- upc: 074646735121 (string, optional)

    Universal Product Code

- release_date: 1995-10-02 (string, optional)
- song_count: 12 (number, required)
- length_seconds: 3006 (number, optional)
- artist(Artist, required)
- songs(array[Song], optional)
- _links (optional)
    - self
        - href: /v1/catalogue/albums/alb000456 (string, required)

Song (object)
- song_name: Wonder wall (string, required)
- song_id: son003456 (string, optional)
- isrc: GBAAW9500189 (string, optional)

    International Standard Recording Code

Artists

albums(array[Album],optional)

Albums

songs(array[Song],optional)

Songs

The `Song` entity is modeled first as this has no dependency with other data objects:

1. Open the `model` folder in any preferred IDE, like IntelliJ IDEA, and create the `song.js` file as illustrated:

2. Open the `song.js` file and include the Mongoose library, previously installed as explained in *Step 2*, that is used to connect with the MongoDB from Node.js:

```
var mongoose = require("mongoose");
```

3. Next, create the **DDL (Data Definition Language)**, starting with the Song schema and attributes defined in the API design. The Song schema is exported to ensure the schema is publicly available. The following code shows the schema and attributes created for the Song entity:

```
var mongoose = require("mongoose");
// create instance of Schema
var schema = mongoose.Schema;
// create schema: more info
// on http://mongoosejs.com/docs/schematypes.html
var songSchema = new schema({
  song_name: String,
  song_id: String,
  isrc: String, release_date: String,
  audio: {
    "format": String,
    "lenght_seconds": Number
  },
  video: {
    "format": String,
    "lenght_seconds": Number
  }
});
module.exports = mongoose.model('Song', songSchema);
```

Notice that the **HATEOAS (Hypermedia as the Engine of Application State)** links are not defined in the data model as these are dynamically constructed in the Controller layer as part of the response. HATEOAS is used to provide means for a client application to navigate through the site's REST interface dynamically by providing links with the response payload. This provides more flexibility as client applications don't need to construct the URI and parameters.

4. The previous step is repeated to create the schema and attributes for the Album entity:

```
var mongoose = require("mongoose");

// create instance of Schema
var schema = mongoose.Schema;

// create schema: more info
// on http://mongoosejs.com/docs/schematypes.html
var albumSchema = new schema(
{
  album_id: String,
```

```
  album_name: String,
  upc: String,
  release_date: String,
  song_count: Number,
  length_seconds: Number,
  artist_name: String,
  songs: [{ type: schema.Types.ObjectId, ref: 'Song' }]
});

module.exports = mongoose.model('Album',albumSchema);
```

5. Next, the `Artist` data object is created:

```
var mongoose = require("mongoose");

// create instance of Schema
var schema = mongoose.Schema;

// create schema: more info
// on http://mongoosejs.com/docs/schematypes.html
var artistSchema = new schema(
{
  artist_id: String,
  artist_name: String,
  country: String,
  bio: String,
  genres: String,
  albums: [{ type: schema.Types.ObjectId, ref: 'Album' }]
});

module.exports = mongoose.model('Artist',artistSchema);
```

Notice that the `Album` schema is referring to the `Song` schema of type `ObjectId`. The `ObjectId` type in MongoDB is the unique identifier for each record created. This is similar to a primary key in a relational database. The Artist refers to the Album using the `ObjectId`.

There are no strict rules on how to store the data in a NoSQL database, unlike traditional relational databases. This means that `Album` can also be put as an array inside the `Artist` object and the `Song` as an array inside the `Album` object. The main advantage of this is that only one query is required to return the data. The disadvantage is that you can't access the embedded data objects as a standalone entity like you can with objects referenced using the `ObjectId`.

Step 6 – code the interaction with the database

After completing the schemas the database logic can be incorporated to interact with MongoDB:

1. Open the file `cataloguedb.js` in the `data` folder. Import the `Artist`, `Album`, and `Song` schemas:

```
var Artist = require("../model/artist.js");
var Album = require("../model/album.js");
var Song = require("../model/song.js");
```

2. Next, the `getArtist` function is coded and exported to be used by the Controller logic. The code is shown in the following code block:

```
module.exports.getArtist = function (request, response) {
  var query = Artist.find({"artist_id" : request},
    {'_id' : 0}).populate({
        "path": "albums",
        "model": "Album",
        "populate": {
          path: 'songs',
          model: "Song"
        }
    })

  query.exec(function (err, artist) {
    var object = [];
    // Mongo command to fetch all data from collection.
    if(err) {
      message = {"code" : "ERR01","message"
        : "Unexpected error. " + err};
      //For the purpose of the book any errors
      //are currently not logged to a separate file.
      console.log(message);
      response(message);
```

```
  } else {
  //return a warning code in case no record can be found.
    if (artist.toString() != []){
      response(artist);
    } else {
      message = {"code" : "WRN01","message"
        : "The artist does not exist."};
      response(message);
    }
  }
});
}
```

The query is constructed using the `find` operation in MongoDB with the addition of the `populate` function. The `populate` function ensures that the attributes for the `Albums` and `Songs` are automatically returned using the reference `ObjectId`. This saves time as no separate queries are required to retrieve the album or song. The query is then executed using the `query.exec` method and the response is returned, either it was successful or has failed.

Step 7 – define the controller function

In this step the `controller` function is created that calls the `getArtist` in the data layer and returns the response using REST:

1. Open the controller file `catalogueController.js`, create a new function `getArtist`, and implement the logic to call the `getArtist` as part of the data layer and return the correct response. Please see a snapshot of the following code:

```
controller.getArtist = function (request, response) {
  data.getArtist(request.params.artistId, function(result){
    var index;
    var albums;
    try{
      //Loop through each album and songs to include
      //HAL and to capture the fields required in the JSON
      //response to the Client i.e. the MongoDB document
      //version field is not returned.
      for(index = 0; index < result[0].albums.length; ++index){ }
      var resource = halson({
        artist_name: result[0].artist_name,
        artist_id: result[0].artist_id,
        country: result[0].country,
        bio: result[0].bio,
```

```
              'albums': album
          })
          .addLink('self', '/v1/catalogue/artists/' +
            result[0].artist_id)
          .addLink('albums', '/v1/catalogue/artists/' +
            result[0].artist_id + '/albums')
          .addLink('genres', '/v1/catalogue/artists/' +
            result[0].artist_id + '/genres')
          response.header("Content-Type", "application/json");
          response.status(200);
          response.send(JSON.stringify(resource));
      } catch(e) {
          //For the purpose of the book any errors are
          //currently not logged to a file.
          if (result.code.match(/WRN.*/)) {
            response.status(400);
            response.send(result);
          } else if (result.code.match(/ERR.*/)) {
            response.status(500);
            var message = responseMessage(result.code,
              "Unexpected error occurred. Please contact
              your system administrator.");
            response.send(result);
          }
      }
    });
  }
```

The logic within the for loop is collapsed so the code snippet is not too large.
The `for` loop contains the logic to include the HATEOAS links, using HAL, for
each album and song within the album. Halson is used to construct the
HATEOAS links at runtime. The code after the loop creates a new Halson
resource, which includes the Album, with the Song, and then the resource for the
Artist is defined. The result is returned with a status code `200` with the payload
including HATEOAS. Errors are captured in the `catch` branch to return a proper
HTTP code and message.

Step 8 – route the incoming request to the new controller function

The last step before testing our logic is to route the incoming request to the new controller function.

1. Open the `catalogueRouter.js` file and include the routing logic shown as follows:

```
const express = require('express');
module.exports = function (catalogueController) {
  var router = express.Router();
  router.route('/catalogue/artists/:artistId')
  .get(catalogueController.getArtist)
  return router;
};
```

The function is called from the `server.js` file passing the `catalogueController` as the input object as shown in a previous step. The `getArtist` controller function is then added to the `get()` method that will forward the request accordingly using the `Router()` method that is available within Express.

These conclude the steps required to build the microservice.

Step 9 – test the microservice

The next step is to test the microservice in the IDE that is explained using Postman.

Postman is a client REST application to create and run tests against REST endpoints. However, Postman does not have the capability to test isolated pieces of code. Unit testing will need to be done with a proper testing framework like Mocha. For more information, see `https://mochajs.org`.

1. Open Postman and create a new collection called `MediaCatalogue` and add a new request called **Retrieve Artist Information**:

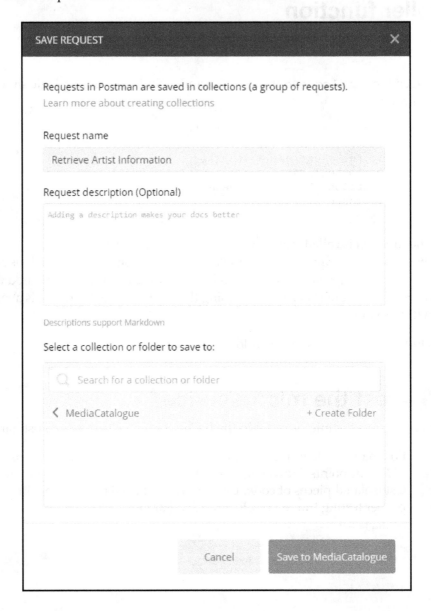

2. Open the request **Retrieve Artist Information** and update in the box, next to the HTTP Verb, the URL with value
   `http://localhost:3000/catalogue/artists/art123456`.
   The `art123456` is the artist ID that is provided as a parameter, which has been precreated in the database.
3. Select in the drop-down list the http verb **GET** and click on the button **Send**. The response is returned with a HTTP 200 and the Artist payload as illustrated:

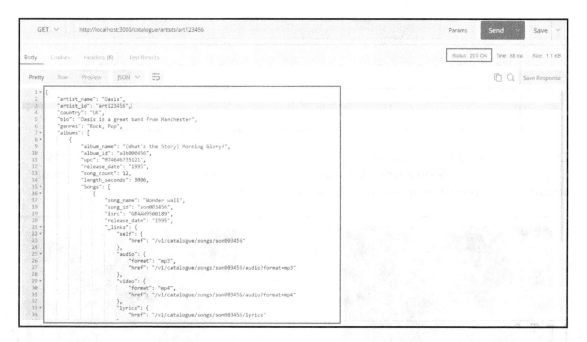

Chapter 6, *Defining Policies for APIs* will explain further testing of the Media Catalogue Microservice and how to incorporate this as part of the CI/CD process.

> It's a good practice to start testing each developed URI with Apiary by running Dredd instead of doing this at the end. This means that step 11, that explains running Dredd, is repeated several times during the development of the URIs.

Step 10 – package and deploy the microservice

The Media Catalogue Microservice is ready to be packaged and deployed to a Docker container that can be called by the API gateway. The MongoDB will be separated and included into its own Docker container, so this can scale independently:

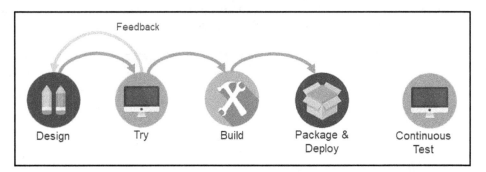

Docker has gained enormous popularity in the last couple of years. The reason is that a Docker container runs on a single OS process and as such is far more efficient in terms of resource allocation in comparison with its VM counterpart:

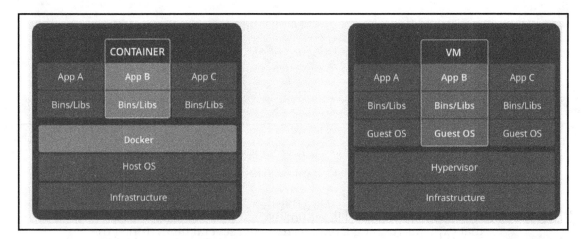

Containers	Virtual Machines
Containers are an abstraction at the app layer that packages code and dependencies together. Multiple containers can run on the same machine and share the OS kernel with other containers, each running as isolated processes in user space. Containers take up less space than VMs (container images are typically tens of MBs in size), and start almost instantly.	Virtual machines (VMs) are an abstraction of physical hardware turning one server into many servers. The hypervisor allows multiple VMs to run on a single machine. Each VM includes a full copy of an operating system, one or more apps, necessary binaries and libraries-taking up tens of GBs. VMs can also be slow to boot.

Source: `https://www.docker.com`.

The other benefit is that multiple containers can be run to provide more flexibility for testing teams to compare different releases and coding issues can be better isolated to debug problems without environment dependencies.

The next steps explain the install and run of containers for the MRA Media Catalogue Microservice with the assumption that Docker and Docker-Compose are installed, for more information, see `https://docs.docker.com/install/` and `https://docs.docker.com/compose/install/`.

After successful installation ensure Docker is started with the following command:

```
sudo systemctl start docker
```

Docker-Compose is a tool that manages the dependencies and links between containers.

Coupling of containers needs to be done with care and consideration to prevent creating a new form of monolith that will impact the scalability and re-use of containers. In the situation that a microservice is dependent on another microservice and both are running in their own containers the question is whether the correct bounded context has been designed or whether both needs to be run in the same container.

The creation of a Docker image is built from a series of layers.

The Docker layers are explained in the Docker documentation: `https://docs.docker.com/storage/storagedriver/#images-and-layers`.

The following is quoted from the Docker documentation:
A Docker image is built up from a series of layers. Each layer represents an instruction in the image's Dockerfile. Each layer except the very last one is read-only. Consider the following Dockerfile:

```
FROM ubuntu:15.04
COPY . /app
RUN make /app
CMD python /app/app.py
```

This Dockerfile contains four commands, each of which creates a layer. The FROM statement starts out by creating a layer from the Ubuntu:15.04 image. The COPY command adds some files from your Docker client's current directory. The RUN command builds your application using the make command. Finally, CMD specifies what command to run within the container.

The MRA Media Catalogue Microservice will be run in two containers. As such, two images are required, one to run the Node.js Media Catalogue Microservice application and one for running the Mongo database.

The first step is to create a Dockerfile that contains a list of instructions that will install and run the container for the Media Catalogue Service.

1. Create a file called Dockerfile, using any text editor, in the root of the project folder and include the following:

```
FROM node:latest
RUN mkdir -p /usr/src/app
WORKDIR /usr/src/app
COPY package.json /usr/src/app/
RUN npm install
COPY . /usr/src/app
EXPOSE 3000
CMD ["npm", "start"]
```

FROM is used to specify what version of Node needs to be installed. The option `latest` means that the newest available version of Node is going to be installed. The first RUN command ensures that the directory /user/src/app is created, which is then set as the WORKDIR in where the package.json file is copied using COPY. The second RUN command is then used to install all the dependencies in the package.json file using NPM. The code of the Media Catalogue Microservice is copied to the working directory. The EXPOSE is then used to bind the Node application to run on port 3000. The CMD command is used to start the node application.

2. Create a file called dockerignore in the root directory where the Dockerfile is located. Edit the file and include any folders or files that don't need to be copied across as follows:

```
node_modules
npm-debug.log
```

The folder node_modules can be ignored as Docker will install the required modules and the npm-debug.log file is not required by the microservice. This will reduce the size of the Docker container.

3. Next, create a **Mongo image**. This could be created from scratch, but there are preconfigured images available that will save time and effort. These can be downloaded from the Docker Hub here https://hub.docker.com/_/mongo/.

4. Next, create a new file called docker-compose.yaml in the root folder of the Media Catalogue Microservice. This file is required by Docker-Compose to understand the dependencies and links between the Media Catalogue Microservice and the MongoDB container. The yaml file is specified as follows:

```
version: "2"
services:
  catalogue:
    build: .
    depends_on:
      - mongodb
    ports:
      - "3000:3000"
    links:
      - mongodb
  mongodb:
    image: mongo:3.6.2
```

```
volumes:
  - ./data:/data/db
ports:
  - "27017:27017"
```

The `services` tag defines the two containers that need to be built, one that is going to be called `catalogue` and the other `mongodb`. The catalogue service is configured with the options:

- `build`: This refers to the location of the Dockerfile to build the container.
- `depends_on`: This specifies the dependency with the MongoDB container. This means that the MongoDB image will be built first.
- `ports`: This is used to map the host machine port to the container.
- `links`: This enables communication between the two containers.

The MongoDB service is configured as followed:

- `image`: This related to an existing image in Docker Hub that will be used to create the container.
- `volumes`: This maps the local directory on your host machine to the directory of the container. The advantage of this feature is that no data will be lost if the container is removed.
- `ports`: This is used to map the host machine port to the container.

The Dockerfile to build the catalogue container can also be uploaded to Docker Hub or your local hub and then referenced using the image tag as shown for the MongoDB image.

5. It's important to realize that the Node.js container running the Media Catalogue Microservice is linked to the MongoDB container named `mongodb`. This means that the MongoDB database can only be accessed on the host MongoDB, as such the `config.js` file in the microservice needs to be updated to reflect this as shown in the following code block:

```
module.exports = {
  server: {
    port: process.env.PORT || 3000
  },
```

```
db: {
  connectString: process.env.MONGODB_URI ||
  "mongodb://mongodb:27017/catalogue_db"
}
};
```

6. Next, start Docker if not already done, with the following command:

```
sudo systemctl start docker
```

7. Navigate to the root folder of the Media Catalogue Microservice where the Dockerfile is located and type the following command to install and run the Node.js and MongoDB container:

```
docker-compose up -d
```

8. Re-test with Postman to confirm that the containers are up and running.

Step 11 – updating the API endpoint and re-test using Dredd

The API endpoint of the MRA Media Catalogue Microservice created in Chapter 3, *Designing the API* needs to be updated from Apiary to the newly implemented Media Catalogue Microservice that runs in a Docker container. The last step is to re-run Dredd to ensure that the service implementation matched with the API design in Apiary. This is the last step in the API design-first approach:

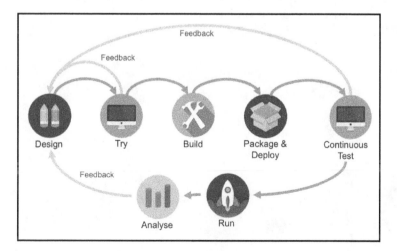

The steps are as follows:

1. Log in to APIP CS, click on the **APIs** tab, and open the MRA Media Catalogue API:

2. In the API, click on **Service Request** and update the Apiary URL to the URL of where the Docker container is running and click on **Apply**:

The API gateway needs to have network access to the Docker container. This might need additional configuration in the network to allow access through web gateways, firewalls, and proxies.

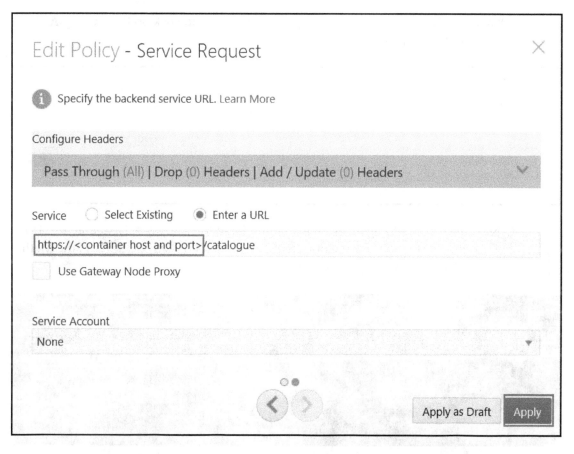

A good practice is to select the option **Select Existing** service instead of the option **Enter a URL**. The reason is that Oracle will soon support multiple endpoints per service to be able to map endpoints to different environments (that is, development and test). The creation and configuration of the service is explained in more detail in Chapter 6, *Defining Policies for APIs*.

3. Save the changes, click on the **Deployments** tab, and click on the **Deploy API** button to deploy the API to the gateway:

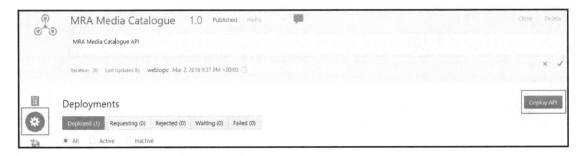

4. Next, re-run Dredd again as explained in detail in Chapter 3, *Designing the API*. This time ensure that for the option URL of tested API endpoint, the Media API URL gateway URL is entered:

5. To execute a test, run the command dredd. The outcome of the execution is 11 failures and 3 passed tests. The reason is that at this point only the GET Artist and Create Artist, Album and Song are implemented. The other URIs are going to be made available as the MRA development team are still implementing these in the parallel. This means that 4 tests should have passed. However, notice that the GET Artist failed:

```
[root@docker MRAMediaCatalogueAPI]# dredd
info: Configuration './dredd.yml' found, ignoring other arguments.
info: Beginning Dredd testing...
fail: GET (200) /catalogue/artists?limit=10&name=Oasis&country=GB duration: 99ms
pass: POST (201) /catalogue/artists?limit=10&name=Oasis&country=GB duration: 31ms
fail: GET (200) /catalogue/artists/art123456 duration: 1542ms
fail: PUT (200) /catalogue/artists/art123456 duration: 10ms
fail: GET (200) /catalogue/artists/art123456/albums duration: 13ms
fail: GET (200) /catalogue/albums?limit=10 duration: 15ms
pass: POST (201) /catalogue/albums?limit=10 duration: 18ms
fail: GET (200) /catalogue/albums/alb000456 duration: 14ms
fail: POST (200) /catalogue/albums/alb000456 duration: 21ms
fail: GET (200) /catalogue/songs?limit=10 duration: 20ms
pass: POST (201) /catalogue/songs?limit=10 duration: 40ms
fail: GET (200) /catalogue/songs/son003456 duration: 38ms
fail: POST (200) /catalogue/songs/son003456 duration: 12ms
fail: POST (201) /catalogue/songs/son003456/media duration: 8ms
```

6. To find out why the test failed and fix the problem, open a browser and enter the URL that appears immediately after the text See results in Apiary at:

```
complete: 3 passing, 11 failing, 0 errors, 0 skipped, 14 total
complete: Tests took 2058ms
complete: See results in Apiary at: https://app.apiary.io/mramediacatalogueapi/tests/run/f5e17cb5-ce41-467a-9ac1-19865ef522a6
[root@docker MRAMediaCatalogueAPI]#
```

7. Once the page is loaded, click on the **GET Artist** URI and see the details. Notice that the genres field is missing in the response as shown in the following screenshot:

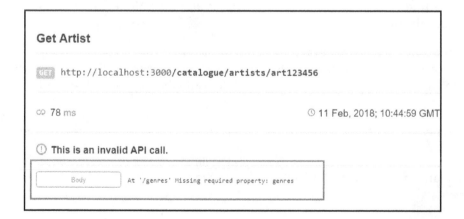

8. Exploring the code confirms that the genres field has not been implemented to be returned as part of the response in the `controllerCatalogue.js` file. Fix the code to include the genres field as part of the response and re-run Dredd. Notice that this time all 4 URIs are successfully passed:

```
[root@docker MRAMediaCatalogueAPI]# dredd
info: Configuration './dredd.yml' found, ignoring other arguments.
info: Beginning Dredd testing...
fail: GET (200) /catalogue/artists?limit=10&name=Oasis&country=GB duration: 57ms
pass: POST (201) /catalogue/artists?limit=10&name=Oasis&country=GB duration: 19ms
pass: GET (200) /catalogue/artists/art123456 duration: 32ms
fail: PUT (200) /catalogue/artists/art123456 duration: 12ms
fail: GET (200) /catalogue/artists/art123456/albums duration: 226ms
fail: GET (200) /catalogue/albums?limit=10 duration: 13ms
pass: POST (201) /catalogue/albums?limit=10 duration: 21ms
fail: GET (200) /catalogue/albums/alb000456 duration: 373ms
fail: POST (200) /catalogue/albums/alb000456 duration: 14ms
fail: GET (200) /catalogue/songs?limit=10 duration: 15ms
pass: POST (201) /catalogue/songs?limit=10 duration: 384ms
fail: GET (200) /catalogue/songs/son003456 duration: 42ms
fail: POST (200) /catalogue/songs/son003456 duration: 14ms
fail: POST (201) /catalogue/songs/son003456/media duration: 384ms
info: Displaying failed tests...
fail: GET (200) /catalogue/artists?limit=10&name=Oasis&country=GB duration: 57ms
```

Summary

This chapter first explained what a microservice is and why Node.js and MongoDB are used to build the Media Catalogue Microservice.

The chapter continued with the steps, as part of the API design-first approach, of how the microservice is built, packaged, and deployed in a container using Docker. The Media Catalogue API is then updated in the APIP CS to route the request to the newly deployed microservice running in a Docker container.

The chapter ended with testing the API design with the backend microservice using Dredd.

The next Chapter 5, *Platform Setup and Gateway Configuration* explains in depth how the APIP CS platform is setup and how to configure the gateways.

Platform Setup and Gateway Configuration

5

In the previous chapters we got an overview of the APIP CS and a use case on which to hang our explanations, along with using the design aspects of the platform. In this chapter, we work through the process of taking the platform from enabling API design, to the point at which real API calls can be received, passed on to an application, and return responses. To produce an appropriately sized and configured environment, a number of questions need to have answers teased out. As the chapter progresses these questions, will be answered and the reasons for asking the questions become apparent.

This chapter won't cover configuring and deploying APIs and their associated policies or anything more than the basic user setup necessary as these areas get covered in later chapters.

As previously shown, APIP has two parts, the managing cloud and deployable gateways. The cloud tier itself needs to be deployed and configured, so we will start this chapter by looking what is involved in the cloud management setup. As the chapter progresses, some recommendations on setup and configuration will be made.

With the cloud tier managed, we will then work through the process of deploying a gateway and connecting it to the cloud management. Of course, through this we will link to our use cases.

Before we start configuring and deploying anything, we should walk through the architecture and its prerequisites.

Platform architecture

The cloud platform has a number of constituent parts as shown in the diagram. So parts have to be explicitly created, others are created as part of the process of creating another service. The following diagram illustrates these elements involved and which ones we will need to create:

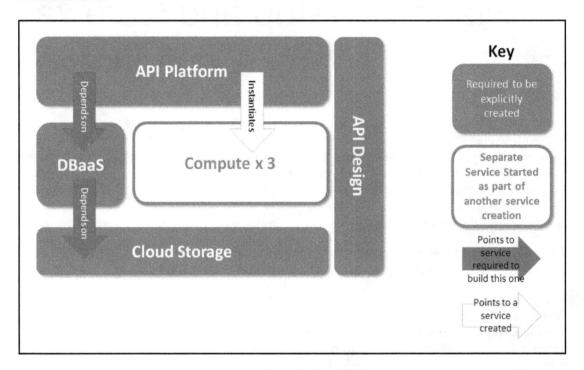

Components services used by API management

A brief summary of the key cloud services involved in providing the API platform:

- **Storage**: The cloud tier needs to keep track of configuration and analytics which needs storage capacity. Obviously for storage to be sized, we need to understand the non-functional requirements from which we can derive volumetric data that will help us complete sizing.
- **Database (DBaaS)-Database as a Service**: This is needed want to perform tasks such as holding analytical data and storing configurations.

- **API Management tier**: This is then made up of several logical component parts. These parts are not identified as when it comes to seeing the basic building blocks in `cloud.oracle.com`, they won't be explicitly identified. These elements are specifically:
    - **API Design**: In the form of Apiary, this is provided in a SaaS style configuration, so no details are needed here.
    - **Developer Portal**: This is the aspect where APIs are made real. The standard developer portal is created during the APIP setup. It is possible to deploy this independently into another location. We will describe what we are going to do here in a moment.
    - **Analytics Portal**: This provides us with the views on the activity of the API gateways. This is separated from the other elements as the amount of activity needing to be analyzed by the cloud can be significant, resulting in the server(s) needing to work hard. Having any analytics processes adversely impacting operational processes is obviously very undesirable.
    - **Management Server**: This is the server that controls what is happening.

Notice how no reference has been made reference to the gateway itself in the cloud. As mentioned in earlier chapters it is entirely possible to host the gateway in almost any cloud or on-premises, as it is designed to be deployed wherever it is most optimally deployed.

The gateway we can treat a single entity, but for purposes of troubleshooting issues, it is worth looking more closely at its composition as it will help if any troubleshooting is required. The parts are:

- **Gateway Engine**: This is the heart of the gateway and executes the policies. This core was originally developed by Oracle for the telecommunications industry to handle things like SMS and call logging. Obviously, this means that it needs to be very capable in terms of throughput, and is configured to be very efficient. The engine has since been developed to support high performance needs like that of the API Gateway.
- **WebLogic Server**: This is responsible for the coordination between the gateway and the cloud management, sending analytical information, and retrieving configuration information.

- **Java Database**: This is usually referred to by its Apache project name, Derby DB. This is used to hold the information needed locally:

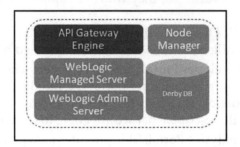

Make up of an API gateway deployment

It is important to understand that despite the fact that the gateway includes elements such as a WebLogic server, the gateway does not make use of WebLogic features such as clustering. As will become clearer as the deployment approach is examined in later in the chapter, the gateway looks towards a microservice architecture of keeping each node simple and then apply a load balancer to spread workload across multiple gateways. It is for this reason that we have the idea of logical gateways and nodes, where a logical gateway is one or more nodes (specific gateway instances) which can be linked to. This means that deploying gateways is not complicated by managing clusters.

Much of this information is presented to help understand what processes will be running and how it is possible to interact the gateway. For the majority of configuration and operational tasks, the gateway should be seen as a blackbox (exceptions to this are things like log harvesting and monitoring to ensure all processes are running).

The concept of logical and physical gateways

The API platform supports the idea of **logical gateways** and **physical gateways**. This concept is important as it has implications on the operational costs. Unlike a number of other products which charge based on the number of CPUs being used, the API platform is priced based on the number of logical gateways and API call volume in blocks.

As the following diagram shows, it is possible to have as many physical gateways deployed as desired within a logical gateway, where a physical gateway represents a single physical deployment of the gateway component. Not only that, the gateways can span as many hosting locations as desired:

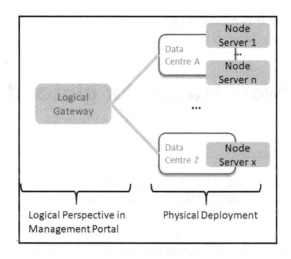

Deployment relationship between logical and physical gateways

The logical gateway, as its name suggests, is an abstract idea (as in there is no software deployed specifically for a logical gateway), which allows us to group collection(s) of APIs that we would want to manage in a similar way. For example, we might wish to manage our development versions of APIs in a different way to production ones so that we can control more tightly who can deploy to production compared to development.

It is important to understand that when more than one gateway is being used to service API calls in a single data center, we need to add some sort of mechanism to spread the load between the servers. Depending upon the deployment location (for example, if using Oracle cloud or running the gateway on ExaLogic servers), a good choice would be **Oracle Traffic Director (OTD)**. However, in other environments, you may need to consider infrastructure elements such as a Cisco Load Balancer or software appliance (https://www. cisco.com/c/en/us/solutions/data-center-virtualization/intelligent-traffic-director/index.html).

In a pure software-driven environment, this can be something as simple as HAProxy (`http://www.haproxy.org`), Nginx (`http://nginx.org/en/docs/http/load_balancing.html`), or Apache HTTP Server with load balancer mod (`https://httpd.apache.org/docs/2.4/mod/mod_proxy_balancer.html`).

It should be apparent that this model means that having hot standby environments only comes at the cost of the machine, not the gateway software.

Avoiding network latency for global deployments

There is an additional upside of this. When offering APIs to support user experience in a global model, it is necessary to consider the user experience including factors beyond your control such as network latency.

If an API application and gateways are deployed in Europe, for example, users in Australia are going to experience some latency. With the fastest, most direct fiber connections, it will take 56 milliseconds for a bit of data to travel from London to Sydney (16,983 km). This is simple physics of the speed of light which travels at 299,792 km/s. This is before taking into account the reality of network traffic going through multiple routing servers and networks.

By having the physical and logical models, we could deploy API gateways around the world and use clever DNS routing to send the API calls to the nearest server (just as Google does, for example) and keep them in the same logical gateway. So, when the API policies are updated, they will get deployed globally.

Deployment for the use case

Before we can start walking through the deployment process, we need to answer a number of questions:

1. How many nodes should we have per gateway?
2. How many logical gateways do we need?
3. How much storage will the database need to account for details such as the volume of analytics needing to be stored?

How many nodes

Stepping back to our use case, MRA identified that they wanted to start small so that they can build experience and confidence. So, we can assume that we are not going to see more than 10 API calls per minute over a 24/7 x 365 period from external sources or internal sources. While workload volumes won't be large, to start the environment needs a reasonable level of robustness so that the external consumers are not impacted by maintenance processes. This points to deploying gateways as two or three nodes depending upon the maintenance strategy.

While the performance of a gateway is somewhat dependent upon the configuration of the hardware it is running on and the number and complexity of the policies an API may require. Oracle has established some benchmarking for the gateway engine, which is responsible for handling the API calls.

Two servers running as a load balanced pair (each server having 2 CPUs with 18 cores per CPU with each core supporting 2 threads, giving us 72 processor threads and 256GB RAM) could handle approaching 50,000 transactions per second in a sustained run. A transaction can be viewed as a basic API invocation, reducing the footprint to a virtualized environment with each server only having 4 logical CPUs (the relationship between a virtual CPU and a physical CPU isn't simple, but as a rule of thumb 1 thread is one logical CPU) and 80GB RAM. At this end of the spectrum, the gateways processed nearly 5,000 transactions per second.

That strategy could be:

1. Run three concurrent nodes, so that there are always two gateways running even during maintenance periods OR
2. Operate with two nodes, but maintenance is done by introducing a new patched node before removing a node to perform patching OR
3. Run with two nodes, and maintenance is performed by patching and restarting one node at a time. This would mean accepting the risk of just one node taking all the load during the patch process, and if it was to fail while performing maintenance, there would be a full outage.

MRA has elected to adopt the 3rd option for simplicity on the basis that the patch process will be quick and rehearsed before execution and future risk will be mitigated against a scale out as load increases.

How many logical gateways

Earlier in the chapter we described the idea of Logical nodes as a means to organize our APIs and their deployments. A key decision is how many logical gateways do we need. Several factors can contribute to the decision here, including:

- Number of development, preproduction, and production environments needed, based on the idea that any policy modifications should be checked before going live. Making live changes can obviously at worst disrupt a service, but worse still accidentally remove security.
- Network traffic routing to the gateway; should internal traffic route through the same policies as external traffic?
- Should the number of security checks conducted within the API policies differ depending on the whether the calls originate from elsewhere within the organization or come from an unknown third party?
- Is it desirable to logically separate the API gateway deployments that server calls from the internet (which would necessitate the gateway being deployed in the demilitarized zone) from internal calls where the gateway could be hosted in a secure zone?
- Is it desirable to protect internal traffic from possibly being impacted by the processing load created from an external attack, such as a denial of service attack?
- Pricing model-as previously mentioned the primary division of cost is through the number of logical gateways. But each gateway is allowed a defined number of calls (at the time of writing this is 25 million per month). If the API calls exceed this then it is effectively having to pay for another logical gateway, even though in deployment and configuration terms it is the same gateway handling all the calls. For example, if we choose to have 3 logical gateways (development, test and production) then we could expect the following costs:

Logical Gateway	Expected API Call volumes per month	No Server Gateway Deployed to	Total Logical Gateways to be purchased
Development	10,000	1	1
Test	1 million (assume we will run short performance tests)	3	1
Production	45 million	3	2 (as we have exceeded the 25 million threshold).

How much storage?

In the ideal view of PaaS, the amount of storage needed for the database supporting the API platform shouldn't be a consideration, as part of the PaaS ideal is that these problems are abstracted away. However presently this isn't the case. As shown previously, we are aware of the underlying elements such as storage.

How much storage to allocate is a difficult value to judge as the key drivers are details such as:

- Number of APIs and the amount of change those APIs undergo.
- The number of API calls that are being recorded into the analytics views.
- How much history is needed to be kept.
- As the database contains the configuration information, space should be allocated for database backups. How far back the backups need to go also impacts the volume of storage.

In terms of backups, as a rule of thumb there is little value in backing up beyond each major release is likely to have limited value as trying to restore a database with a schema that may have changed as part of the major release is likely to create problems.

Currently the authors have configured the databases to be oversized in the 50-100 GB range with a view that if in the unlikely event that more capacity is needed the storage will be added. As storage is not a significant element of the cloud cost over sizing isn't costly, but also allows the database to use the storage more effectively. It also means the analytical data history can go back a long way.

Gateway design decisions in our use case

MRA determined that their internal traffic should flow regardless of any outward facing service impacts, nor did they want the internal traffic passing into the DMZ. To accommodate this a common pattern of having an external logical gateway to face external users and an internal logical gateway is adopted. This model not only allows a gateway to operate unaffected by possible external attacks but allows us to define different policies for an endpoint depending on the traffic origin. For example, an API call with external origins is more likely to need checks on the payload and perhaps multiple security checks such as whitelist, user credentials, and application token. Whereas for internal traffic, it may be preferable to only confirm the user has the permissions to invoke the API and trust the payload won't be malicious.

The following diagram illustrates their logical model with respect to the use of APIs. The initial focus given the bulk of systems are on-premises will be to build gateways there. This does of course allow for when the cloud solutions come into the scope to add additional gateways to be delivered:

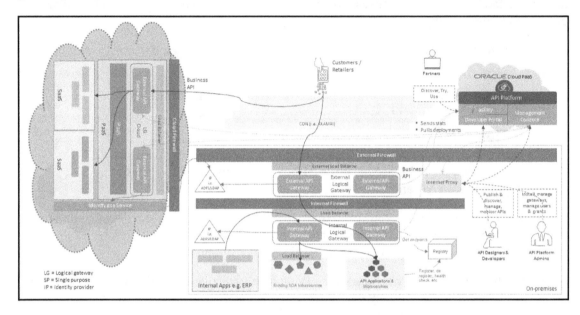

Logical solution design

One cloud management or several?

The cloud management tier which we will establish shortly can handle as many gateways as needed. Obviously very large numbers of gateways will require additional compute nodes, but this has little impact in terms of setup that we need to do. But, do we want to separate our development configuration from our production configuration?

Single management instance

It is not unusual for organizations to create separate instances of solutions for the different stages of development such as functional test, performance test, training, preproduction, and production support. The following diagram illustrates the two ends of the spectrum in terms of decoupling environments:

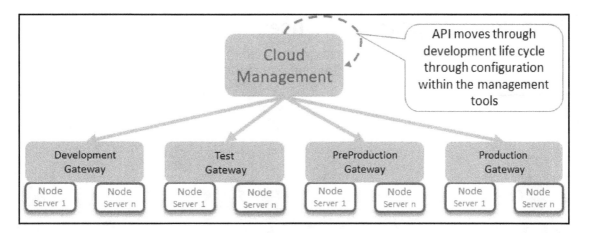

Single cloud management model

In this scenario, we have a single management cloud which manages gateways deployed into the different environment stages. Each environment's gateway(s) belong to separate logical groupings. For example, if we decided to separate our gateways based on whether they supported internal APIs or external (internet) facing APIs. Then each environment would have 2 logical gateways. This makes it important to establish a strong naming convention. For example:

- Dev-Internal
- Dev-External
- Test-Internal
- Test-External
- Preprod-Internal
- Preprod-External
- Prod-Internal
- Prod-External

In terms of naming, experience has shown that using hyphenated naming has made for easier reading (and for the platform's search mechanisms) particularly for non-developers who may find camel case types harder to read
https://techterms.com/definition/camelcase.

Multiple management instances

We will look at the advantages and disadvantages and the recommended approach shortly. Let's compare this with the more development centered approach, as follows:

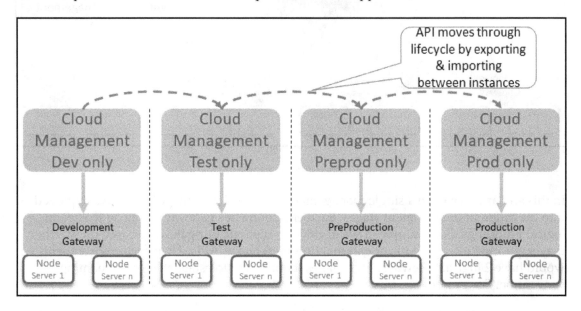

Multi-cloud management model

This model can be seen as simplifying the gateway configuration as we can have just two logical gateways (internal and external) and the gateways are configured to connect to their relative management clouds. The cost is now in the process of migrating approved APIs through the different stages by copying the API configuration from one management cloud to the next.

In both single instance and multi instance management clouds, by using the management APIs that the platform offers, it is possible to automate necessary configuration for both approaches. In Chapter 1, *Platform Overview*, a range of the API REST endpoints where illustrated. This means that for example, the following script could retrieve a named API policy and push it into the next management cloud.

```
curl -k -i -X GET -u myUserNameCloud1:myPasswordCloud1 https:// <my mgmt
svr>/apiplatform/management/v1/apis/103 --output api.json

curl -k -X POST -H "Content-Type: application/json" -u
myUserNameCloud2:myUserNameCloud2 -d @api.json https:// <my mgmt
svr>/apiplatform/management/v1/apis
```

As the preceding script shows, to achieve this an understanding of the REST endpoints in depth is essential. There have been utilities built to simplify this mechanism of pushing and pulling versions of the API definitions in the API management. These can be found at:

- Managing API Versioning (`https://blog.mp3monster.org/2018/02/27/apiversioning/`) while this focuses on version management the capabilities described here can be achieved using the tooling (produced by one of the authors of this book)
- API Platform Cloud Service REST API scripts and REPL using Python (`http://www.ateam-oracle.com/apip-rest-python/`) produced by the Oracle A-Team

Although it may be preferable to keep things simple with a single management cloud and allow a configuration manager to promote APIs through the environments.

Before we look at all the pros and cons of the options described (and by implications the variations), it's worth considering Oracle's recommendations. Oracle will typically advise that it is better to have a single cloud management instance. This recommendation is based on the fact that the API policies that are being transferred around will typically contain a lot of security considerations, for example, how an API is authenticated, what information needs redacting, how are malicious payloads detected. Adopting the transfer model, then it is likely storing this information somewhere as staging would be necessary. Perhaps, a configuration repository such as GIT or SVN for example. While there is nothing fundamentally wrong, typically a GIT configuration is not as secure as the database repository being used by the API platform. Oracle are also ensuring that the API management layer can provide all the necessary tools to complete all the configuration and management tasks that maybe needed.

The following table layouts the pros and cons:

Multiple Management Environments		Single Management Environment	
Pros	**Cons**	**Pros**	**Cons**
Closer to traditional development frameworks	Not aligned with Oracle's recommendations.	Aligned to Oracle's recommended approach.	Configuration for a *lower* environment, for example, Development could be perceived as potentially compromising *higher* environments, for example, accidentally allowing developers to change production.

The management tier, needs to be upgraded-separately for each environment means it is possible to verify the process before changing production	Upgrade Process needs to be repeated on each environment	Only one environment needs to be patch managed making it easier to implement patching more frequently.	A failed patch process can directly impact the ability to at least manage production.
Configuration of access controls is simpler, and the impact of an error can be limited	Additional cost for increased resources to apply configuration to multiple environments	Only 1 environment needs configuring and validating.	Perceived risk of not having a more *physical* isolation as such more error prone.
The logical gateway names remain the same through all the environments when it comes to policy configuration.	Moving APIs between environments is enduring process of importing & exporting policies and configuration.	Gateway configuration simpler as only referencing one cloud.	Gateway deployment needs to be more advanced in terms of associating to the correct logical gateway
End point URLs can be different to point to different environments for API Apps being developed without needing advanced routing	No overloading of the target URL to remain unchanged	No changes needed between routing for different environments as masked elsewhere.	
	More cloud server capacity required (API Platform has a base footprint of 4 nodes plus a database).	Smallest number of cloud management resources required	

The two options described are very much the extremes. There is a middle ground that allows the core concerns (security, making full use of API platform management capabilities and so on) that are likely to be expressed without compromising the recommended practices.

The middle ground position is two have two instances of the cloud management and gateways as follows:

1. A single instance of the management cloud and associated gateways that support normal development to production.
2. A second small instance of the management cloud and one or two gateways that are used to pilot the patching and maintenance activities such as changing JREs and OS before being applied in the dev to production. There are additional benefits of having this instance we'll see later in `Chapter 9`, *Implementing Custom Policies*.

MRA's approach number of cloud management instances

Looking at our use case, MRA wants to adopt the Oracle-recommended Single Management cloud model, but are concerned about the implications it has in terms of:

- Possible impact of an upgrade or a patch process creating a disruption to their production processes
    - Discovering that an OS security patch disrupts the gateway from running
    - Making sure they can run the API Platform maintenance process without issues
- Risk of creating a security vulnerability while people are learning to use the product trying out changes to permissions management

Therefore, MRA has elected to adopt the single cloud model with one key variation.

In addition to the main management cloud, a second cloud and logical gateway will be used. This second environment will be used to dry run patching and maintenance processes and experiment with new API platform features before going to the real environments. With this, they would select a set of APIs that are being developed that represent the APIs most likely to be impacted in the event of an API change and manually migrate them into this test environment. Manual migration process means that any sensitive information does not need to be persisted anywhere outside the API platform and important security keys, and so on can be removed.

The following diagram illustrates the approach to be adopted:

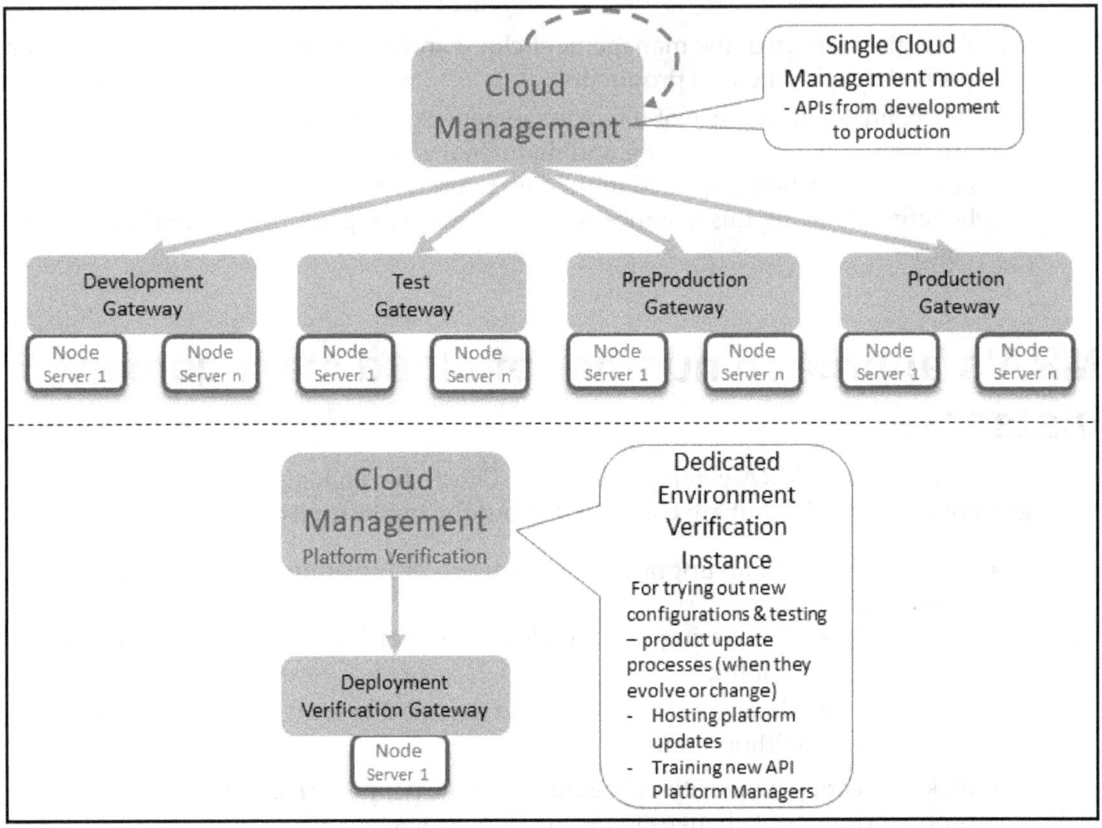

MRA's API platform approach

Firewall or no firewall

Arguably as the API gateway is a frontline component with security features, it may not be necessary to deploy a firewall. That said, given the licensing model which includes the API call count including rejected calls, there is sense in exploiting the fact that people will have invested in some way in a dedicated firewall capability as this means that simple probing and attacks can be easily deflected without calls to the gateway and incurring cost. This approach also means that the network contact with the outside world passes through a managed point of contact to the outside world. If a firewall is available (even if it is an open source software only solution), we would recommend using it for these course grain protections.

Load balancing

As previously described in preproduction and production environments it is advisable to have multiple nodes operating to provide higher levels of resilience and the ability to perform maintenance activities without having down time for the API services. We would therefore recommend that a normal web load balancer be placed in front of the API Gateways even when starting with a single node configuration as introducing the load balancer later is far more disruptive.

Load balancing capabilities often come as part of network tools such as firewalls and routers (for example, Oracle Traffic Director is provided in its cloud and for Exalogic, Exadata appliances), so introducing load balancing is likely to be relatively easy to achieve. Even without advanced technologies simple load balancing of the web traffic can be achieved with software such as HAProxy, Nginx and Apache HTTP Server.

Web proxies

Some organizations like to incorporate web proxy tiers within their network to allow traffic to be routed through specific parts of the network where additional security checks can be implemented between the different zones of their network including out to the internet. Proxies may also be used to help shape traffic within an organization to optimize how it travels. To this end API gateway configuration allows for proxies so that the *phone home* need is not impacted. Proxy support is also provided for the calls to the target API implementations.

In our use case MRA don't make use of proxies as their network is not deemed big enough to demand such requirements and feel that the use of proxies is perceived as a potential impediment that encourages people to adopt practices to circumvent the constraints.

Content Delivery Networks (CDNs)

CDNs provide means to push static content to the *cloud edge* so it is nearer to the consumers. To do this, the CDN provider will have lots of caches distributed around the world. This provides several benefits:

- Reduced network load into the data center (not having to return the static content repeatedly to different clients)
- Improved customer experience as the static content will download a lot quicker as the latency of the traffic is minimized

CDNs can be used to cache and return the results of APIs without the call going all the way back to an API gateway and into an application. This benefits us by reducing the workload of the API gateway. However, the use of CDNs needs to be handled with care as it is undesirable for the CDNs to be storing and returning results of API calls that should retrieve dynamic data.

Prerequisites to allow the API platform to be built

Before anything can be created and configured, first it is necessary to establish an Oracle cloud account (`https://cloud.oracle.com`) either in a trial form or a full account with appropriate credits. Currently there are two account types and we would, given the option, recommend using **Cloud Account with Identity Cloud Service** as this is the strategic account model for Oracle.

Background to the account types

The reason for two different account types is largely historical and relates to how Oracle have developed their cloud offering. The accounts types are presented as:

- Cloud Account with Identity Cloud Service
- Traditional Cloud Account

Over time we can expect to see the **Traditional Cloud Account** to become unavailable. The **Cloud Account with Identity Cloud Service** is also sometimes referred to **UCM** (referring to the new accounts can use the **Universal Credit Management** approach to pay for cloud services).

With the new model comes the provision of limited version of the **IDentity Cloud Service** (**IDCS**) cloud service. The **Traditional Cloud Account** does not provide this and offers different more restrictive model.

Existing Oracle cloud customers will in due course be migrated from the traditional account to the new model.

Details from Oracle on setting up the cloud can be found at `https://docs.oracle.com/en/cloud/paas/api-platform-cloud/apfad/how-begin-oracle-api-platform-cloud-service-subscriptions.html`.

Building the cloud

Setting up the cloud management needs to be completed before we can start deploying gateways. The cloud setup is more like SOA Cloud Service than Integration Cloud Service. This means that rather than commissioning a single service, several pieces need to be setup.

During the setup, it will be necessary to provide some user credentials with associated email addresses. We would recommend that these credentials are *system* accounts with group email addresses associated with them. This is necessary as the account creator will want to receive notifications, not to one individual but all the addresses, so that even if one addressee is on leave or is away, this will not result in the details not being addressed:

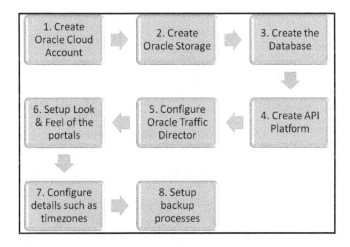

Cloud build flow

The process of getting setup are as follows:

1. Create users that can use the API platform. For this, we will be adopt a simple approach by creating the users within the API Platform WebLogic environment that underpins the management cloud. Other approaches available would involve exploiting IDCS, but we don't want to get too sidetracked by IDCS. More on this shortly!

2. It is possible to configure the storage needed for the database and related services independently or allow the setup to create the storage required.
    a. In many of the Oracle cloud services configured that an email account is needed to send notifications and alerts to. With this in mind, we recommend the use of a group or shared email address, and ideally shared credentials for the administrators. The following screenshot illustrates this in the database configuration page:

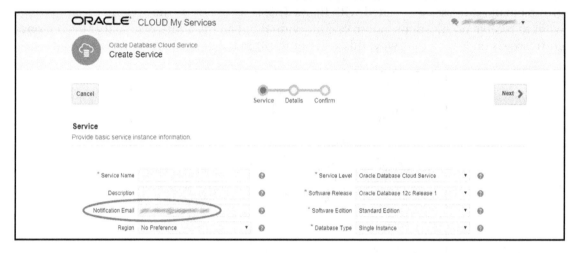

Create service – step 1

3. The database will hold both configuration information but also the analytics data.
    a. The amount of storage will be influenced by the application of the API platform; for example, in a development context we do not need too much storage. But production will need a reasonable amount of space as there will be a lot more data generated in forms of analytics.
    b. At this stage, consideration to what kind of database is needed. We would recommend a standard edition or better. For development a standard edition is fine, but for production it may be better to make the database more resilient through the use of options such as **RAC**. As the gateways can function without the cloud management and storage it may be preferable to keep things simple. However, the loss of the database, would impact the ability to manage the gateways centrally.
    c. Many of the configuration values needed to provide when establishing a DBaaS are the same as when establishing a normal database instance.

d. In the following screenshot, we have highlighted (solid line ellipse) where to provide a prebuilt storage information. Note the need for credentials, so ideally don't use an individuals' account. The alternative is to ask the DBaaS creation process to create the storage (options highlighted with a dashed ellipse):

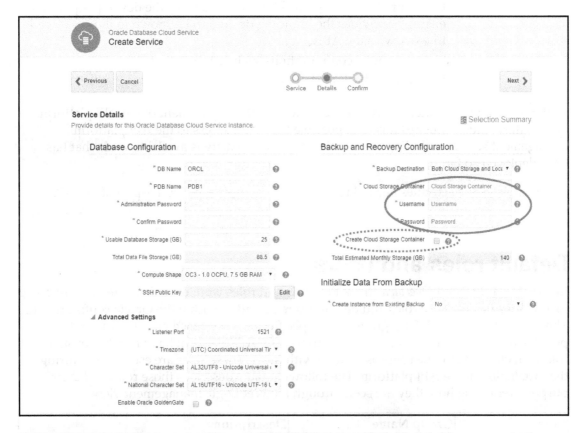

Create service – step 2

4. With the database established, we can then instantiate the API platform itself and complete the configuration in the API platform, this covers a number of activities:

a. WebLogic server authentication details (configuration of a WLS external authentication provider) or basic users necessary. Note that during this process, the compute resources that will have had to have been purchased being consumed as this will be executing the different portal services.

    b. Configure the **Oracle Traffic Director** to provide DNS addressing and associated certificates.

    c. Define any security rules for allowing traffic into the APIP portals, such as perhaps restricting traffic from a narrow range of origins such as the external IP for in our example MRA.

    d. Configure the look and feel for the portals. So, the developer portal for example provides the branding desired to be shown to those allowed to work with the APIs.

    e. Setting general configurations such as time zones.

    f. Establishing backup processes.

With the storage and database in place. Let's look at the deployment of the API platform. Within the cloud dashboard it is now possible to see the access to the API platform management screen, including information on what capacity is available, and what has been deployed so far.

This completes the activities needed to create the management cloud aspect of the API platform.

Default roles and users

In Chapter 1, *Platform Overview*, the API grants and roles were described. Here, we're going to look specifically at the roles and default users provided within the Oracle configuration. The API platform will default grants to do specific activities based on roles. But is it possible to assign some grants to specific users. The API platform has a number of standard roles, which need to have users associated with them. These roles are established during the installation of the API platform. The following table describes those roles and their purpose, reflecting how they are seen through the WebLogic management view:

Role	Group Name	Description
Gateway Manager	APIGatewayManagers	Those who perform this role have ability to manage the deployment and registration of gateways, including removing gateways. In addition to this management of grants can also be done by these users.
Gateway Runtime	APIGatewayRuntimeUsers	This role is used to perform the communication between the gateway and the cloud management tier.

API Manager	APIManagers	Members of this role have the means to manage the APIs through their life cycle such as development, deployment, versioning, deployment and so on.
Application Developer	APPDevelopers	Members of this group can view the documentation of an API, request to use the APIs.
Administrator	APICSAdministrators	Administration of the APIP. This role inherits all the capabilities of the other APIP roles.

For development environments, it may be easier to add the same user to be both the Gateway Manager and Gateway Runtime roles.

Using a credentials management solution such as IDCS or Azure Active Directory Federated Services within the enterprise that include people such as developers then it is worth considering linking the API platform cloud management directly (via OAuth 2) or indirectly via IDCS federation capabilities, as this provides:

- Centralized role and credentials management.
- Opportunity to provide people with developer-based roles easy access to the developer portal.
- Developers within an organization working to implement the backend services for the published API are also likely to be the people defining the API policies. Using such identity management will make configuration easier.

To start with, let's simply configure the users within WebLogic as the use of OAuth and services such as the Oracle Identity Cloud will come in a later chapter, not to mention configuring Identity Manager will distract from the goal of this chapter. The following steps will walk through the simple process of establishing users within WebLogic.

 Oracle's documentation relating to cloud setup can be found at
https://docs.oracle.com/en/cloud/paas/api-platform-cloud/apfad/creating-api-platform-cloud-service-instance.html.

Creating users inside API platform

With the cloud management services built, navigating to the home page of your Oracle cloud (**My Services**) and a dashboard something like the following screen will be visible where the different cloud services are displayed.

Before starting the following steps, it should be noted that if the cloud account created supports the use of IDCS then it is recommended that users be configured within IDCS rather than using the following steps. For IDCS users the following maybe of interest to understand the art of the possible.

 More information about using the WebLogic management console can be found at `https://docs.oracle.com/middleware/1221/wls/INTRO/adminconsole.htm`.

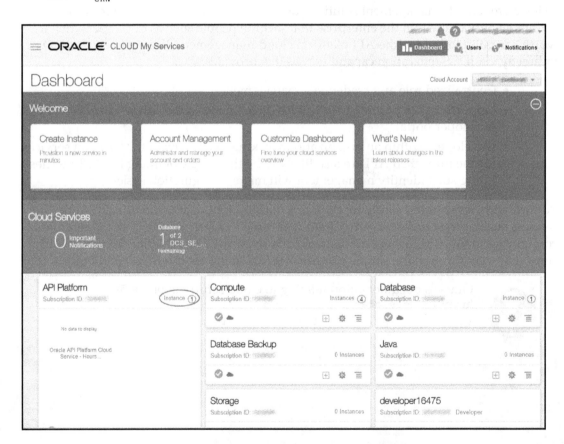

Oracle cloud – my services dashboard

1. As the next step requires use to find our way to the WebLogic servers the API platform. Oracle cloud like any good user interface provides a number of ways to do this. But the simplest is to click on the **Instance** count for the cloud service desired. In the preceding screen shot the count for API platform has been highlighted. This action will then result in the following screenshot being presented:

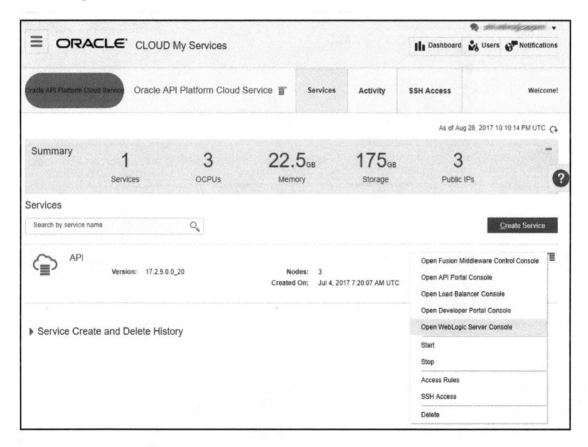

API Platform Oracle cloud dashboard

As the previous screenshot shows from within the core Oracle cloud management it is possible to access a drop-down menu listing all the different UIs to managing the different parts of the APIP CS. To manage users, like a basic WebLogic solution it is necessary to get at the management console.

2. Select the **Open WebLogic Server Console** option. This will result in a standard WLS login screen being presented. It is necessary to now login with appropriate credentials from the Oracle cloud.

With those credentials provided, a standard WLS Management Console as shown in the following screenshot should be accessible:

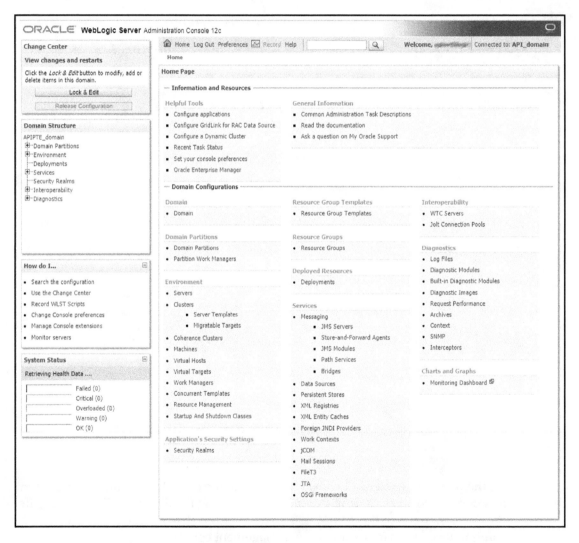

WebLogic admin console

3. The **Security Realms** option needs to be accessed, this can be done from the left-hand menu tree, or from the **Domain configuration** options in the central panel as shown in the preceding screenshot. Note for the subsequent steps the navigation steps will relate to what is presented in the central part of the screen. With the **Security Realms** option selected, the screen will appear as shown in the following screenshot:

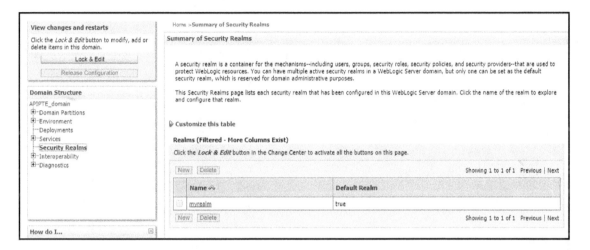

WebLogic security realms

As the default Security Realm is displayed, all the relevant users and roles are within this realm.

4. Select **MyRealm**. This will result in the settings options for **MyRealm** to be presented as shown in the following screenshot:

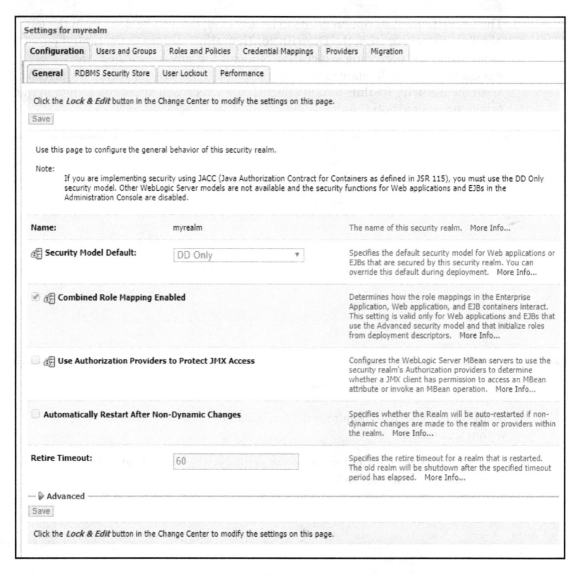

WebLogic MyRealm configuration view

5. The settings for what is needed can be accessed from the **Users and Groups** tab. Select this tab; then the following screenshot should be presented (any variation will be down to presentation configuration, or additional greps created to support new features):

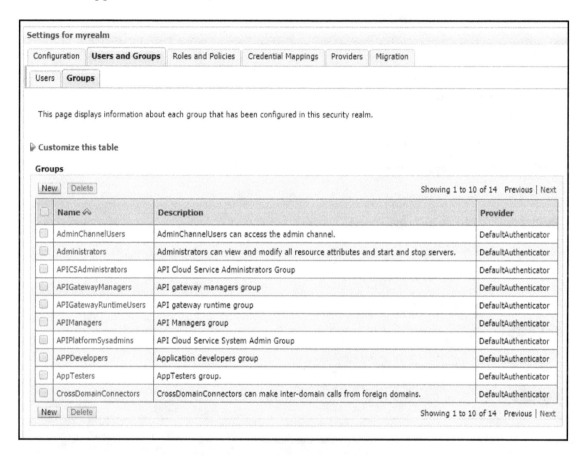

WebLogic groups

The preceding screenshot shows the **Groups** that have been created during the deployment group. These reflect the groups that were created as part of the APIP deployment process. However, we need to create users.

6. Click on the nested tab labelled **Users**. With that, it is possible to see the existing users. Like the **Groups** shown in the preceding screenshot, below the table is a **New** button. This will then allow use to create the relevant user using the screen as shown in the following screenshot:

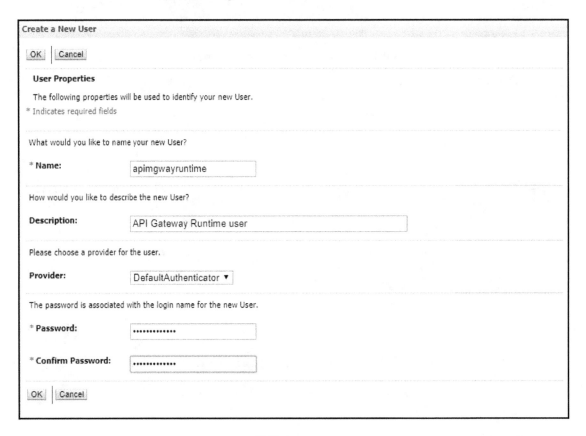

WebLogic create user

As shown in the preceding screenshot the basic details of the user have been defined, including:

- Username
- Password
- Authentication provider, which has the default set (which is the WebLogic Server)

7. Complete the user credentials. With these details then saved (using the **OK** button), it is necessary to associate the user with the desired groups.

Configuring Oracle traffic director

Within the APIP dashboard, as part of the Oracle cloud management, is the option to see the **Load Balancer Console**. The load balancer is provided as there are several servers created immediately to give us:

- The means to cope with a potentially high volume of activity, such activity is to primarily cope with potential workload created by API gateway nodes *phoning home* with very short heartbeats. If the Gateway nodes are very active then there will also be a reasonable amount of traffic being sent to the cloud management in the form of analytics data.
- Provide greater levels of resilience.

The load balancing capability is provided through the use of an **Oracle Traffic Director** (**OTD**) instance.

The Oracle Traffic Director is a very mature product and is provided with many of Oracle's cloud products by default as well as part of a number of on-premises solutions. To find out more about OTD visit
`https://docs.oracle.com/cloud/latest/as111170/TDADG/get_started.htm#TDADG102`.

Network-based access controls

In addition to load balancing, an API platform like other Oracle cloud services allows the network to be configured with routing and access controls. For example, it is possible to define rules such that traffic to the management console may only originate from a specific part of the internet and only letting traffic through that originates from MRA's public internet address.

The following screenshot shows the standard rules. Note that some of the rules include those between the different services needed for the APIP capability to function, for example the database. In the **Description** column, the most critical have the label **DO NOT MODIFY**.

Regardless of the cautions in the configured elements is still necessary to be careful with making changes, as it is possible configure the network in a manner that will prevent operating even accidentally.

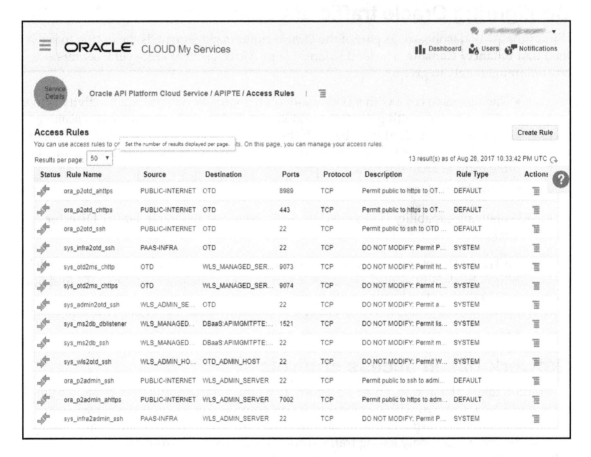

Access controls

Let's create a new rule that directs all HTTP (port 80) traffic from the internet go to the load balancer:

1. To navigate to this screen, select the drop-down menu on the API Platform dashboard screen. Click on the **Access Rules** option so the previous screen can be seen.

2. The first step in then creating a rule is to click on the **Create Rule** button on the top right of the screen. The following screenshot represents the result of this action:

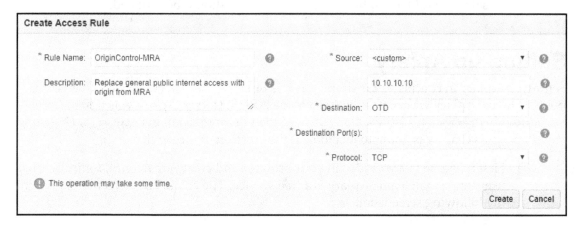

Create access rule screen

3. With the screen displayed it is possible to complete a rule, by adding the following values:

Screen Field	Value	Explanation
Rule Name	HTTP to OTD	As shown in the rules list.
Description	Direct all internet HTTP traffic to OTD	An explanation of what the rule is meant to be doing so others can understand the purpose of the figuration. Helps if changes need to be applied.
Source	Select **PUBLIC-INTERNET**	This describes the network traffic origins which will be determined via Internet addresses.
Destination	Select **OTD-OTD-SERVER**	The web traffic to goes to the engine of OTD, so select the execution part of OTD (rather than the Admin side)
Destination Port(s)	Set this to be 80 (the port for HTTP traffic)	As the OTD should consume the traffic as HTTP traffic the port is configured to be 80.
Protocol	Select **TCP**	Standard HTTP traffic is carried using TCP.

4. With these values applied the rule can be created. Click on the **CREATE** button.

5. The rule will be in the list now and can be enabled or disabled using the **Actions** drop down menu that can be accessed from the right-hand end of the row. But to be safe the **DELETE** option to remove the rule should be actioned.

Setting up Apiary

Setting up Apiary in contrast is far simpler as it is offered as a discrete service (that is, it is possible to use Apiary without having the Oracle API Platform). Apiary was first introduced in Chapter 1, *Platform Overview* and then in more detail in Chapter 3, *Designing the API*. So, this chapter is going to just look at the creation of the service.

1. First navigate to Apiary.io in your browser and create an account, for individual users and small teams Apiary is a free service. The create user screen is shown in the following screenshot:

The Apiary creation screen

2. Complete the registration using either GitHub, Twitter, or using an email address. If the APIs are intended for public consumption, then a social credentials option is probably a better option as any integration with these channels can be exploited to promote the APIs.

3. Once the registration is completed the Apiary editor is displayed (shown in the following screenshot). From here, it is possible to expand the number of people editing the API by establishing a team. Depending upon the team size there will be a cost involved. These options can be accessed through the **People** menu:

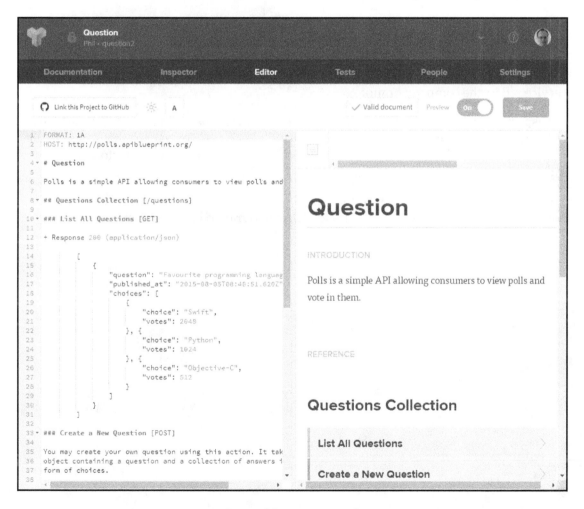

Apiary appearance

The remaining setup relating to Apiary is to connect Apiary to the developer portal. This connectivity then allows API definitions and documentation to be drawn into APIP and linked to the API policy.

 Note to integrate Apiary with the API platform it is necessary to have the **Team Edition** of Apiary.

Configure developer portal look and feel

With the **developer portal** being used by internal staff as well external users such as partners and maybe even the public, it is obviously desirable that at least this part of the service reflect the company brand.

All aspects of the core API platform (administration, developer, and analytics portals) are delivered through the use of APIs on the platform's backend. This means that it is possible to develop automation processes if wanted, or even go as far as creating custom user interfaces if wanted.

This approach does mean that it is possible to write a CURL script that will call the management cloud APIs and configure the UI with our own logo and name.

The following screenshot illustrates the use of Postman to make the necessary web calls to achieve this:

Postman configuration

The call to apply the changes, obviously needs a JSON payload that tells the API Platform where to retrieve the different images from, which images to use where and details such as the default font and copyright statements. The following illustrates the configuration:

```
{
  "language": "en",
  "branding": {
    "vendor": "",
    "product": "MRA API Services",
    "product_short": "API Platform",
    "title": "Developer Portal",
    "logo": {
      "url": " https://github.com/APIPlatform/blob
        /master/PortalCustomisation/logo.png",
      "width": "auto",
      "height": "30px",
      "alignment": "center"
    },
    "login": {
      "logo": {
        "url": " https://github.com/APIPlatform/blob
          /master/PortalCustomisation/logo.png",
```

```
      "width": "200px"
    },
    "splash": "oap/css/images/login/productLogo.png",
"productLogo": "oap/css/images/login/productLogo.png",
    "background": {
      "desktop": "https://github.com/APIPlatform
        /blob/master/PortalCustomisation/desktop_background.jpg",
      "tablet": {
        "portrait": "https://github.com/APIPlatform
          /blob/master/PortalCustomisation/portrait.png",
        "landscape": " https://github.com/APIPlatform
          /blob/master/PortalCustomisation/landscape.png"
      },
      "mobile": {
        "portrait": "https://github.com/APIPlatform
          /blob/master/PortalCustomisation/mobilePortrait.png",
        "landscape": "https://github.com/APIPlatform
          /blob/master/PortalCustomisation/mobileLandscape.png"
      }
    },
    "css": {}
  },
  "copyright": "Copyright © 2017 Monster Recording
    Artists and/or its affiliates. All rights reserved."
},
"css": {
  "*": {
    "font-family": "\"Helvetica Neue\",Helvetica,Arial,sans-serif",
    "font-size": "13px"
  }
}
}
```

Gateway life cycle and deployment

The way gateways are being deployed is developing and expanding, still. Early releases provide the gateway through a ZIP file, which contained all the jars and configuration files but had a number of prerequisites such as **Python** and **OpenSSL**. This has evolved to a model more like the agent deployment used by Integration Cloud Service using a Bash executable shell. It can be reasonably expected that Oracle will probably offer additional deployment options through, for example, Docker in the future.

In all of this, the information the gateway needs and the deployment life cycle has not fundamentally changed. So, for the rest of this section the life cycle will be explored, along with the data needed in the configuration.

Regardless of how the deployment works, the gateway offers a key security element, therefore it is always recommended that the use of the latest and highest release of Oracle Java. This removes chances of any vulnerabilities that have been identified being there for someone to exploit. The Java deployment needs to be a **JDK** rather than the **JRE**.

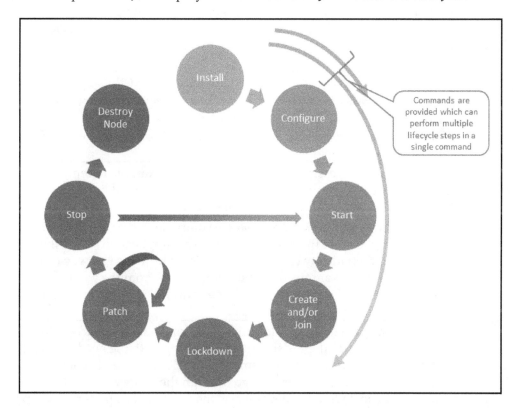

The gateway life cycle

As the gateway goes through its life cycle, regardless of how it may be packaged for different environments it is fair to expect the deployment to change a bit, but fundamentally it will need to be possible to manipulate the gateway through the phases described in the following table:

Phase	Description
Install	This is the phase most likely to change over time as this performs the task of unpacking the components and laying them out for use.
Configure	It is necessary to configure the gateway to provide information such as where the management cloud is, which ports to be listening for API traffic. This provides the means to configure aspects of the gateway building blocks to use different ports if required for example.
Start	With a configured gateway, the next step is to start it up so it can either operate in its normal life cycle of phoning home for API policies, report its data, and so on. But the gateway needs to be started before it can be joined to a logical gateway.
Create	This step is optional, depending upon whether an existing logical gateway is being connected to or not, as the process will create a logical gateway.
Join	With a logical gateway established, then the node needs to be connected to it. There are necessary specific values needed for this step, to identify the logical gateway properly.
Stop	Sometimes it is necessary to stop a gateway, for example to remedy a problem such logs growing too big. Using the command line, it is possible to issue the actions to start and stop as necessary.
Lockdown	As the gateway maybe used as *frontline* component, that is, Between the unrestricted world of the internet and internal applications, once the setup is satisfactory, then ideally controls are restricted how the gateway can be manipulated (for example, only issue commands from the gateway locally, no access to consoles provided by the gateway). To apply these restrictions, the lockdown command should be used.
Patch	Overtime the policies available will be developed and enhanced, along with the possible need to deploy security fixes, along with the need to keep the gateway in step with the management cloud. As a result, it is necessary to be able to patch a node. Rather than go through the process of patching manually by installing the new binary, the gateway can perform the update process itself once it receives a patch command.
Destroynode	There will be a time when a node will need to be decommissioned, for example deploying a replacement gateway onto s newer server. In which case, it must be possible to decouple node from the management tier.

As illustrated gateway has a life cycle. The gateway comes with the means by which it can be commanded through that cycle. The command mechanism requires a number of parameters to describe the configuration and tell the gateway what to relate to, and how.

In addition to the gateway life cycle, the gateway needs to be able to receive instructions during its operational life, such as the change of credentials. Ideally the passwords for the different system roles don't want to remain unchanged for ever. As a result, the following commands to allow these details to be changed.

Command	Description
`updatecredentials`	This command allows us to inform the gateway of the change of credentials for the Gateway Runtime user. This is one of the credentials that is used to help communicate with the cloud management tier.
`updateoauthprofile`	If the details of connecting to the OAuth provider change then the configuration needs to be updated.
`applypatches`	As the command name says, this triggers the patching process on the gateway.

Both the life cycle controls and the above commands are issued using the `APIGateway` script as will be illustrated later in the chapter.

Gateway configuration

Deployment of the gateway, regardless of whether one or multiple steps are executed, a JSON configuration file is used. This is then in turn used to populate the values in a significantly larger configuration file, which provides information for all the different parts of the gateway.

While it maybe be appealing to configure all the parameters by copying and editing the master, it can be easy to get things wrong as an element in the smaller configuration file can impact multiple parts of the master. Further, it will become difficult to understand what elements have been changed.

The configuration attributes can be characterized into several groups:

- **Mandatory values**: These are values that are essential to various configuration stages and should be defined in the configuration.

- **Key values**: These values will influence the gateway performance and need to be considered for each deployment; for example, the size of the heap being made available to the gateway. It is possible to get a gateway up and running without changing the defaults to these values.
- **Optional values**: Theese are configuration values for specific behavior of the gateway. These typically relate to the way components will be used; for example, which ports will be used for the gateway's own management UI, data cache behavior. It is recommended that these values be defaulted, unless there is a security policy that directs that standard/default ports should never be used.

While Oracle documentation will identify the mandatory configuration elements, it doesn't necessarily provide the clarity for the key values and optional values.

Oracle documentation on the configuration data can be seen at
`https://docs.oracle.com/en/cloud/paas/api-platform-cloud/apfad/installing-gateway-node.html#GUID-A02059C9-37B4-40F0-9FEA-C648804BB98F`.

Within the configuration values it is necessary to be able to define the network ports to be exposed and used by the gateway. MRA have decided that for internal operations, using default ports are fine. However, public internet facing traffic should not be on standard ports. By doing this, it increases the effort involved in locating the APIs through which attacks could be started. The one exception to this is for serving static content such as web pages.

The following table shows the configuration values that MRA have identified from the documentation as mandatory or key. With each configuration item, the purpose of the value has been described:

Property Name	(M)andatory (K)ey (O)ptional	Description	Suggested Value
gatewayInstallDir	K	This is where the gateway will be deployed. It is recommended that this is different from the installer location. This should be wherever the recommended 30GB of storage is available. The following diagram shows the suggested directory structure.	`/u01/oracle/api/gateway-installer`

prevInstallCleanupAction	K	It is possible to define what happens when deploying/patching/updating a gateway. A simple **clean** will result in previous deployment being deleted. The alternative id to **archive**, which allows the opportunity to restore state.	`Archive`
opatchesFolder	K	This defines the location to store patch resources for patching the gateway.	`u01/oracle/ api/gateway/ patch`
installationArchiveLocation	K	This only needed if the *prevInstallCleanupAction* is archive	`/u01/oracle/ api/gateway/ archive`
GatewayMServerPort	M	This defines the port that API calls can be received on using HTTP. While the value defaults to `8011`. It is recommended that based on good security practice to use ports that cannot be used to infer the underlying technology. Using industry standard ports, such as `80` therefore makes good sense. It should be noted that ports below 1024 often get treated differently in Linux environments for reasons of security. In this case another common port should be adopted. A common alternate port is `8080` for HTTP traffic (`https://www.iana.org/ assignments/service- names-port-numbers/ service-names-port- numbers.xhtml? search=http-alt`).	`8080`

listenIpAddress	M	This should be the public IP address of the machine the node is installed to. Trying to use IPs such as localhost will cause problems.	The server's IP as identified across the network and internally
publishAddress	M	This is the URL that will be published to the management server to identify this server instance. Typically, this would be the same value as the *listenIpAddress* unless there is an unusual network configuration that would make it hard to relate back.	The server's URL as identified across the network and internally
gatewayMServerSSLPort	M	This is the SSL/TLS alternative to *GatewayMServerPort*. Following the same principle and IETF guidance port 8443 will be adopted.	8443
gatewayAdminServerPort	O	The non-SSL version of port that provides gateway admin server. Like a number of other ports this is provided so different parts of the gateway can talk to itself (and users if necessary). The configuration is used so possible port clashes, and so on, can be addressed.	
gatewayAdminServerSSLPort	O	The SSL version of *gatewayAdminServerPort*.	
logicalGateway	M	When a logical gateway is created it needs to be provided with a name, which is taken from this configuration item.	For the MRA use case we will use gate names based on <environment name>-Internal / <environment name>-External. Environment name represents dev/test/ preprod/prod

gatewayId	M	When joining a gateway node to the logical gateway the numeric identifier of the logical gateway needs to be provided. This Id is provided when a create process is performed but can also be obtained through the UI. This value typically starts at `100` and increments every time a gateway logical or otherwise is provided.	`100` if not known
gatewayDomainName		This provides the WebLogic container that forms part of the gateway with a name for its default domain. Although defined as mandatory, the value is also defaulted. Unless there is going to be the co-deployed multiple Gateways (a model that wouldn't recommend). Your gateway logs default to be inside this folder. To use monitoring of the log files keeping the file path consistent across your servers makes life easy. But monitoring your gate with OEM or another such tool means domains need to be unique. Therefore, it is suggested that a symbolic link be established. For MRA the decision is to implement monitoring through the use of more contemporary log analytics model, so the same name in the configurations be used.	Gateway1

gatewayNodeName	M	This helps us identify in the management portal a specific gateway node. The easiest thing to provide here is the host name of the server running the gateway, assuming host names are set uniquely within the organization's deployment scope.	
phoneHomeProxy	O	This allows a proxy to be defined if the outbound traffic needs to pass through a web proxy layer on the way to the cloud management layer.	In the case of MRA, no outbound proxy exists
nodeProxy	O	This allows a proxy to reside between the gateway and the address of the service that will realize the API. Typically, this will occur if the proxy needs to do some additional routing to accommodate network structures, for example, network proxying between different network zones or segments for security.	In MRA there is no internal proxies to segment the network.
coherencePort	O	With WLS part of the gateway, the option to configure the Coherence port provided with WLS. Typically, this will only change if: • A port conflict is occurring as the default port is assigned something else • Security policy dictates default ports can never be used	Leave defaulted
gatewayDBPort dbHostName	O	As with the Coherence port it may be necessary to configure the DB to run on a different port to normal.	Leave defaulted

nodeManagerPort	O	This provides the means to address possible port conflicts that could occur by moving the Node Manager to a different port.	Leave defaulted
heapSize	O	Depending upon the server configuration and scaling strategy (scale up vs scale out) it may be able to provide the gateway with additional memory to work with.	MRA have elected to adopt a scale out strategy-so it can be left defaulted.
maximumHeapSize	O	Defines the maximum Heap the gateway can use. To handle throughput through larger gateway nodes rather than more gateway nodes, then this value like **heapSize** needs to be modified to ensure resources are used.	MRA have elected to adopt a scale out strategy-so can be left defaulted.
gatewayExecutionMode	O	Configure the gateway to run one of two modes- **Development** (default) and **Production**. In the Production state hostname and certificate verification is performed.	Preproduction and Production servers are set to Production as a value
loadBalancerUrl	K	A JSON array defining the HTTP/HTTPS URLs of the load balancer that frontends the gateway node. This can be configured through the Gateway UI which is recommended as it allows the config file to remain as simple as possible-and therefore the greatest chance of automation.	Only needs to be defined if there is a load balancer with the, as recommended for production.
mangementServerHost	M	This is the address to phone home to.	The DNS address of our management server
managementServerPort	M	This is the port to be used when phoning home.	Set to 443 as SSL is being used.

registryManagementUrl	O	If the number of gateways and frequency of phoning home is high, then it is possible to configure the gateways to talk to a different node in the management cloud. Like the analytics cloud settings this would only need to be done in special circumstances.	Leave defaulted
nonProxyHosts		This provides a means to configure proxy host information in the same way as Java VM can be configured using `http.nonProxyHosts`. More information can be found at `https://docs.oracle.com/javase/8/docs/technotes/guides/net/proxies.html`	Leave defaulted
oauthProfileLocation	O (mandatory if using OAuth2)	Describes where the OAuth profile information is either `OAuth2TokenLocalEnforcerConfig.xml` or `OAuth2TokenLocalEnforcerConfig.xml`. This configuration information tells the gateway where it can obtain authorization of an API call from.	MRA initially don't have OAuth2 capabilities, but will configure this once ADFS is adopted.
analyticsManagementUrl	O	In very high-volume cases (lots of gateways producing analytical information) it will become preferable to separate the analytics server from the management server. This address is then used. Without it, it is assumed to have the same address as the management server.	Leave defaulted

The following diagram illustrates the directory structures that will be made use of:

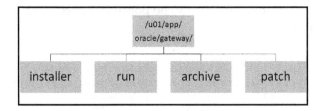

The recommended filesystem layout for gateway deployment

Where to get the logical gateway ID

The ID of a logical gateway is displayed in the **Gateways** part of the management portal when the top level is displayed showing the logical gateways. The following screenshot fragment highlights the logical gateway ID:

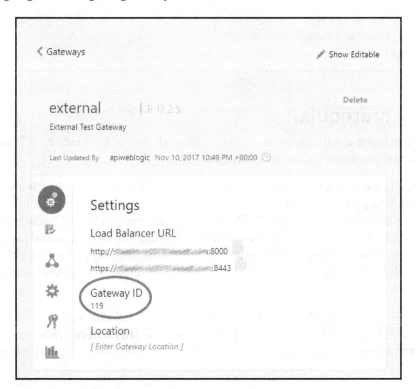

The gateway ID

Configuration JSON properties

With this information, the properties file can be populated accordingly, and get something like the following example:

```
{
    "gatewayInstallDir" : "/u01/app/oracle/gateway/run/",
    "installationArchiveLocation" : "/u01/app/oracle/gateway/archive/",
    "prevInstallCleanupAction" : "clean",
    "gatewayNodeName"    : "Svr1234",
    "managementServerHost"    : "https://oracleMgt.APIPlatform.cloud",
    "managementServerPort"    : "443",
    "nonProxyHosts"           : "localhost",
    "listenIpAddress"         : "1.1.1.101",
    "publishAddress"      : "1.1.1.101",
    "gatewayExecutionMode": "Development",
    "gatewayNodeDescription" : "API Platform Gateway for book",
    "gatewayDomainName" : "gateway1",
    "logicalGateway" : "DevGateway",
    "opatchesFolder" : "/u01/app/oracle/gateway/patch",
    "gatewayMServerPort" : "8080",
    "gatewayMServerSSLPort" : "8443",
    "gatewayId" : "100"
}
```

Gateway prerequisites

So now there is some clarity on what will be deployed. Before we execute, it is necessary to ensure the target platform for the gateway is ready.

First of all, the node will need sufficient storage, as it will be holding effectively up to four copies of the gateway (install, run, archive, and patches) plus all the logs. It is recommended there be a minimum 10 GB of storage for the gateway (Oracle recommend allocating 30 GB). As writing to logs files will be a valuable operation-something that will become clearer in later chapters. The faster the I/O when running production, the better (think about high performance disks, RAID, or SAN managed storage that exploits concurrent disks).

When it comes to memory, Oracle defines a minimum of 6GB although to provide increased throughput working with 10-12GB of available this will provide head room for all the policies, OS overheads and monitoring utilities, while not being excessive.

Finally, with respect to CPU and network, as the licensing model is not linked to CPU but to API calls and logical gateways, so it is possible to apply as much compute power as desired.

When it comes to the server environment itself, a Java JDK is needed as the gateway is likely to be applying security checks. It is best that the latest certified version of the Oracle JDK is used so that any Java identified vulnerabilities can't be exploited. With this the **JAVA-HOME** environment variable needs to be set.

Earlier gateway versions also needed Python to be preinstalled as the API platform deployment tools are written in Python. If Python is deployed, ensure it is a recent build with **OpenSSL** included. Although more recent editions have changed how this dependency is addressed. The Python version to use has changed over a number of releases as a result of needing to include updates in dependent libraries to address security vulnerabilities. Therefore, it is recommended that the adoption of the latest version of Python possible, or at least refer to Oracle's published guidance for the gateway version being deployed.

 The latest deployment requirements can be seen at https://docs.oracle.com/en/cloud/paas/api-platform-cloud/apfad/system-requirements-premise-gateway-installation.html#GUID-45E866FB-A8E3-4DF3-A031-21ADBADC674D.

While experimenting and learning to deploy the gateway, shortening the deployment processes can be made to run far more quickly (moving from tens of minutes to tens of seconds). This can be done by changing the way certificates are created for security purposes. As this impacts security, it is recommended the change if applied is not used for production gateways.

The performance gain can be obtained by changing how certificate keys are seeded. When generating keys, the seed random value is taken from a memory buffer that is involved in receiving physical events such as mouse movement events. As it is likely the deployment of the gateway is to a server with only a command-line shell, and potentially virtualized (both of which reduce the rate of change in the buffer). The rate that the buffer changes is a lot slower, resulting in making the key generation longer. By changing the randomness process (that is, the use of the buffer) with the following command, the key generation will be made quicker.

```
export CONFIG_JVM_ARGS=-Djava.security.egd=file:/dev/./random
```

A power user account will be needed to run the gateway. It's not good to run as root. Consider the risk if a vulnerability was to be found in the gateway that meant the attacker could get access to the operating system. But the account does need to be able to write to the file system.

Finally, link the gateway start to the OS restart. If for any reason the server restarts, then the gateway will restart. This can be done by creating a script to contain the start process (as seen later in this chapter) and incorporating it into /etc/init.d.

Retrieving the gateway deployment package

The last preparatory step for deploying the gateway is to retrieve the gateway deployment package. This can be obtained through the management portal:

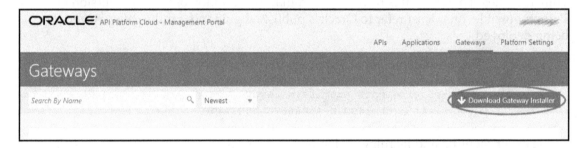

Gateway download

If the deployment is to a server with only command-line access, then the binary can be retrieved to the target machine by downloading to a browser enabled desktop and then using FTP or better still SCP to transfer the file. An alternative to this is to utilize the wget tool as shown here:

```
wget --keep-session-cookies --save-cookies cookies.txt --post-
data='j_username=######&j_password=########' --no-check-certificate
https://1.2.3.4/apiplatform/public/j_security_check
wget --load-cookies cookies.txt --no-check-certificate
https://1.2.3.4/apiplatform/downloads/ApicsGatewayInstaller.zip
```

The download is not small, so a single step transfer is far more desirable.

Actioning the gateway deployment

Let's look into actioning the gateway deployment.

Unpacking

To start, the installation bundle retrieved from the management portal needs to be unpacked. It is recommended that this be done this in the gateway installer folder previously mentioned. Precisely how this is done will be dependent on the cloud version of the portal being run. The following command shows the ZIP deployment. In future, the deployment process will become a Bash shell that simply needs to be executed in the correct part of the directory tree:

```
unzip . ApicsGatewayInstaller.zip -d /u01/app/oracle/gateway/installer
```

The outcome of the process should be that there is a directory structure populated with jars, various scripts, and configuration file resources. The majority of the steps will result in log files being created in a folder called /logs in the directory being installed to, using the outlined tree that would be called run. If there is any concern over the processes being executed this is where to start.

Install

There are several important preparation steps to complete before performing the installation step. This includes setting up several environmental variables. The first step is to prepare the configuration values to be applied. This is done by copying our gateway-props.json file described earlier in the chapter into the installation folder. The file is needed here as this will provide the installer script with the information necessary to perform the next steps. The following shows the command that needs to be run:

```
./APIGateway -f gateway-props.json -a install
```

Configure

The configuration process sets up the domains, database, and other related details on the gateway such as local key stores. As previously mentioned, if the deployment is to a development environment it is desirable to first modify the entropy configuration:

```
./APIGateway -f gateway-props.json -a configure
```

Start

With the various parts of the gateway configured, everything needs to be started up. The `start` script will use the properties file to determine things like the domain to start-up and so on.

If there is any concern about processes having started properly, it is possible to list all the Java processes (`ps -ef | grep Java`). The command should show up four distinct processes relating to the WebLogic server and Java database. The command for this step is:

```
./APIGateway -f gateway-props.json -a start
```

Create

The first time a gateway is deployed for a new logical gateway, it is necessary to perform the create command so that the logical gateway is setup and configured in the cloud management tier ready to connect the gateway to.

The ID of a logical gateway is displayed in the **Gateways** part of the management portal when displaying the top-level gateways. The following screenshot fragment highlights the logical gateway ID:

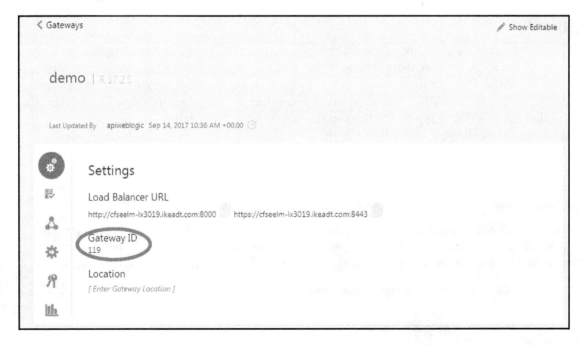

Gateway ID

By clicking on the gateway as illustrated in `Chapter 1`, *Platform Overview*, more information can be seen. In the preceding screenshot the ID for the gateway is highlighted. It is this information that needs to be plugged back into the configuration file: `gateway-props.json`.

If the `create-join` operation is executed, then the script actually captures the ID and uses it in the second step automatically. The steps have been separated here so that more of what is happening and when it happens can be seen.

With this ID the JSON file needs to be amended to set the **gatewayId** value to be the same. Unless by chance the right ID is in the file already. It is possible to guess what the ID will be as the numbering of gateways is managed by an algorithm.

Once the `gateway-props.json` file is modified then run the following command:

```
./APIGateway -f gateway-props.json -a install
```

Join

The final step is to connect or join the gateway to the correct logical gateway. This step allows us to connect one or more gateway nodes to a single logical gateway. The command to perform this step is:

```
./APIGateway -f gateway-props.json -a join
```

With this completed, it is possible to publish API Policies to the gateway to execute.

Making the gateway production ready

With the gateway up and running it is desirable to tune the configuration of the gateway, for example:

- Modify the heap space available as the environment is better understood
- Configuration of features such as OAuth 2.0 validation for the APIs

But to make the gateway production-ready, it is recommended several things be considered:

- Is the file system in which the gateway is installed secured, so that the gateway can be run, log files generated but nothing else? This is part of good Linux security.
- If HTTPS is being used, are good certificates properly deployed?
- Execution of the lockdown process.

Linux security

Securing Linux is a whole subject in its self, and too big to do justice in this book. So, it is recommended that other good sources for information available on securing Linux including books, such as *Practical Linux Security Cookbook* by *Tajinder Kalsi* published by *Packt Publishing*, be reviewed and recommendations applied. It should be noted that part of the filesystem to allow logging policies to work requires the permissions to write files, and for these to be retrieved.

Log analytics

It is recommended that the API platform is supported with the deployment of a log analytics solution that can gather the contents of the log files. Just a few solutions in the area include:

- Oracle Log Analytics Service: `https://cloud.oracle.com/log-analytics`.
- Splunk: `https://www.splunk.com`.
- Elastic Stack (sometimes referred to as ELK): `https://www.elastic.co`.
- These tools bring all the logs together and allow them to be analyzed together. When combining logs from the gateway(s), applications and other systems it becomes a lot easier to understand what is happening across the environment and easier to determine cause and effect. For example, if the gateway starts failing, combining these logs with those from the operating system may show a disk issue occurring when the gateway starts failing to work correctly.

Dealing with certificates

As part of the gateway is actually a WebLogic server, handling TLS/SSL certificates is the same process as configuring WebLogic which out of the box uses the demo java key store (demo.jks). While OK for development, the credentials to demo.jks are openly published. This makes the key store very insecure and it is recommended that a secure keystore is used for certificates, and so on.

To do this a new keystore needs to be created—an explanation of this can be seen at https://docs.oracle.com/middleware/1213/wls/SECMG/identity_trust.htm#SECMG365.

Then the WebLogic server will need to be configured to use the new key store, and will also need the credentials needed to access the key store. There are several approaches to this either through the local user interface or via the command-line tool WLST. Configuring WLS with key store information:

- Using WLST: http://bit.ly/WLST-SSL or https://docs.oracle.com/cloud/latest/fmw121300/IDMCR/ssl_config_wlst.htm#IDMCR11784
- Using WLS Admin Interface: http://bit.ly/WSL-SSL-UI
  or https://docs.oracle.com/cd/E72987_01/wls/WLACH/taskhelp/security/ConfigureIdentityAndTrust.html

Gateway lockdown

As mentioned earlier in the chapter, the gateway has a lockdown command. The lockdown command makes the gateway a more secure by greatly restricting where the gateway can be commanded from through the user interfaces or command line tools such as those provided with gateway and WLST.

While it is possible to reverse the actions of a gateway **lockdown**, for obvious reasons these are not simple. As a result, it is not recommended that a gateway be locked down until such time as the setup established as complete and stable. The command to lockdown the gateway is:

```
./APIGateway -f gateway-props.json -a lockdown
```

Summary

In this chapter, the design decisions involved in how the API platform were implemented. The makeup of the different parts of the solution have been examined, both in the cloud layer and the gateway.

This has included exploring the pros and cons of different options and the possible constraints. This has extended to considering aspects of the infrastructure around the gateway such as load balancing and firewalls. With these considerations, the approach has been outlined for our use case—MRA.

The setup of the cloud elements of the solution and the configuration of users and their roles have been walked through. From there the design considerations of the *engine* of the API platform, the gateway nodes (or just gateways) were explored.

The configuration parameters and various deployment configurations, such has handling web proxies, have been described. A standard configuration of a gateway has been provided. With the configuration defined, the steps necessary to deploy a gateway have been described including the differences in process when connecting more than one physical gateway to a logical gateway. The entire gateway life cycle has been examined. The final step was to look at how to make the gateway production fit with the last stage of the life cycle.

In the next chapter, we will look at the development of the API policies and deployment to the gateway.

6
Defining Policies for APIs

Chapter 3, *Designing the API* introduced the concept of API design-first and described how Apiary can be used to define, document, and negotiate API contracts with consumers. It also detailed how to create and publish an API to the developer portal for consumption. This chapter will focus on securing APIs before they are exposed to developers on the public internet or indeed to internal developers. It will describe how to create managed APIs using APIP CS and apply policies to control access and monitor usage, thus providing a secure environment for API access.

Background

APIs can be created and exposed to consumers directly without the need for an API platform. However, this is highly unadvisable as it requires a high level of effort and diligence in terms of network security and firewall configuration, while still exposing organizations to a significant level of risk. Instead, API managers need to ensure their APIs are secured against all common threats and provide facilities to manage a community of developers using a user-friendly portal. By providing a central point of access, together with full API documentation, API managers can create a controlled environment that will promote API usage for an organization. When a service endpoint is accessed using an API Gateway that enforces security policies, then it becomes a **managed API**.

APIP CS policies are defined centrally in the management portal, meaning that service implementations, such as the Microservices described in Chapter 4, *Building and Running the Microservice*, do not have to be modified in any way to deal with security issues; the gateway will act as the point of enforcement.

API Gateways can be deployed on the cloud or on premise. Chapter 5, *Platform Setup and Gateway Configuration*, described in detail how to set up an APIP CS environment and how to configure gateways. It also showed how logical gateways are used to group collections of APIs that should be managed in a similar way. For example, separate gateways can be configured for production, development, and test environments.

This chapter discusses the steps required to create and configure security policies and recommends policies that should be enforced both internally and externally. It also shows how to implement gateway-based routing, which can be used to direct API requests to the correct backend service implementation depending on the gateway that the request has passed through; this can be used when supporting multiple environments such as development, test, and production.

Common security threats

Exposing APIs to consumers, especially external consumers, creates an inherent risk of attack for an organization. While there are no guarantees that an attack can be thwarted, every effort should be made to secure APIs using APIP CS. There are several policies that can be applied out of the box, which will help circumvent the most common types of attack. These policies will be described in more detail later in the chapter. This section will discuss several common threats that the reader should be aware of.

 Further details of common threats can be found at **The Open Web Application Security Project (OWASP)** `https://www.owasp.org/index.php/Main_Page`.

Denial-of-service attacks (DoS)

In a denial-of-service (DoS) attack, the perpetrator attempts to prevent legitimate users from accessing a service, usually by sending excessive messages to a service endpoint. DoS attacks may be distributed in nature, meaning that the excessive traffic is directed from multiple attack systems. While DoS attacks originating from a single source can be easier to mitigate because defenders can block network traffic from the offending source, attacks directed from multiple attacking systems are far more difficult to detect and defend against because it can be difficult to differentiate legitimate traffic from malicious traffic and filter malicious packets when they are sent from all over the internet.

Rate limiting policies can be defined to protect backend APIs against these sorts of attacks and should be used for the following purposes:

- Enforcing security to prevent denial-of-service (DoS) attacks impacting backend systems
- Supporting capacity management so that when APIs are being serviced by solutions running on a shared API platform, that one application cannot swamp the platform and thus impact other users

The gateway acts as an agent to protect the API in this case and will return an error when the number of requests exceeds a certain limit.

API applications running on platforms that are not configured to be dynamically scalable should have a rate limit specified. These rate limits can then be modified in different environments based on the available capacity provided.

Payload attacks

Payload attacks result from malicious content being sent in a request payload. Common attacks include SQL injection, XML injection, recursive payload attacks, and oversize payload attacks.

SQL injection attacks work similarly to cross-site scripting. However, in this case, it is malicious SQL statements that are inserted into the site or payload. Data is injected into the payload that can result in data leakage, removal, or manipulation of stored procedures.

XML injection is an attack technique that is used to manipulate or compromise the logic of an XML application or service by injecting additional XML content and/or structures into an XML message. This can alter the intended logic of the application. Further, XML injection can cause insertion of malicious content into the resulting message/document.

Recursive payload attacks involve attempting to create a denial-of-service by using recursion of XML elements resulting in excessive processing overhead that will bring down a service.

The key point here is that the payload should be examined in the gateway to confirm that such attack vectors are not incorporated into it.

Role of the gateway

API Gateways are policy enforcement points that can protect backend APIs from the types of attacks discussed above. API Gateways should be designed to be fast and lightweight. To keep the API gateway as lean and performant as possible it is important to remember where the gateway fits into the overall Enterprise IT architecture and what roles it should play. Gateways should concentrate on determining whether a consumer has the rights to access a service, protect endpoints from malicious requests, routing, throttling, and facilities to analyze and monetarize API calls. They are not meant to replace traditional service buses as they play an entirely different role.

Integration platforms, on the other hand, such as **Oracle Integration Cloud service** (**OIC**) offer facilities to handle more heavyweight operations, such as message transformation and protocol conversions. Modern architecture design paradigms, such as those proposed by OMESA, consider that the service itself should be responsible for payload transformation and enrichment. Alternatively, a callout could be used to encapsulate the message transformation, which again can be implemented in a separately scalable microservice.

 Further details on OMESA can be found in Chapter 2, *Use Case* or at http://omesa.io.

Routing should be limited to restructuring HTTP headers and URLs. Orchestration is the domain of middleware or handled within the service implementation itself. Therefore, it is important for organizations to evaluate and consider best practices when implementing an API platform and to define a reference architecture to consider these principles.

This does not mean that an API gateway should never offer these features. There may be a good reason why an organization adopts certain exceptions, such as when integrating to a third party which has no middleware. However, the recommendation is that care should be taken to restrict the gateway to lightweight transformation if at all.

HTTP and HTTPS

An organization's security policy will provide a more concise guide on whether to use HTTP or HTTPS to access an API. However, the following guidelines should generally be applied:

- Always use HTTPS if there is doubt regarding security
- Use HTTPS if the header or body is carrying data that is commercially sensitive (such as pricing data or financial transactions) or personal data
- If the external communication is via HTTPS then the internal security should also utilize HTTPS

Throttling

Throttling, which limits the number of requests to a service to a manageable level, can be used to protect resource limited services such as compute intensive tasks or backend services with underlying resource restrictions, such as those making use of an FTP server for example. When many requests flood into an FTP server, the server will inherently slow down as the underlying storage system needs to perform expensive disk searches.

There are many examples of systems overloading due to high demand, none more so than those observed on Black Friday in 2016. Throttling is used to prevent systems from going down especially at peak times, which can be very costly for the reputation of a business.

 Further details on the Black Friday melt down can be found at the following URL:
`https://www.forbes.com/sites/tompopomaronis/2016/12/01/black-friday-and-cyber-monday-2016-lets-just-say-there-were-scary-moments/`

Implementing APIs for MRA

Referring back to the use case being followed by this book, by now the desired APIs for MRA will have been reviewed by potential developers and contracts agreed and tied down. It is now time to start to expose these APIs using APIP CS. API managers utilize APIP CS to create, manage, secure, and publish APIs using the management portal. This topic was extensively covered in Chapter 3, *Designing the API*.

This chapter will focus on the policies that can be applied to an API to secure it. It assumes that the microservices that implement the APIs have been created to support the use cases. These are described in detail in Chapter 4, *Building and Running the Microservice*.

API managers are also responsible for managing API grants and application registrations and they may also deploy or request deployment (depending on privileges) of their APIs to gateways. The design of the gateways is an important part of the overall security design and is discussed in detail in Chapter 5, *Platform Setup and Gateway Configuration*.

Understanding policies

Policies are a powerful capability provided by the API cloud platform that allow a designer to change the behavior of an API through declarative configuration. They are a collection of statements that are executed sequentially on the request or response of an API, allowing the API designer to secure, throttle, route, or log requests sent to the API. This will result in a request being rejected should policies be contravened. Policies are reusable and can be applied across multiple APIs, independent of the domain in which the API resides.

APIP CS allows the designer to apply security checks using one or more policies that are configured as part of the request or response pipeline. Policies are executed in the order that they are specified in the API management portal, so careful consideration should be made for most likely failure scenarios and these should be placed first in the flow. Also, a policy can only be placed in certain locations in the execution flow. While most policies can be used in request flows, only the redaction, logging, and groovy script policies can be placed in the response flow.

APIP CS provides policies for the following areas:

- **Security**: Policies that determine who can send requests to a service.
- **Traffic Management**: Policies that manage the volume of traffic sent to services.
- **Interface Management**: Policies that manage the service interfaces clients are permitted to access.
- **Routing**: Policies that route requests to different service URLs depending on the requesting application, the resource requested, and other conditions.
- **Other**: Policies not belonging to one of the above categories and covering concepts such as service call-outs, logging policies and bespoke Groovy script and custom java policies. These are covered in detail in `Chapter 9`, *Implementing Custom Policies*.

General guidelines for designing policies

Policies should be configured to be naturally defensive, meaning that if access is not explicitly granted then it is denied. The degree to which this is done will depend on the nature of the API call and what data it exposes. Careful consideration should be given to ensure that the correct level of security policies is set, as even innocuous looking API calls can result in damage to organizations. For example, an API call that records the last login date and time of a user may seem harmless, but it will presumably store the login details into a database and therefore, this API could be used to direct potential SQL injection attacks, which if successful could result in serious damage.

The focus will naturally be on network level security and common attack vectors initiated over the internet, such as denial of service, brute force attacks, and vulnerability detection. In addition, simple malicious content checks should be provided. While it is correct to concentrate on external threats, API policy designers should also consider internal attacks as well since many security breaches originate from within the organization; here a user or administrator with malicious intent may call API endpoints in order to gain access to key information or personal details. Thus, a defensive posture should be applied to both internal and external resources alike.

The API platform layer should provide technical security and not incorporate business rules. So, for example while it is legitimate to apply policies for detection of injection attacks and authentication, the gateway should not generally apply rules to filter data or access to data based on the payload values. These business rules should be applied within the service implementation itself.

Security should also consider the data being returned from an API call and how sensitive that data is. Therefore, the response should be considered to be as important as the request. An API that is used internally may return more information than that required on public site, such as price-sensitive data. Where a public-facing API utilizes the same underlying service implementation, redaction will be required to ensure that important information is not accidentally leaked outside of the organization.

Certain security checks should be applied early in the request pipeline to identify obvious security breaches. This includes checks like the presence of a valid application token or key or IP whitelisting. These security checks provide a quick and efficient initial filter on API invocations before applying more computationally intensive user-based authentication as they only require the simplest of lookup mechanisms within the gateway. API key/token based authentication, however, is a weak security option since:

- It does not identify an individual making the call
- Traffic sniffing may be used to identify the key as it will be a common string pattern
- The token can be reverse engineered out of an application since it is likely to be hardwired into it, unlike for example credentials for an individual user

When API keys are utilized, they should be removed from downstream application API calls. This prevents security information being accidentally exposed elsewhere in the solution space. This also means that traffic can be passed over HTTP rather than HTTPS where the API key is the only sensitive piece of information in the call downstream. Switching to HTTP means there is the potential simplification of not needing to manage a deploy certificates. A small reduction in communications and compute overhead of the SSL handshake and encrypt/decrypt activities.

This chapter will outline how to apply the relevant policies necessary to deliver a secure solution.

Request and response pipeline policies

Request policies are applied to the request flow and are enforced between the request being received from a client and the request being forwarded to the backend service endpoint. Any number of policies can be defined but policies execute in order, with the uppermost policy first, followed by the next policy, and so on, until the request is either rejected or forwarded to the backend service if all policy conditions are met. The service request URL is where requests meeting the policy criteria are sent, that is, the service endpoint:

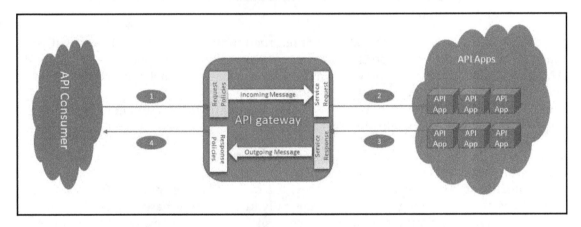

Request and response policy enforcement

Response policies behave in a similar manner but apply from the point where the service endpoint responds up to the point where the response is sent back to the consumer from the API. The response from the backend service is always the first entry in an outbound flow. Additional policies can then be applied with the policies executing in the order that they are specified.

APIP CS provides four built-in policies that are automatically added to the pipeline and cannot be removed. These are:

- API Request
- Service Request
- Service Response
- API Response

The API Request, which is always first in the pipeline, is used to define the API Request URL, which is the endpoint that the consumer uses to call the API. The Service Request, which is the last policy in the pipeline, specifies the endpoint for the service implementation. The Service Response and API Response policies are not editable.

The following table describes all the policies that can be applied to request and response pipelines:

Policy type	Description
Basic Auth	The basic authentication policy is used to secure an API using the basic authentication protocol. The policy validates the value of the authorization HTTP header against the identity store that the gateway node is configured against.
Key Validation	Use a key validation policy to reject requests from unregistered (anonymous) application.
Oauth 2	Use this policy to enforce OAuth 2 authentication.
API Rate Limiting	The API rate limiting policy limits the total number of requests an API permits over a specified time period; in seconds, minutes, hours, days, weeks, or months.
API Throttling - Delay	The API throttling-delay policy is used to control the global volume of requests to an API by delaying requests exceeding a threshold you set.
Application Rate Limiting	The application rate limiting policy is used to limit the number of requests an API allows from each application over a specified time period: in seconds, minutes, hours, days, weeks, or months.
Interface Filtering	The interface filtering policy filters requests based on the resources and methods specified in the request.
Service Callout	The service callout policy can call an external service from an API's request flow. The gateway can pass or reject the request based on the status code received from the external system.
Method Mapping	Method mapping can be used to change the HTTP method, resource, query parameters, headers, and fields of a request to another specified value before passing it to a service.
CORS	The CORS policy is used to specify which domains a request can be sent based on the value of a header element-*Origin*.
Redaction	Use a redaction policy to manage the fields and headers that appear in the request or response payload. You can explicitly include or exclude the headers and fields sent to the backend service (from the request flow) or sent to the client (from the response flow).

Header Validation	Use this policy to pass or reject a request based on the presence of or value of headers sent with the request.
IP Filtering	This policy is used to control which IP addresses can send requests to an API.
Service Level Authorization	Use this policy to pass credentials to backend services secured with basic authentication or OAuth 2.0.
Header Based Routing	Use the header-based routing policy to route incoming requests to a specific service request URL based on the presence or value of a specified header.
Resource Based Routing	This policy can be used to route a request based on the resource path to different service implementations.
Application Based Routing	Use this policy to route a request from a specific application or application type to the required service endpoint.
Gateway Based Routing	This policy is used to route requests to different service request URLs based on the gateway to which the API is deployed.
REST to SOAP	Introduced in 18.1.3, this policy can be used to expose a SOAP service as a JSON REST service.
Groovy Script	Use a groovy script policy to pass or reject a request by examining the request context or to manipulate the request context.
Logging	Use this policy to log custom messages for APIs deployed to specific gateways.

Since policies are executed sequentially, the order in which they appear is important. Certain policies are only applicable to the request or response pipelines, whereas others can apply to both, such as redaction and logging. The following table specifies the valid policies for each pipeline and the order in which Oracle specifies that they should be applied out of the box. Notice that certain policies can be placed at the same point. Later in the chapter, a preferred order is specified by the authors.

Order of request policies:

Order	Policy type
1	API Request
2	Key Validation
3	Basic Auth
3	Oauth 2
4	API Rate Limiting
4	API Throttling-Delay
4	Application Rate Limiting
4	Interface Filtering
4	Service Callout
4	Method Mapping
4	CORS
4	Redaction
4	Header Validation
4	IP Filtering
5	Service Level Authorization
5	Header Based Routing
5	Resource Based Routing
5	Application Based Routing
5	Gateway Based Routing
3,4,5	Groovy Script
3,4,5	Logging
6	Service Request

Order of response policies:

Order	Policy Type
1	Service Response
2	Redaction
3	Groovy Script
4	Logging
5	API Response

The policies defined in the preceding table can be applied at the same point in the pipeline. Further details can be found in the Oracle documentation:
`https://docs.oracle.com/en/cloud/paas/api-platform-cloud/apfad/i`
`mplementing-apis.html#GUID-E3BBFD46-BD95-41E6-9BB1-03E8AD860106.`

Defining polices

Previous sections of this chapter have discussed the types of threats that are likely to be encountered by an organization and the policies that can be used to defend against them. This section will discuss how policies are defined using APIP CS.

The type of policy used will depend on whether APIs are being exposed on an internal gateway or an external gateway. Policies are designed by the API Manager in conjunction with Enterprise Security Architects. Generally, more consideration needs to be given to external-facing APIs as they will almost be certainly subjected to attack over the course of their life time. However, internal policies are still important, albeit that they are usually limited to authentication and authorization. The use of API gateways internally also helps to decouple and abstract systems, particularly for COTs functionality, since the APIs act as a central point of access and route to the appropriate backend implementation.

The following table identifies recommended policies that should be used, their sequencing and the gateways that they are expected to be in.

The policies have been classified here as:

- **Mandatory**: Should be implemented
- **Recommended**: Not enforced but would be recommended
- **Optional**: Considered as useful

Inbound policies

Policy name/type	Elaboration	Sequence	Internal Mandatory / Recommended/ Optional	External Mandatory / Recommended/ Optional
Throttling	Control the amount of workload coming into the environment	1	R	M
Lightweight Authorization checks	Simple checks such as application key/token; white and blacklisting	1	R	R
Authentication (by Certificate)	This can be against a certificate	2	O	
Authentication by Id	App Key or User credentials	3	M	R
Logging	Record the payload that has been received	4	R	R
Redaction	Remove or add header or body data if required	4	O	O
Payload Check	Examine the payload to confirm that content is not malicious, for example, doesn't contain SQL injection	5	O	R
Transaction Id Header	Ensure the tracing Id is in the payload header	6	R	R
Gateway Routing	Header tag to show which gateway the request has passed through	7	O	O

The **Payload Check** feature is not available in initial product releases.

Outbound policies

Policy Name/Type	Elaboration	Sequence	Internal Mandatory / Recommended	External Mandatory / Recommended
Redaction	Remove header or body data from response if required	1	O	O
Logging	Record the response that has been sent	1	R	R

To configure and apply policies for an API, the user must be granted the **Manage API** grant. Further details of grants can be found in Chapter 3, *Designing the API*.

Defining rate limiting policies

Implementing rate limiting policies on the external gateway should be considered mandatory to prevent attacks such as denial of service and where backend solutions are not elastically scalable, to prevent overloading that would result in possible loss of service. In Chapter 5, *Platform Setup and Gateway Configuration*, the assumption was made by MRA that it is unlikely to observe more than 10 API calls per minute over a 24/7 x 365 period from external or internal sources. To enforce this condition, a rate limiting policies can be applied.

A rate limiting policy should be defined at the application level as a preference. Where APIs are single use in nature, they should be associated with just one application and use a single **Application Key**. However, where an API is multi-purpose, and thereby shared among many applications, the rate limit should be applied to the API itself as it is the total use that will impact the back-end platform.

API rate limiting policies

An API rate limiting policy can be configured to limit the total number of requests to an API over a specified period, which can be seconds, minutes, hours, days, weeks, or months. In the case of the MRA use case, this must limit the number of requests to ten per minute.

Steps to create a rate limiting policy

1. To define a policy, select the required API in the management portal, select the required policy from the **Available Policies** list and hit **Apply** as shown in the following screenshot:

The API management portal

2. In the screen that pops up, enter the name of the policy. This should be as descriptive as possible and convey the purpose of the policy. The comment should describe what the policy is meant to do and mention any important considerations, such as exception conditions for example. The screen also allows the API manager to specify where the policy should sit in the pipeline. The reader is referred to the section on *Request and Response Pipeline Policies* for the recommendations on policy placement. In this case, after the request as shown in the following screenshot:

Rate limiting policy definition

3. Hit the arrow icon to proceed to the next screen.
4. On the next screen, configure the policy to limit calls to 10 per minute as shown in the following screenshot and hit **Apply**:

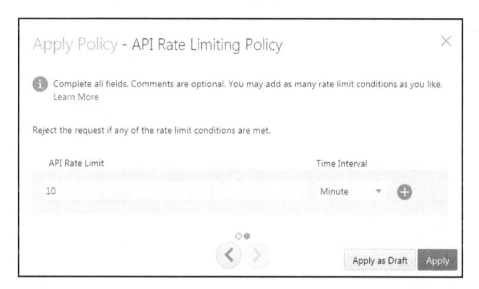

Apply Policy - API Rate Limiting Policy   ✕

Complete all fields. Comments are optional. You may add as many rate limit conditions as you like.
Learn More

Reject the request if any of the rate limit conditions are met.

API Rate Limit	Time Interval
10	Minute ▾ ➕

Apply as Draft   Apply

Rate limiting policy limit

Application rate limiting policies

The application rate limiting policy is used to restrict the number of requests to a given API from each subscribed application. This policy is different to an API rate limit policy where all requests are counted independent of the application. Subscribed applications are displayed in the **Registrations** tab in the management portal. The rate limit can be set over time periods which are specified in seconds, minutes, hours, days, weeks, or months.

Rate limits can be applied to the entire gateway or to each node within a gateway. If a gateway has two nodes and you wish to set a limit of 50 requests per minute for an application, this can be configured at node level such that each node can furnish a maximum of 50 requests per minute. Alternatively, the limit can be set at the gateway level, so that each node can serve a maximum of 25 requests per minute. The gateway will reject requests that exceed the threshold value.

Creating an application rate policy

1. To create an application rate limit, select the API and then **Traffic Management**. Select the **Application Rate Limiting** policy and click on **Apply**:

Defining application rate policy

2. On the screen that pops up, complete the details for the policy name and description as follows:

Application rate policy description

3. Hit the arrow icon to proceed to the next screen and on the screen that follows enter details for the limit to be imposed; in this case, 10 calls per minute:

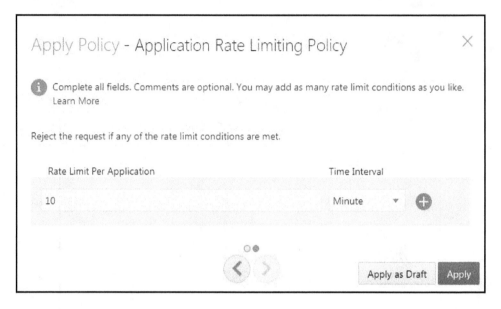

Application rate policy limits

4. Hit **Apply** to create the policy.
5. With the rate limiting policies applied, the API can be deployed to the gateway. To deploy, select the **Deploy** icon from the left-hand pane while the desired API is selected. The deploy icon is a cog with an embedded arrow. The following screen will appear:

Deploying policies

6. Hit the **Deploy API** button to deploy to the required gateways.

Testing the policy

The policy can now be tested. Here, the API is invoked using **Postman**. In the following example, a call is made to the **Search Artists** operation, which is exposed as part of the API. Before the API can be called, you must set the required parameters for the call. The developer portal can be used to view the Apiary documentation to determine the required parameters as shown in the following screenshot:

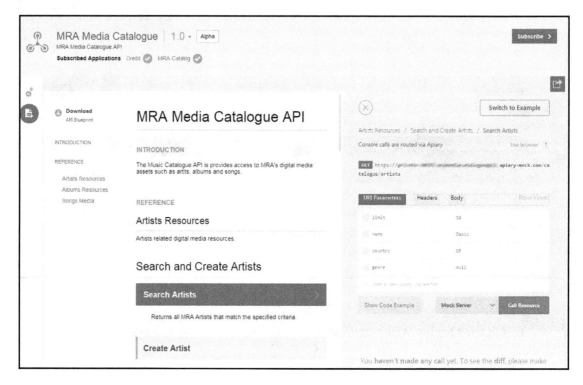

Apiary documentation access via the development portal

In this case, parameters were configured in Postman as follows:

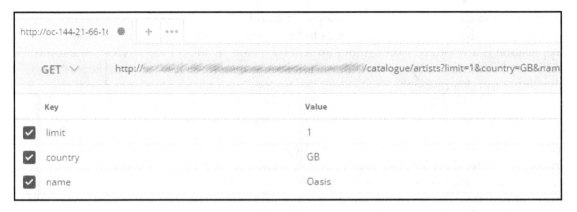

Passing parameters using Postman

The HTTP method for the call is set to **GET**. The call can be executed multiple times and after calling the API for the 11th time in a minute, an error is received as follows:

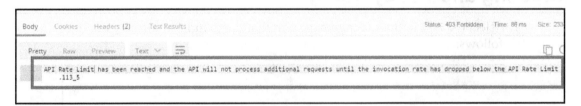

API limit Postman response

This book strongly advocated using API Fortress for testing please refer to `Chapter 7`, *Testing APIs with API Fortress*. However, any tool that can invoke REST APIs can be used for initial testing. For convenience, this chapter makes use of Postman but there are other tools that are equally suited for the task.

Lightweight authorization checks

Authorization checks should be considered as mandatory in the API security policy pipeline. In order to call an API, it needs to be associated with an application. The application is authorized to consumer an API by means of an API key. Indeed, the same API may be consumed by multiple applications and therefore have multiple keys. A developer can determine the application key by logging into the developer portal. The APIP CS platform will check all the associated keys when an API is invoked and if the consumer passes a key in the list, it will allow the call to proceed.

Where APIs are single purpose in nature, they should be associated with just one application (and therefore one application key) and the rate limiting should be defined at the application level. However, when an API is multi-purpose (that is, shared among many applications) then the rate limit should be applied to the API as it is the total use that will impact the backend platform. This section shows how to enforce application key validation to consume the service endpoint.

Creating an API key policy

1. Select the API in the management portal and expand the security nodes as follows:

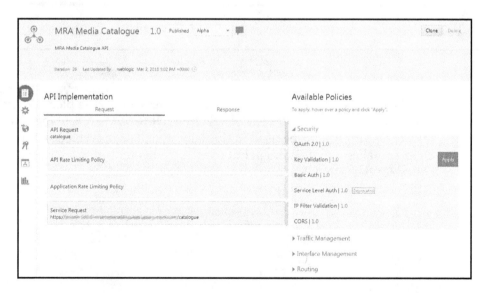

Key validation definition

2. Select **Key Validation** and hit **Apply**.
3. On the screen that pops up, enter details for the policy and hit the arrow icon to proceed to the next screen:

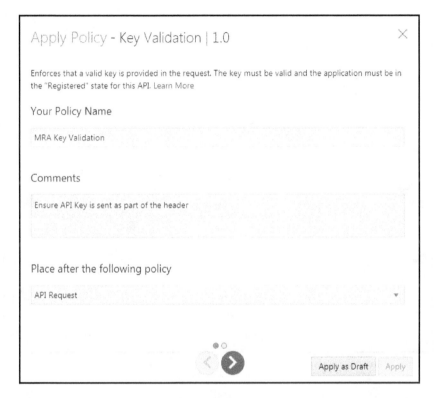

Key validation policy description

4. On the screen that follows, select the **Header** tab to ensure that the app key is passed as a header element and specify the name of the key; in this case, `api-key`:

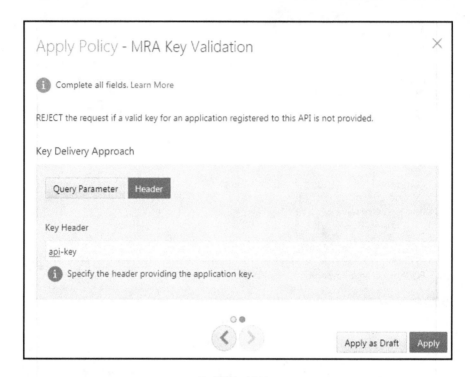

REJECT the request if a valid key for an application registered to this API is not provided.

Key Delivery Approach

Query Parameter | Header

Key Header

api-key
Specify the header providing the application key.

Apply as Draft | Apply

Key validation definition

The api key can either be passed as a query parameter on the URL or as part of the header. It is not advisable to pass it as part of the query since it is visible as part of the request. Passing a key as a header variable ensures that it is hidden during the call.

5. Hit **Apply** to and then save the API policies.
6. Deploy the API to the required gateway to activate the policies.

Testing the API key

1. The API can then be tested using Postman. Here the same parameters are used to invoke the API as used previously. The following screenshot shows the error that is observed when an application key is omitted from the call. It is important to note that the platform gives no details about the gateway in the response but only a 401 error. This is critical to ensuring that no information can be gleaned, which could result in a different attack being launched:

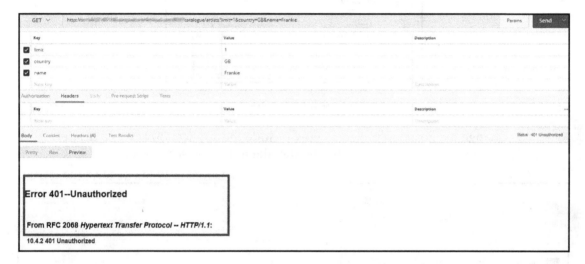

Key validation result

2. The Postman parameter list needs to be amended to include an API key value. The application key can be found in the developer portal as shown in the following screenshot:

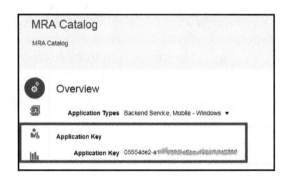

Application key in the development portal

3. Change the Postman project to now include the application key as a header parameter (`api-key`) as highlighted in the following screenshot:

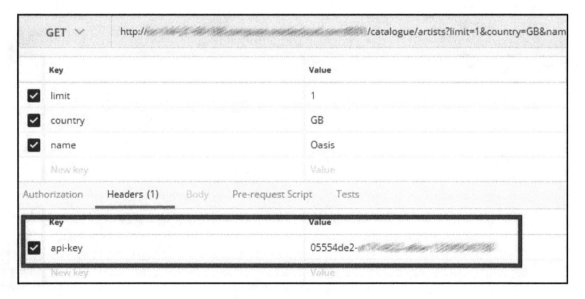

Define the API key in Postman

4. Execute the query. This time the call is successful and the results are returned.

Logging

Logging allows the API manager to log and store custom messages for APIs that are deployed to a specific gateway.

Enabling logging

1. The enable logging, open the manager portal and select the required API. Expand the **Other** menu and select **Apply** on the **Logging** option as shown in the following screenshot:

Define the logging policy in the management portal

2. On the screen that displays, enter basic details for the logging policy as shown in the following screenshot:

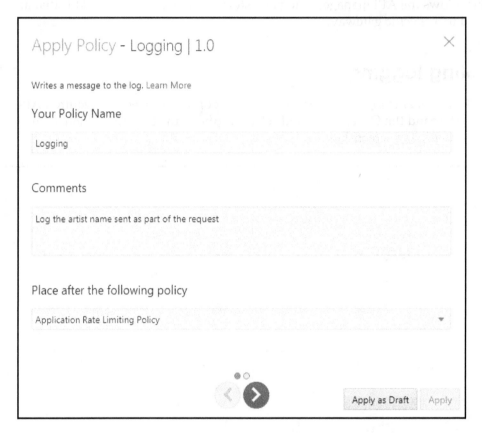

The logging policy description

3. Hit the arrow icon to proceed to the next screen:

Apply Policy - Logging   ✕

  ⓘ Complete all fields. Comments are optional. Learn More

Logging Conditions

Log Level Info   ▼

Log Message

${payload.artist.artist_name}

Example Invoice number is ${payload.salesOrder.invoiceNumber} Learn more

Log File Path

mra_catalog.log

    ◌ ●

    ❮ ❯   Apply as Draft   Apply

Logging policy details

4. In the **Log Message** field, enter the message to be written to the log. Using **Groovy**, it is possible to derive and log values from headers, fields, or other values from the inbound request or response. For example, to log the inbound artist name, enter the expression:

```
${payload.artist.artist_name}
```

Generally, it is not a good idea to log the entire payload as it may contain sensitive information such as personal data. In this case, it is best to choose which parts of a payload should be logged.

In the **Log File Path** field, enter the location of the log file that messages are written to. This path is relative to the following path on the gateway node domain:

```
domains/<name of the gateway domain>/apics/customlog
```

For example, in the preceding screenshot we set the log path to `artists.log` so events will be written to:

```
domains/Production Gateway/apics/customlog/artists.log
```

Further details of using Groovy can be found in `Chapter 9`, *Implementing Custom Policies*, which covers the creations of custom policies.

Interface filtering

Interface filtering can be used to filter requests based on the resource and methods specified in the invocation. This means that it can be used to pass or reject requests to a resource based on the method employed. For example, for resources that should only support a `GET` method, the policy might reject all other method calls, such as `UPDATE` for example. In the case of MRA, the artists resource supports `GET`, `POST`, and `PUT` operations but not `PATCH`. To enable interface filtering, the following steps should be applied.

Creating an interface filter

1. First, select the API from the management portal. Expand the list of policies, find `Interface Filtering`, and select **Apply**.

2. In the pop up, enter the basic details for the policy and hit the arrow icon to proceed to the next screen:

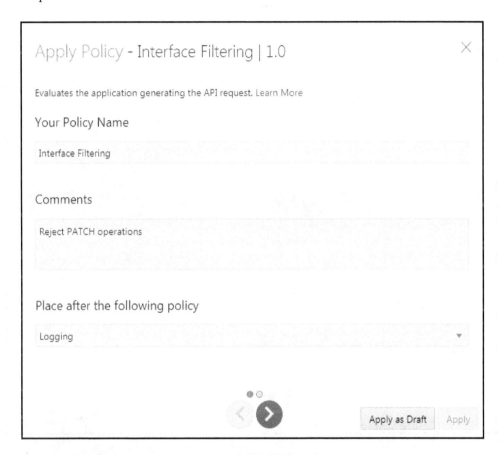

Apply Policy - Interface Filtering | 1.0   ✕

Evaluates the application generating the API request. Learn More

Your Policy Name

Interface Filtering

Comments

Reject PATCH operations

Place after the following policy

Logging   ▼

Apply as Draft   Apply

Interface filtering description

3. On the next screen create the filter condition; in this case, PATCH on all the resources.

4. Choose **Reject** from the dropdown:

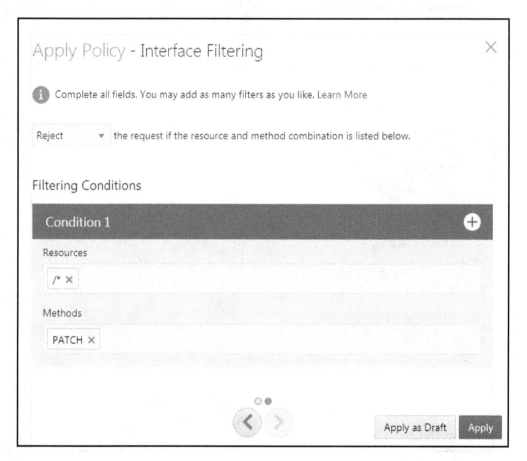

Apply Policy - Interface Filtering   ✕

 ⓘ Complete all fields. You may add as many filters as you like. Learn More

Reject   ▼ the request if the resource and method combination is listed below.

Filtering Conditions

Condition 1   ⊕

Resources

/* ✕

Methods

PATCH ✕

○ ●

‹ ›

Apply as Draft   Apply

Interface filtering details

5. Save the policy and hit **Apply** to create the filter.
6. Finally, deploy the API to the required gateway.

Testing the policy

This policy can now be tested using Postman. The following output shows a failed call when the HTTP method is set to PATCH. Notice that a 403 error is returned:

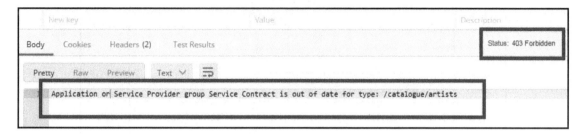

Interface filtering enforcement

Cross origin resource sharing (CORS)

CORS is a mechanism that can be used by web applications to request resources from another domain outside of the domain from which it was first served. For example, a web page may request images, stylesheets, or videos from a URL in another domain. Certain cross domain requests could be exploited to attack a site, and are therefore not allowed by default. However, CORS defines a way for a browser and server to interact to determine if the cross-origin request is safe and therefore allowed. For HTTP request methods that can modify data, such as POST, the specification mandates that browsers check with the server first to determine whether the request is allowed; browsers initiate what is referred to as a *pre-flight* check of the request before sending it using an HTTP OPTIONS request method. Once the approval is obtained, the actual request can be sent.

 A fuller description of CORS can be found at the following URL: https://www.w3.org/TR/cors/.

The following diagram illustrates the typical request and response required:

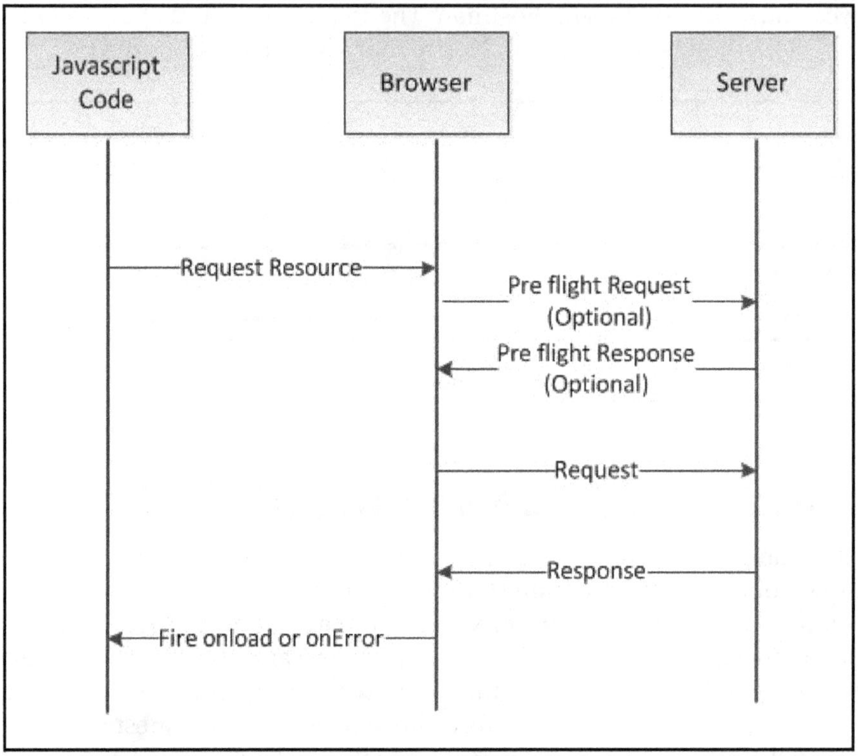

A typical CORS request and response

CORS allows more functionality than would be possible with same-origin requests, but nevertheless enforces a more secure environment than that provided by allowing all cross-origin requests. The CORS standard works by prescribing HTTP headers, which provide a mechanism for browsers to determine whether they have permissions to request remote URLs or not.

A CORS policy can be used to specify which domains are allowed to send requests to a service. By default, a gateway will only accept requests from its own domain and thus prevent potential CORS attacks. However, many use cases exist that require services to be invoked from other domains particularly where resources are shared between environments. Requests can be sent with an **Origin header** that includes the requesting domain. The CORS policy reads the value in the Origin header and compare this to a list of allowed domains. The policy can be configured to allow requests from specific domains or from all domains.

 This feature is not available in initial product releases.

The role of the CORS API gateway policy is to interpret HTTP request header elements and apply declarative filters for the call. However, the policy does not handle the pre-flight check; this needs to be allowed to pass through to the API service to handle. The pre-flight request will inform the consumer if the operations can be accepted by the service, which is relayed back to the consumer using HTTP headers in the response as follows:

- Access-Control-Allow-Origin
- Access-Control-Allow-Methods
- Access-Control-Max-Age

The API gateway's CORS policy doesn't handle the subsequent filters of the different HTTP verbs (Allow-Methods) and this needs to be defined through the Filter policy. This also means that the Filter policy should allow the **OPTIONS** verb if there are to be pre-flight calls on an endpoint.

The recommendation regarding the use of the CORS policy depends upon whether the policy is being used on an internal fateway or an external gateway. Generally, CORS is likely to be secure on the internal gateway but is riskier on the external gateway.

Creating a CORS policy

1. To create a CORS policy, open the API manager portal and select the required API. Choose the CORS policy from the **Security** policies and hit **Apply**:

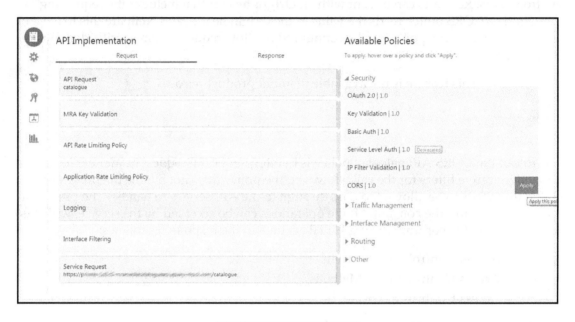

Define CORS policy in the management portal

2. On the window that pops up, enter the basic API policy details and hit the arrow to proceed to the next screen:

CORS policy description

3. In the next screen, enter a list of one or more allowed domains. In the case of MRA, the main root URL is used as follows. This means that all requests from the domain are allowed:

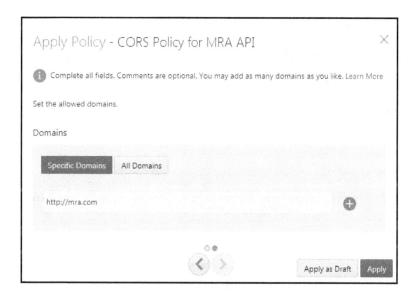

CORS policy definition

4. Finally hit **Apply** and save the policy. The API can now be deployed for testing.

Testing the CORS policy

To test this policy, a simple web page can be created as follows:

```
<?xml version="1.0" encoding="UTF-8"?>
<!DOCTYPE html PUBLIC "-//W3C//DTD XHTML 1.0 Strict//EN"
"http://www.w3.org/TR/xhtml1/DTD/xhtml1-strict.dtd">
<html xmlns="http://www.w3.org/1999/xhtml" xml:lang="en" lang="en">
<head>
  <title>Simple use of Cross-Site XMLHttpRequest (Using Access
Control)</title>
  <script type="text/javascript">
    var invocation = new XMLHttpRequest();
    var url = 'http://xxxxx.compute.oraclecloud.com:8001/catalogue/artists?
      limit=1&country=GB&name=Frankie&api-key=05554de2-a17f-4822-a6be-
      1330f9540780';
```

```
function callOtherDomain(){
   invocation.open('GET', url, true);
   invocation.onreadystatechange = handler;
   invocation.send();
}
function handler(evtXHR)
{
   if (invocation.readyState == 4)
   {
      if (invocation.status == 200)
      {
         var response = invocation.responseXML;
      }
      else
         alert("Invocation Errors Occured");
   }
   else
      dump("currently the application is at" + invocation.readyState);
}
//]]>
</script>
</head>
<body>
   <form id="controlsToInvoke" action="">
      <p>
      <input type="button" value="Click to Invoke Another Site"
         onclick="callOtherDomain()" />
      </p>
      </form>
</body>
<html>
```

In the preceding code snippet, the IP address has been replaced by xxxxxx.

When rendered in a browser, this web page has a single button that when invoked will execute a XMLHttpRequest method to call the MRA API. Since the call is initiated from a PC (in this case), which is in a different domain to the API platform, the invocation will fail. API analytics charts can be viewed to show the error being trapped as follows. The CORS error count increases each time the button is pressed:

CORS policy count in analytics chart

Gateway analytics is covered in more detail later in the chapter. Not all browsers support CORS. This testing was done using the Chrome browser.

Further details of browser support for CORS can be found at https://enable-cors.org/client.html.

Gateway-based routing

The gateway-based routing policy is utilized to route requests to different service request URLs based on the gateway to which the API is deployed. Chapter 5, *Platform Setup and Gateway Configuration* dealt with the concept of handling different environments such as development, test, **user acceptance test** (**UAT**), and production. This policy is an important policy as it allows the API manager to define a policy once and tailor it for different environments based on the gateway from which it was routed. As APIs move between environments, the policy will be released to a new environment but it is not necessary to change any endpoints. So, for example, in a development environment, a request will come from the development gateway. This should route requests to the development service implementation. When a request is received from a UAT gateway for example, it should go to the UAT service implementation instead. This policy can be added only to the request flow.

Creating a gateway-based routing policy

To enable gateway-based routing, follow the steps below.

1. Select the API in the management portal and expand on the policies to find the **Gateway Based Routing** policy. Hover over and press the **Apply** button.

2. On the screen that pops up, enter the policy details as follows:

Gateway-based routing policy description

3. Once the details have been entered, hit the arrow icon to proceed to the next screen.

4. On the screen that follows configure the routing based on the gateway. This screen is included as an example only and the URLs will depend on your own environments. Here, a policy is defined for a **Production Gateway**, but it is possible to add additional policies for each gateway:

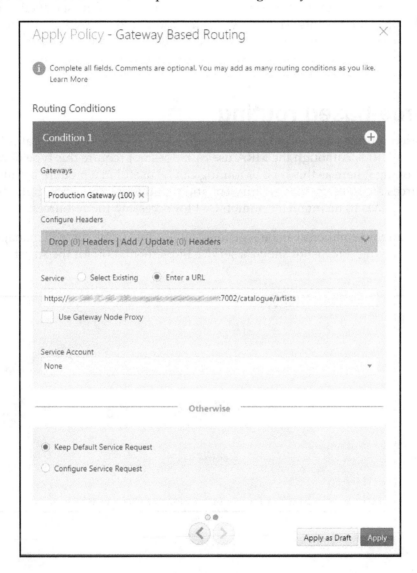

Gateway-based routing definition

5. Finally, hit **Apply** and then save the policy. The policy is now ready to be deployed to the gateways as required.

As can be seen from the preceding screenshot, the **Otherwise** section is used to route all requests not matching the conditions specified in the preceding points. This allows for the routing to a default endpoint or to a specific service request, which might be a generic catch-all endpoint for example.

Resource-based routing

Resource-based routing can be used to direct requests to specific resource paths to different service request URLs. Although the MRA use case does not require this type of routing, it is worth mentioning it here as this type of routing can be useful in a modern architecture where resources are implemented in different and separate microservices but where the API manager wishes to maintain a common URI for accessing the resources.

Microservice implementations can be registered as services using the API management portal. The following screenshot shows a service implementation for the Artist microservice:

Defining a service in the management portal

Resource-based routing can then be set up to direct requests to the correct service implementation based on the relative URI. For example, requests to the /artists URI can be directed to the Artists microservice. This is illustrated in the following screenshot:

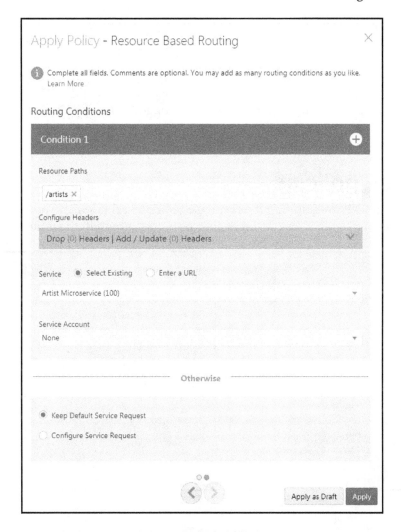

Resource-based routing definition

More details on resource-based routing can be found at https://docs. oracle.com/en/cloud/paas/api-platform-cloud/apfad/implementing-apis.html#GUID-314DC178-0491-4034-A5FC-6080B9C592A4.

Groovy policies

While there are a lot of out-of-the-box policies already provided with APIP CS, API managers can also take advantage of Groovy to create their own policies. The policy can be added to the request or response flows. Since Groovy is a programming language, there are no boundaries to what can be implemented (subject to what is supported by the specification). `Chapter 9`, *Implementing Custom Policies* of this book covers Groovy in detail, so this chapter will only introduce the concept. It should be noted that care must be taken when creating and applying these policies; the gateway must remain a lightweight perimeter security engine and should not become bogged down by CPU-extensive algorithms.

Response policies

It is also worth quickly mentioning the response policies at this stage. These are entered by selecting the **Response** tab in the API manager portal as shown in the following screenshot:

Response policies

While the use case for MRA does not require any response policies, there may be situations where redaction is required to prevent external users from seeing sensitive data. This policy can be used for example, to ensure that when a backend service, which exposes price sensitive data, is invoked externally via an API gateway, that the pricing data is redacted and not sent back to the consumer. A logging policy could be used in conjunction with the redaction policy to store the response sent back to the client to ensure that the redaction policy is being executed correctly.

API policy iterations

When an API is changed, even to add a comment, APIP CS will increment a unique number called an **iteration**. The iteration number can be used for configuration management. The iteration can be viewed in the API manager portal as illustrated in the following screenshot:

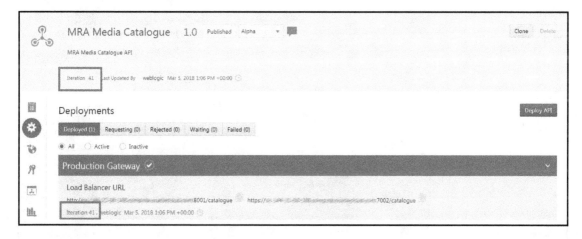

API iterations

Iteration details can also be obtained using APIP CS APIs. Further details on managing API policy versioning can be found at `https://blog.mp3monster.org/2018/02/27/apiversioning/amp/`.

The preceding screenshot also shows the deployed iteration of the API; in this case **Iteration 41** has been deployed to the **Production Gateway**. So in this example, the latest version of the API is clearly deployed to production. As the API is developed and tested, the API will be promoted between environments (development, test, UAT, and production) and the iteration ID can be used to ensure that the correct version of the API is deployed to each environment.

Monitoring APIs

The management console in APIP CS allows the API manager to analyze service requests based on a given time frame. It is possible to view API requests based on calls today, in the last 24 hours or a custom date range. As can be seen in the following screenshots, graphs are available to view various metrics:

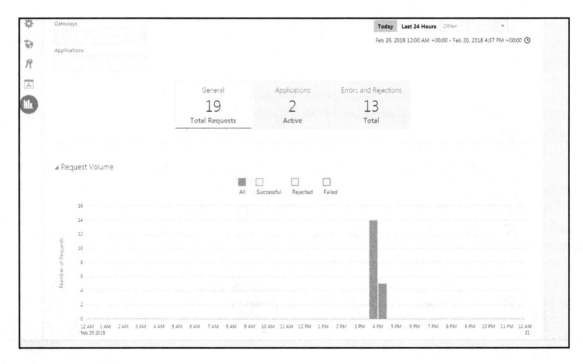

API analytics

The chart legend is dynamic. Selecting the rejected legend for example will change the report output accordingly to show rejected requests only:

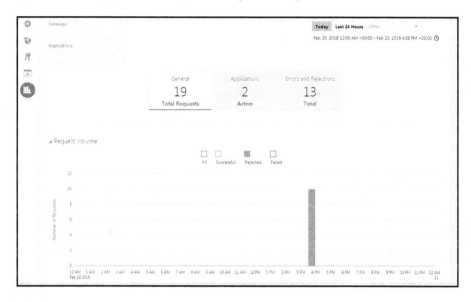

Rejected requests

Other charts available include response times and payload sizes. These are shown as follows:

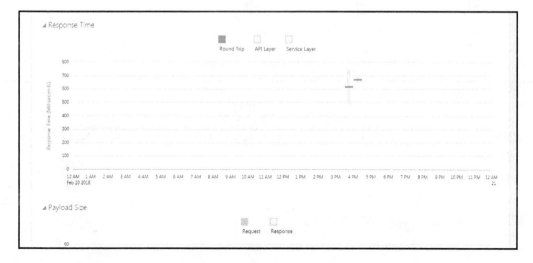

Request response time

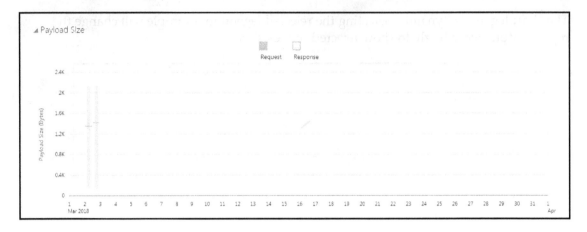

Request payload size

Finally, there is a summary by resource chart shown as follows:

Request Path	Requests		Rejections		Errors	
	Volume	Distribution	Volume	Distribution	Volume	Distribution
/catalogue/songs/son003456/	4	0.8%	4	1.0%		
/catalogue/artists	294	60.0%	242	60.8%	8	100.0%
/catalogue/artists/art123456	16	3.3%	7	1.8%		
/catalogue/songs	15	3.1%	8	2.0%		
/catalogue/catalogue/artists	13	2.7%	13	3.3%		
/catalogue/albums/alb000456	10	2.0%	3	0.8%		
/catalogue/songs/son003456	10	2.0%	5	1.3%		
/catalogue/albums	10	2.0%	3	0.8%		

Request by resource

This chart is useful as it shows a summary of all requests, rejections, and errors by each resource.

It displays the volume and distribution of requests (as a percentage) to resources for an API. The request by resource chart displays the following data:

- The volume of requests sent to each resource
- The percentage of requests sent to each resource
- The volume of rejected requests for each resource
- The percentage of rejected requests for each resource
- The volume of errors processed by each resource
- The percentage of errors processed by each resource

These reports can be used as the basis of management reports, although at present they do not print out very well. Oracle are planning to improve the analytics in future releases and provide charts and metrics to enable monitorization of APIs and to provide advanced reporting and report publication features.

Finally, the response payload size details can also be view by changing the dynamic legend from request to response. This allows the API manager to view payload sizes that can indicate a leak of data for example due to a successful SQL injection attack:

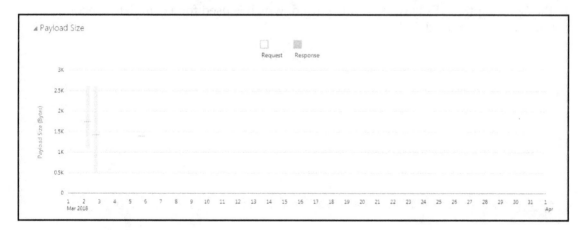

Response payload size

Summary

This chapter explored the various in-built security policies available with API-CS and how these can be used to mitigate against threats that can be exploited on exposed APIs. It is the job of the API gateway to implement these policies. Gateways can be installed either at the external perimeter of an organization or to provide protection from internal attacks, depending on how the logical gateways are configured. Further information on how to define and configure gateways can be found in Chapter 5, *Platform Setup and Gateway Configuration*.

The chapter also looked at how policies can be tested using tools such as Postman. However, this was for illustrative purposes only and Chapter 7, *Testing APIs with API Fortress* shows how to configure and use API Fortress for more complete functional testing of an API.

Finally, this chapter briefly touched on the analytics available in the management portal, and how these can be used to understand and monitor API usage and detect error conditions.

In the next chapter, **API Fortress** is introduced, which is used for a complete functional testing of the developed APIs.

Testing APIs with API Fortress

7

The previous chapter explained the implementation of the Media Catalogue API and the importance of configuring policies to ensure information is logged, secured and routed accordingly to the back-end Microservice implementation.

In this chapter the Media Catalogue API is going to be put to the test using **API Fortress**. The chapter starts by walking through the key features of API Fortress and illustrate some of these features in more detail including a run through of how test conditions can be created from an existing **Postman collection** and **Apiary** document.

The chapter continues to explain how to add new test **assertions**, and how to transfer the result of one test case to be used as the input in another.

The chapter concludes with running the test cases in a Continues Delivery setup using the **Jenkins plugin**.

What is API Fortress?

API Fortress is an automated testing platform run as a Cloud Service, which can also be run on-premises and it allows development, test and operational teams to create, run, validate and monitor tests. This platform allows teams to ensure that APIs are behaving in accordance with the contractual agreement between the client application and the back-end API implementation.

API Fortress simplicity, although it is a feature-rich platform, increases the speed of delivery by automating the creation of test cases from API description formats designed in Apiary and Mashery. It has the ability to create test cases from predefined document specifications like API Blueprint, RAML, Swagger (including Open API), and Postman Collections. It allows for validation of test cases using business rules, Continuous Development support, features to support performance testing and ability to monitor the outcome of each test run. This means that all test phases are supported in API Fortress. API Fortress offers a 30-day trial version and afterward a monthly fee needs to be paid based on the number of users. For more information see `http://apifortress.com/`.

The following is an overview of the current features of API Fortress. As the product is still developing rapidly, more features will be added to what has been written about in this book:

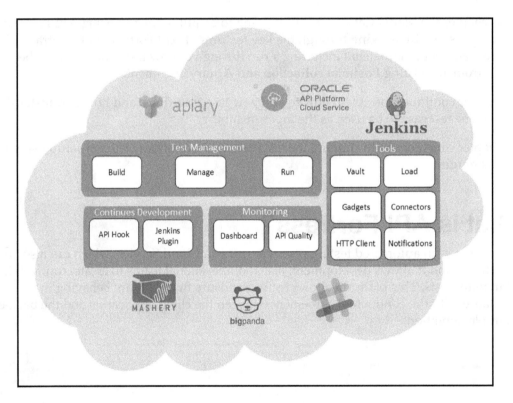

1. **Test Management**: This is the core functionality of API Fortress to build, manage, and run tests.
2. **Monitoring**: Tests executed can be monitored against KPIs to determine the result of your test cases.
3. **Continues Development**: API Fortress has strong Continuous Development support to automate tests using API Hooks and Jenkins.
4. **Tools**: API Fortress' toolbox that can be used while defining your test cases. This includes the ability to use Vaults, Gadgets, HTTP Client, Load Testing, Connectors, and Notifications.

 BigPanda creates tickets and notifications based on correlated incidents, rather than each individual alert. Tickets are updated in real time and enriched with contextual information such as runbooks, configuration items, code deployments, related incidents, and more. For more information see `https://bigpanda.io/`.

Test management

This is the core functionality of API Fortress with three main components:

1. **Build**: With the build component manual test cases can be composed with an option to use the *Generate Test* feature to autocreate test cases from a predefined API URI. The other options provided are to create test cases from an API description format using RAML, Swagger, I/O Docs, API Blueprint, and the possibility to create test cases by importing Postman collections and WSDLs for testing SOAP services. API Fortress can also link with your API description format designed in Apiary (Swagger and API Blueprint) or Mashery (I/O Docs). The test cases created from an API description format can be amended and enriched using the visual composer.
2. **Run**: Each test created can be run on its own merits, run as part of a CI/CD process (Jenkins, CircleCI, and so on), or scheduled to run at a preset time and date for monitoring.
3. **Manage**: Tests can be published, deleted, and existing working copies of your tests can be removed, and other related resources can be added.

Monitoring

API Fortress has monitoring capabilities to understand the result of tests that have either passed or failed. There are two main components:

1. **Dashboard**: The Dashboard consist of three main areas:

   - **Logs** show the history of the test cases/events run with the option to select specific events between a date and time period. Each event is listed in a table with information about the status, date, time, and location of where the event happened. The result of each event can be viewed in a test report that can be exported to PDF format.
   - **Metrics** section shows the performance of the API call. The data is shown in a table with information about the footprint, date, time, latency, fetch (number of instances run), location and status of the event. For each event, an alert can be triggered when for example the latency is not within the expected threshold.
   - **Availability** section shows the availability of the API endpoint with the number of success, failure and scheduled runs against the total of tests created per project. The data is listed in a table showing the endpoints, date, time, location and status of the event.

2. **API Quality:** This provided a high-level view about the quality of the API. The API Quality consist of two main views:

   - **Functional View** shows the total number of successful or failed events and the success ratio per month with the option to compare the results with previous runs to predict a failure trend.
   - **Performance View** shows per endpoint the response time, successes/total hits and the overall success ratio with the option to compare the results with the previous run to understand whenever the performance is improving.

Continuous deployment

API Fortress has strong capabilities to support Continuous Deployment using API Hooks and Jenkins support.

1. **API Hook**: Some of the features that can be done from the front-end are also made available through the use of APIs. These APIs are referred to as **API Hooks** and are used to run test cases, update test cases and return insightful information for monitoring purposes.

   The APIs supported are documented using Apiary. Details can be found here: `http://docs.apifortressv3.apiary.io/`.

2. **Jenkins Plugin**: The other option is to use the API Fortress **Jenkins Plugin** to run automated tests. This plugin uses an API Hook to automate tests in Jenkins and is explained in more detail further in this chapter.

Tools

API Fortress also comes with a toolkit that includes:

- **Vault** to store variables and fragments of code that can be reused across the tests in a project. This is useful for example when communicating the application key that will be re-used across multiple APIs.
- **HTTP Client** can be used to manually test an API with the ability to import Postman collections.
- **Gadgets** contain out-of-the-box features to use a variety of cryptography algorithms like MD5, SHA256, or the ability to generate a symmetric key. This might be useful when parts of the payload are encrypted that needs to be validated to pass a test. Gadgets also support base-64 encoding/decoding and signatures. These features might be useful to decipher JWT tokens.
- **Load** refers to the performance testing feature with the ability to performance test APIs and injecting high volumes of data to ensure the API meets the KPIs set by the business.
- **Connectors** are used to configure alerts to be sent to an external application like BigPanda or to a messaging application like Slack.
- **Notifications** that is used to administer who is notified of alerts and reports.

Test the MRA Media Catalogue API

MRA has traditionally done a lot of manual testing to deliver code changes in their existing on-premise solution. The time spend for testing was in many situations under-estimated and consequently ended up being rushed to meet deadlines. This resulted in code being released into production to early, which has caused some serious issues in the daily operation of MRA. The main problem was that code fixes introduced new issues and kept being repeated like a vicious circle that was difficult to break.

MRA recognized this problem and decided to setup a Continues Delivery capability with an important focus on test automation to ensure that APIs are regression tested after each code fix with the aim to reduce the risk of defects being introduced and the time required for testing to ensure that deadlines can be achieved.

MRA have been on the lookout to find a testing framework that can support their needs to reduce the time in executing the tests, deliver high-quality code, and to ensure that fewer defects are found. A good testing tool should also be able to schedule tests in production on a periodic basis to alert the operational team of any problems. The goal is to remain a step ahead of the users. **API Fortress** is such a tool and compliments APIP CS very well due to the ease of testing the APIs and the integration capabilities with Apiary. The other point is that API Fortress has excellent support for reporting and sending notification to inform people when tests fail and the ability to run performance testing. MRA has decided to use API Fortress as their strategic product to test APIs and to incorporate this into their Continuous Delivery process.

The MRA Media Catalogue API that has been designed and implemented in Chapter 3, *Designing the API,* Chapter 4, *Building and Running the Microservice,* and Chapter 6, *Defining Policies for APIs* will be used throughout this chapter to explain some of the main features of API Fortress. This is explained by creating two test cases:

- **Create Media Catalogue**: This test case will create the Song, Album, and Artist catalogue
- **Get Artist by id**: This test case will retrieve the artist information by artist ID

Create Media Catalogue test case

This paragraph starts to explain the steps to create a new project before the Create Media Catalogue test case is added. The steps then continue with explaining how to create predefined test condition, assertions, from an existing **Postman collection**. The assertions are then updated to ensure that the unique identifiers $artist\_id$, $album\_id$, and $song\_id$ contain unique values, so each run of the test creates a new resource. The paragraph ends by testing the newly created Create Media Catalogue test case.

The detailed steps are explained as follows:

1. Log in to the API Fortress console at `https://mastiff.apifortress.com/app/web/login/auth` with a valid username and password. The main page is opened as illustrated in the following screenshot:

2. Next, from the main page, click on the **Create Project** button and name it
   `MediaCatalogue` with an appropriate description. The **Notes** field can be left
   empty. The default **Alert Distribution lists** that is configured in the
   `Distribution group`. Save it by clicking on the green tick. The project is now
   visible from the main page as shown in the following screenshot:

3. Next, from the main page create a new test case and click on the **Test Case**
   button. Assign the test case to the project `MediaCatalogue` and save by clicking
   on the green tick:

4. In the **Test name** field, type `CreateMediaCatalogue` with a suitable description. The **Tags** field can be left empty. The value of the **Tags** field can be used to search test results on the dashboard or to run multiple test cases at once that has the same tag name. The following screenshot illustrates this step:

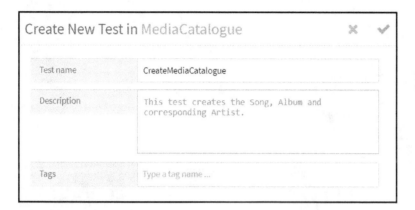

5. Once the test has been created, the main page of the **Tests** tab is opened. This page shows:

   - At the top an option to edit the test case information, that is, name, description, and tag
   - **Test status** whether the working copy has been completed, the test has been published, and if the test has been scheduled to run on a specific date and time
   - Information about when the current working copy and published version were modified

- The menu bar at the bottom to create, edit, or remove the test case

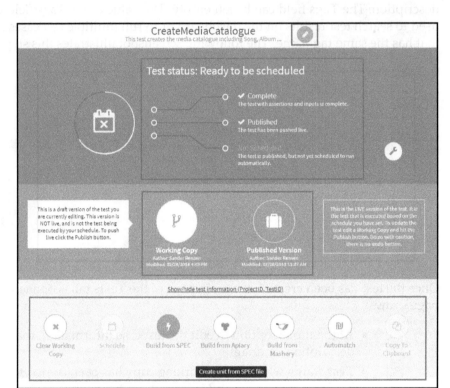

6. Click on the **Build from SPEC** option from the main page as shown in the preceding screenshot. Select the **Postman Collection** as the file type and click on **Drag a file here or click to upload**:

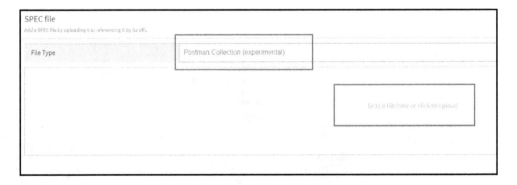

7. Upload the Postman collection that has been used in Chapter 4, *Building and Running the Microservice* and confirm by clicking on the **Save** button:

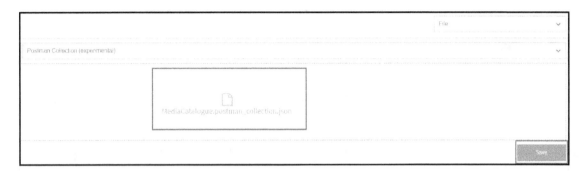

8. In the next screen, **Build options**, select the URI for which the test case needs to be created. In the following example, the URI is /catalogue/artists. Confirm to create the test case from scratch:

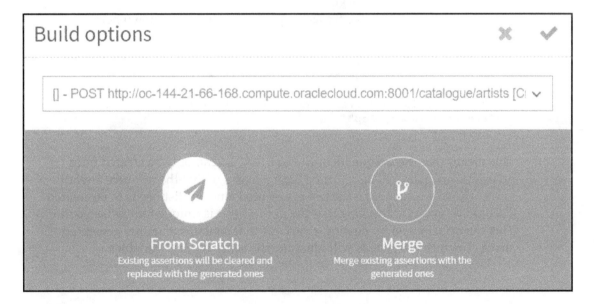

9. This creates the test case with the payload, **Content-Type**, and **api-key** that is required to successfully create an Artist:

10. The test case can only run once as the payload is static, as shown here:

```
{
    "artist_name": "Oasis",
    "artist_id": "art123456",
    "country": "UK",
    "bio": "Oasis is a great band from Manchester",
    "genres": "Rock, Pop"
}
```

This means that the unique identifier `artist_id` can only be created once otherwise an error will be returned with a message that the resource already exists. However, each time the test is executed a new artist needs to be created. This can be done by ensuring that the `artist_id` is unique for each execution. This can be achieved by passing a variable that contains a unique generated string. The following steps will illustrate the setup of such variables.

11. Click on **Vault** in the menu above and select the **MediaCatalogue** project. Then click on **Variables** and **New Variable** as shown in the following screenshot:

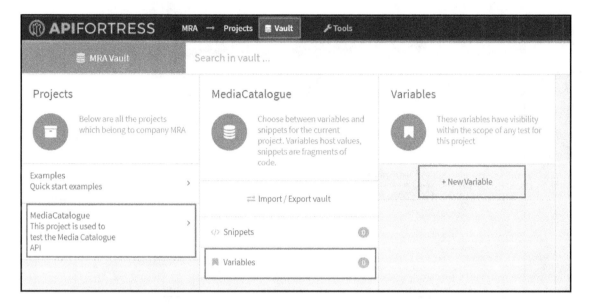

12. Name the variable `ArtistId` with the value `none` because the value will be overwritten. Click on the green tick to create the variable:

 Updating the vault `ArtistId` variable won't work when launching a test from within the composer. Run the test from outside the composer or schedule the test to update the value and from that initially test the composer can be used again.

13. Go back to the `CreateCatalogue` test case and click on the list button in the **Request Post component** and select **Add component before** as shown in the following screenshot:

14. Next, confirm the component to add. There are four different type of component groups:

- **System components**: These are system-driven components, for example, to change dynamically a vault variable to be re-used across other tests or to tag the result of a test in order to search for this test more easily in the dashboard or test report.
- **Requests components**: These are used to send a new request to a different API endpoint, JDBC Connection, or GitHub.
- **Assertions components**: These are the rules that can be asserted to validate the response. This can be to validate that an element exists in the response or to validate that the data contains a certain value.
- **Control components**: These components can be used to control the behavior during the test execution, that is, **loop component** to loop through one or more elements, **if component**, **flow component** to control the flow of execution, or simply to **add comments** to a test condition.

Refer to the following screenshot that provides all the components that can be selected within the group:

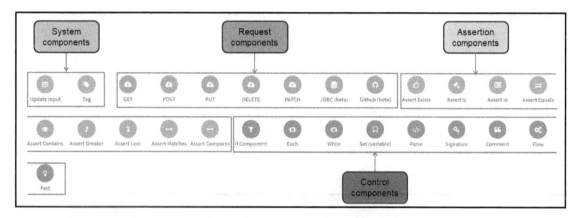

Select **Set (variable)** from the component.

15. In the **Variable** component update the field **Var** with artistId, **Variable mode** with String, and **Value:** ${WSCrypto.genUUID()}. The function genUUID() will create a unique value. Confirm the changes and click on the green tick in the top-right of the **Variable** component as shown next:

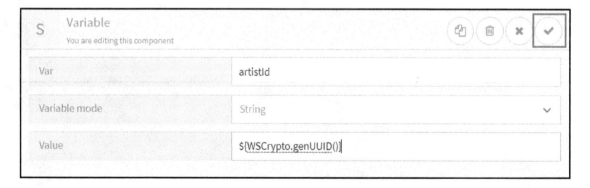

16. Next, click on the **POST** body component within the request **POST** component and click on **Edit**:

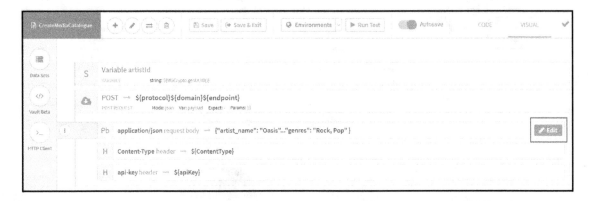

17. In the **Content** field, update the value to `"${artistId}"` and confirm the change by clicking on the green tick as illustrated in the following screenshot:

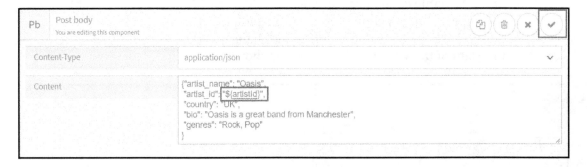

18. Next, run a test to see that the artist has been successfully created with a unique generated string identifier. Click on the **Run Test** and select a time zone as illustrated in the following screenshot where **EU West** is selected:

19. Click again on **Run Test**, which will open a test report. The test has passed with the unique string identifier as `artist_id` as shown in the following screenshot:

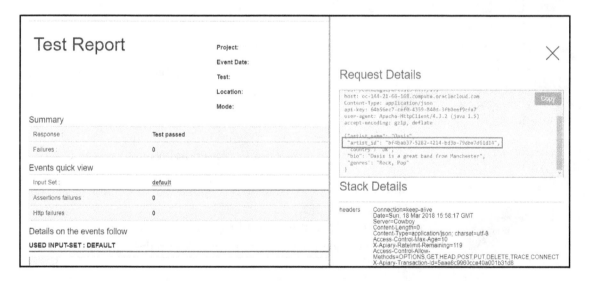

20. Next, the Album and Song post requests need to be created in the same
`CreateCatalogue` test case. The variables are similar, which means that the
Artist Post Request can be copied and updated. Click on **POST REQUEST** for
the artist, click on the drop-down list, and chose the option **Clone Component**:

21. The cloned Post Request needs to be updated to ensure that it invokes the correct
URI and payload. The following points explain what needs to be updated, which
can be done in any following order:

- The endpoint needs to be updated to `/catalogue/albums`. This
  can be done by adding a **Set Component** before the cloned post
  request.
- A new vault variable needs to be created with the name `albumId`
  similar done for the `artistId`. This needs to be updated with a
  unique string identifier by adding a new **Set Variable** component.
- The body payload needs to be updated with the following
  payload:

```
{
    "album_name": "(What's the Story) Morning Glory?",
    "album_id": "${albumId}"
    "upc": "074646735121",
    "release_date": "1995",
    "song_count": 12,
    "length_seconds": 3006,
```

```
        "artist": {
          "artist_id": "${artistId}"
      }
    }
```

See the result in the following screenshot:

22. Repeat the same steps to clone a new post request to create a new song and update as followed:

- The endpoint needs to be updated to **/catalogue/songs**. This can be done by adding a **Set Component** before the cloned Post Request.
- A new vault variable needs to be created with name songId. This needs to be updated with a unique String identifier by adding a new **SetVariable** component.
- The Body Payload needs to be updated with the payload below:

```
{
  "song_name": "Wonder wall",
  "song_id": "${songId}",
```

```
      "isrc": "GBAAW9500189",
      "release_date": "1995",
      "audio": {
        "format": "mp3",
        "lenght_seconds": 259
      },
      "video": {
        "format": "mp4",
        "lenght_seconds": 279
      },
      "album": {
        "album_id": "${albumId}"
      }
    }
```

23. The test case has been successfully created. Publish the Media Catalogue from the **Tests** main page by clicking on the **Publish** icon as shown in the following screenshot:

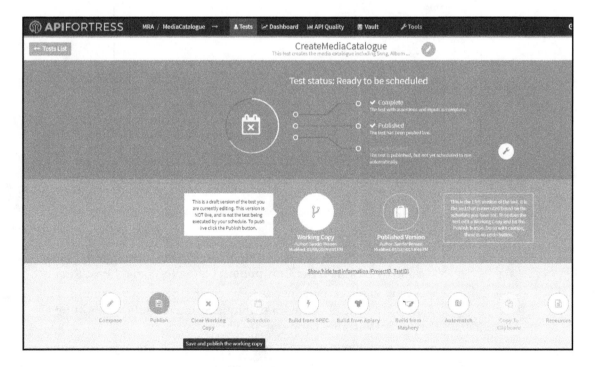

24. Next, run the test case. This time not from the composer view but in the main **Test** page as shown in the following screenshot:

The GetArtistById test case

This paragraph starts to explain the steps to add the **GetArtistById** to the existing Media Catalogue project. The test conditions, assertions, are then created from an existing URI designed in Apiary. The next steps explain how to update the URI parameter `artist_id` for which the value has been previously generated by the Create Media Catalogue test case. The reason is to ensure that the artist exists as a resource in the database that has been created by the Create Media Catalogue test case. The steps continue by adding an additional test condition, the **Assert Contains** component, to validate the HATEOAS links in the response payload. The paragraph ends with testing the newly created `GetArtistById` test case.

The detailed steps are explained as follows:

1. Go to the project home page and click on **Create Test** and select the `MediaCatalogue` project.
2. In the field **Test name** type `GetArtistById` with a suitable description as illustrated in the following screenshot:

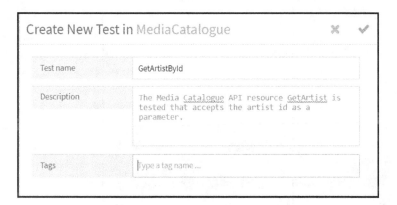

3. Once the test has been created the main page of the **Tests** tab is opened as shown here:

4. In the **Tests** main page select the **Build from Apiary** option as highlighted in red in the preceding screenshot. This will open a new prompt and confirm to continue. In the next window, confirm to **Allow** API Fortress access to the Apiary account as illustrated in the following screenshot:

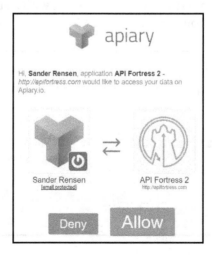

This will import the APIs that are created with a standard paid membership account as shown in the following screenshot:

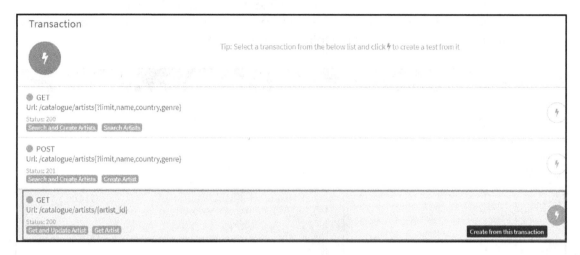

5. Select the GET /catalogue/artist{artist_id} and click on the lightning icon on the right **Create from this transaction** as shown in the preceding screenshot. This will create for each element in the Apiary document a test condition (assertion) that opens in the composer visual viewer as shown in the following screenshot:

6. The default test conditions created validates the multiplicity, optionality, and data accuracy. This can be immediately run to validate that the default interface specification in Apiary works as expected. However, notice that the URL condition contains global parameters `${protocol}`, `${domain}`, `${basePath}`, and `${endpoint}` as per the following screenshot:

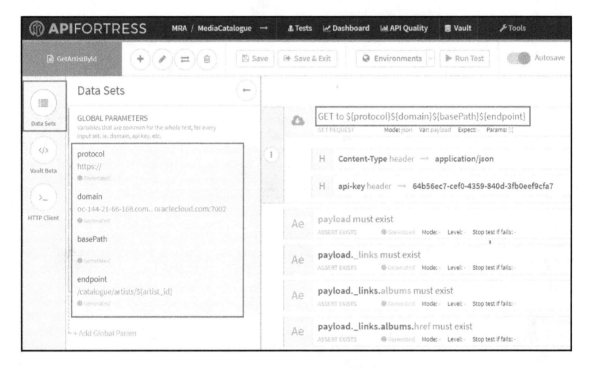

The endpoint inherited from Apiary contains the URI: `/catalogue/artist/{artist_id}`. The endpoint needs to be amended to remove the `{artist_id}` parameter and include this as a variable in the Get request. This can be done by clicking on the **Data Sets** and edit the endpoint variable. To update the Post request, click on the component and **Edit** and change the URI and **Save**. See the following result:

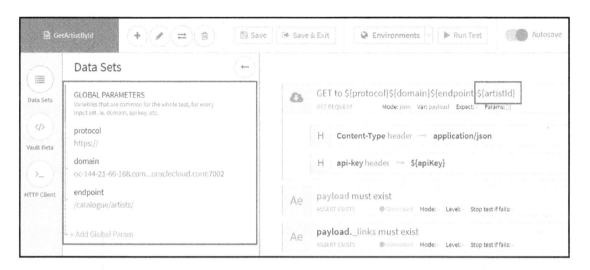

Note that the `basePath` global parameter is not used and has been removed.

7. The value of the `artistId` variable provided in the URI of the Get request is retrieved from the vault. The `artistId` in the vault is updated by the `CreateCatalogue` test case to ensure that the `artistId` contains a value that exists in the back-end database.

8. Next, an additional assertion needs to be included to validate the artist HATEOAS links returned as per expected response message is shown here:

```
"_links": {
    "self": {
      "href": "/v1/catalogue/artists/art12345"
    },
    "albums": {
      "href": "/v1/catalogue/artists/art12345/albums"
    }
  }
}
```

The `artistId` variable passed into the request parameter needs to exist as a substring in `href` for both the `self` and `albums` JSON elements as in previous example `art12345`.

9. To create new assertion, click on **+ Add Request/Assertions** that can be found at the end of the assertions or select an existing assertion and click on the drop-down list and select to add the new assertion component either before or after as shown here:

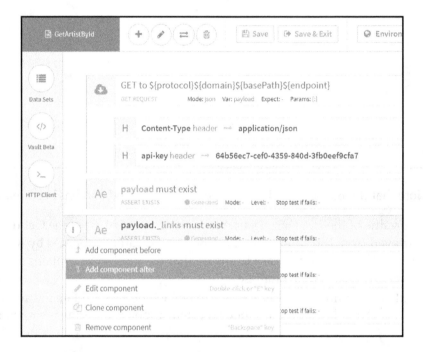

10. Next, select the **Assert Contains** components. This component is used to validate that a value contains a specific substring. The component needs to be updated as follows:

- **Expression**: This field can be updated with `payload._links.self.href`. This is the path to retrieve the HATEAOS link in the response.
- **Value**: In this field type `${artistId}`. This means that the existence of the value is checked against the link.
- **Mode**: This field can be left empty. This is used in the situation when all the repeated payload elements need to match the same condition or only one. In our case, there are no repeated elements.
- **Level**: This field needs to be updated to `error`. This to ensure that an email is triggered. The other value is a warning, which will not trigger alerts such as an email.

- **Modifier**: This can be used to ignore the assertion if the test fails.
- **Execute if item exists**: This won't trigger the assertion if the item does not exist in the response. In our case the value is mandatory, so this can be left empty.
- **Stop test if fails**: This is updated with `false` to ensure that when the **Assert** matches fails that other assertions afterward continue to be validated.
- **Assertion comment**: This is used to include a comment.

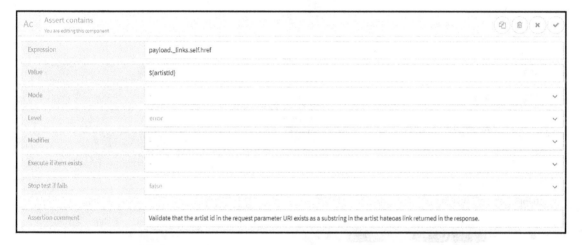

11. The previous step needs to be repeated but this time to validate the album URI "href", `"/v1/catalogue/artists/art12345/albums"`:

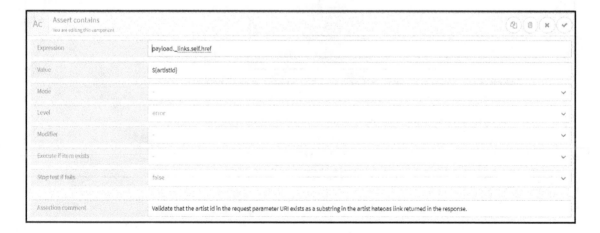

12. The `GetArtistByID` test case is ready. Publish the test and run them from the **Tests** menu as shown previously for the `CreateMediaCataloague` test case. See the results here:

The test fails and on closer inspection the return value of the artist ID is `art12345`. This is a different value then provided in the URI parameter as shown in the screenshot. It turns out that a developer hardcoded the artist ID in the response. After fixing the value the same test is run again. This time the test is successful as illustrated in the following screenshot:

Test using the Jenkins plugin

The challenge of an API-led architecture is that each change to an API or microservice requires a separate deployment. This can quickly become a huge undertaking if not automated.

MRA has streamlined their development using **Continuous Integration** (**CI**) and **Continuous Delivery** (**CD**). CI ensures that code is automatically compiled and packaged from GitHub, a code repository in the Cloud. CD ensures that the packaged code is automatically deployed to the correct environment including the automation of running Unit and Integration test and often performance tests.

API Fortress has strong capabilities to support CD with the use of **API Hooks** and the **Jenkins plugin**.

 Jenkins is an open source server and offers a simple way to set up a CI/CD environment. For more information see `https://jenkins.io/`.

The **Jenkins plugin** is explained in automating the test cases created in API Fortress as explained previously as part of the CD process. The steps to run the test cases are explained as follows:

1. Open Jenkins and update to use the API Fortress plugin. From the Jenkins menu click on **Manage Jenkins** and then **Manage Plugins** as shown in the following screenshot:

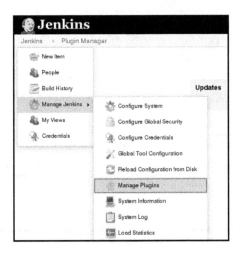

2. In the plugin manager screen, search in the **Available** tab for API Fortress and select to install API Fortress. Restart Jenkins and confirm that the plugin has been installed in the tab **Installed** as shown in the following screenshot:

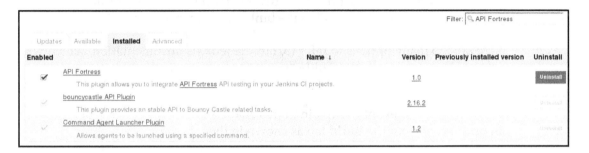

3. Click on **create new jobs** on the main page and select the name MediaCatalogue and select **Freestyle project**:

4. The Jenkins job has a lot of different options that can be configured such as:

   - Linking the Jenkins job to a code repository
   - How to trigger the build either by a script, based on the latest code checked into the code repository

- Configure the build environment like deleting the workspace after a successful build, include time stamp into the console output and so on
- Post-build actions like creating a Junit test report, email notifications, calling the build of another project and so on

There are too many options to refer to, but the Jenkins documentation, which you can view here, is an excellent guide `https://jenkins.io/doc/book/getting-started/`.

The only option relevant to explain in this chapter is the API Fortress plugin. This can be selected from the **Build** tab as shown in the following screenshot:

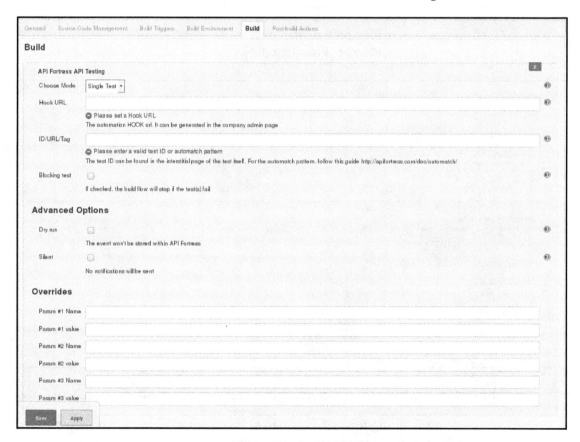

5. The options that can be selected are:

- **Choose Model**: The options are **Single Test**, **Match**, **By Tag**, and **By Project**. The **Single Test** option can execute one test at a time, **Match** run tests that match a specific URI, **By Tag** runs the test cases with the same tag, and **By Project** to run all the test associated with a project.
- **Hook URL**: This needs to be activated from API Fortress to ensure tests defined in a project can be called using **API Hook**. The format of the URL is `https://mastiff.apifortress.com/app/api/rest/v3/[unique id related to the project]`.

For example, `https://mastiff.apifortress.com/app/api/rest/v3/856be30c-bb7e-4f39-8d3b-b4876bb15f0246`.

The activation of **API Hook** will be explained further in this chapter.

- **ID/URL/Tag**: When running in **Single Test** mode, you need to provide the ID of the test you want to run. This ID can be found in the test case as shown in the following screenshot:

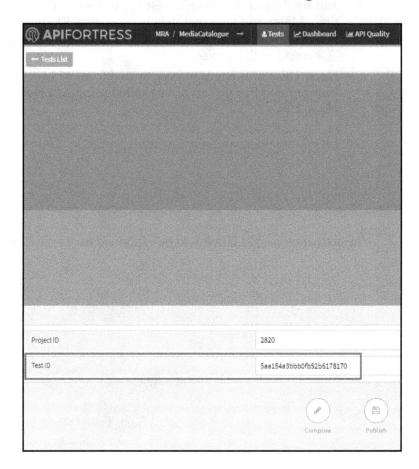

URL is used to call an endpoint directly and when specifying a **Tag** one or more tests are run that have been tagged with the same name. This option is explained in more detail later.

- **Blocking test**: If checked the build flow will stop if the test fails.
- **Dry run**: If checked the test result won't be recorded in the API Fortress Dashboards.
- **Silent**: If checked no notification will be sent.
- **Overrides**: This can be used to overwrite any variables that have been used in the test case.

6. The MRA test cases created previously will be called from the Jenkins plugin with the **Tag** mode enabled. Before this can be configured using the Jenkins plugin ensure that the **API Hook** is activated. Log in to API Fortress and click on the **MRA Settings** in the top-right menu. The MRA settings page is opened and click on the **API Hooks** in the left menu, and then click on the **+API Hook** to create a new Hook as shown in the following screenshot:

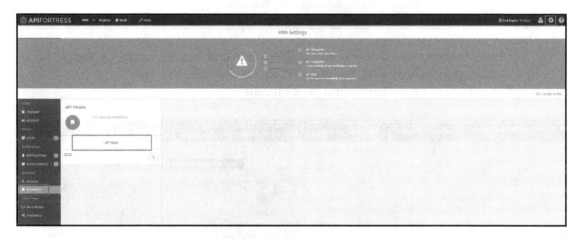

7. In the new window confirm to create an **API Hook** for the `MediaCatalogue` project:

8. Confirm the user associated with the API Hook:

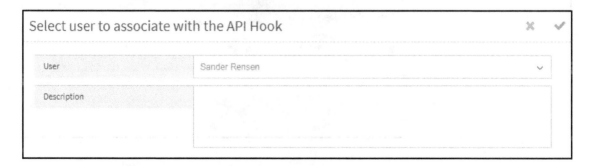

9. The API Hook is created and can be copied to be updated in the API Hook field in the Jenkins plugin:

10. Next, the test cases `CreateMediaCatalogue` and `GetArtistById` need to be updated to include a tag named `artist`. Click on the test case `CreateMediaCatalogue` and click on **Edit**:

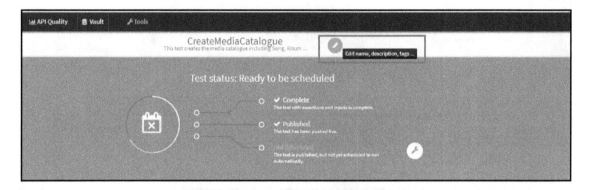

11. Update the `CreateMediaCatalogue` test with the value `artist` in field **Tags**:

12. Repeat the same for the `GetArtistById` test case to update with the tag name `artist`.

13. Next, update the Jenkins plugin as per following screenshot:

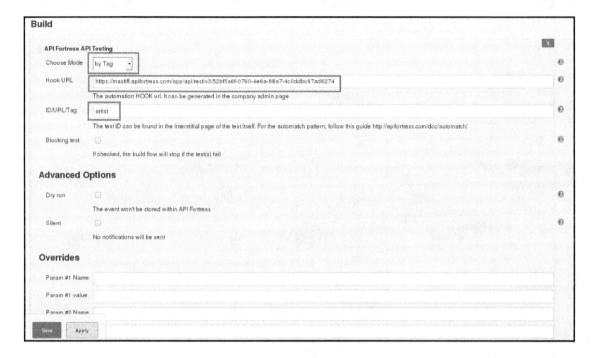

14. Run the job from Jenkins by clicking on **Build Now**:

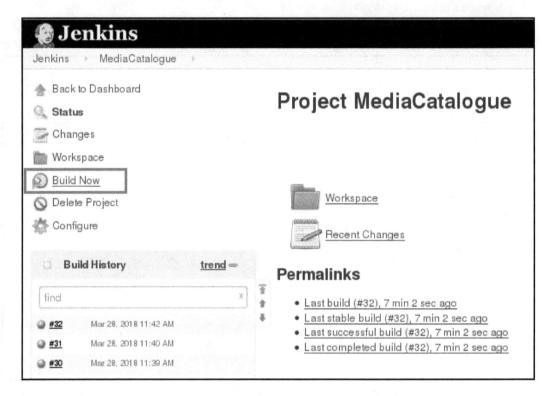

15. In API Fortress, the event of calling the tests should have been recorded in the Dashboard, as seen in the following screenshot. Notice that the tests are successfully run:

Summary

This chapter starts by explaining the high-level features of API Fortress and continues to explain some of the features in more detail by testing the MRA Media Catalogue API. This includes the creation of two test cases. The assertions of one test case are created using an existing Postman Collection from Chapter 4, *Building and Running the Microservice* and the other test case assertions are created from importing the interface definition from Apiary as designed in Chapter 3, *Designing the API*.

The test cases created include additional assertions to validate the HATEOAS links in the response, and include the use of variables to dynamically update the request payload with unique identifiers to ensure the resources of Artist, Album, and Song can be re-run without receiving an error that the resource already exists. The Vault is used to forward the artist id that has been newly created in one test case as a parameter in the request to retrieve the artist information in another test case.

The chapter concludes with automating the test cases using the Jenkins plugin.

In the next Chapter 8, *Implementing OAuth 2.0*. The authorization model OAuth 2.0 is explained and how to configure and add this as a policy to the Media Catalogue API.

8
Implementing OAuth 2.0

This chapter's focus is on explaining how **OAuth 2.0**, one of the most popular **authorization protocols** that is used today in many modern applications, can be implemented using the **Oracle API Platform CS** alongside **Oracle Identity Cloud** to enforce OAuth authorization policies to different API resources.

The chapter starts off by covering key authorization concepts such as **OAuth Grants** and its different **Grant Flows** and then continues to explain how to:

1. Configure **Oracle Identity Cloud (IDCS)** as an **OAuth 2.0 Authorization Server** to issue **JSON Web Tokens (JWT)**
2. Configure **Oracle APIP CS API Gateway** as an **OAUTH 2.0 Resource Server** to accept JWT's issued by IDCS
3. Configure the **OAuth 2.0 API Policy** in Oracle's API Platform Management Service to enforce the presence of specific **Scopes** within the JWTs

OAuth 2.0 overview

Authentication and Authorization always has and continues to be a critical aspect of systems design in the context of APIs, even more so as Web APIs provide access to HTTP resources, many of which contain sensitive or personal information that should only be accessible by authorized individuals.

OAuth 2.0 is an **Authorization Framework** that enables third-party applications to obtain limited access to HTTP resources, either on behalf of the resource owner or by allowing the third-party application to obtain access on the owner's behalf. The specification replaces and obsoletes OAuth 1.0 protocol.

It is worth noting that OAuth 2.0, as opposed to SAML, does not deal with authentication. Its main purpose is to provide a mechanism for client applications to gain access to protected HTTP resources by obtaining valid tokens following pre-defined authorization flows, referred to as **Grant Types**.

Furthermore, OAuth 2.0 is better suited for modern internet-based applications as it does not impose some of the limitations that can make the use of SAML impractical. For example, the use of XML instead of JSON which is favored by the vast majority of modern application developers, or the use of HTTP POST in redirect bindings which assumes that all client applications can make use of HTML forms, therefore representing a problem to native applications and forcing overcome with workarounds.

 Note that OAuth 2.0 is not meant to be a replacement for SAML. In fact, there are multiple scenarios whereby an organization may decide to implement OAuth 2.0 to deal with authorization, but maintain SAML for authentication and enterprise single sign-on across.

OAuth 2.0 defines the following roles:

1. **Client**: An application that wishes to access a protected HTTP resource and thus requires authorization from the resource owner. For example, a native iOS mobile app or an Oracle JET application wishing to access a protected HTTP resource.
2. **Resource Owner**: An user (system or person) that owns a HTTP resource and thus can grant access to it.
3. **Authorization Server**: A server responsible for authorizing users and issuing authorization grants and access tokens. For example, Oracle identity cloud comes with an OAuth 2.0 authorization server that can issue access tokens.
4. **Resource Server**: The server that exposes protected HTTP resources (for example, a REST endpoint) and therefore also verifies that valid access tokens are present when a clients tries to access a protected resource. For example, an Oracle API platform API gateway implements an OAuth 2.0 policy to verify presence of a valid **Access Token** in any client call trying to access a HTTP resource.

5. **User-Agent**: Although this is not explicitly described as a role in the OAuth specification, because of the critical role in plays in the flows, it was therefore described here. It's basically the software used by a user (resource owner in the majority of cases) to access a client application (for example, a web application or a mobile native app) and through it a HTTP resource. For example, a web browser or a mobile device.

 For full details of the OAuth 2.0 authorization framework refer to, `https://oauth.net/2/`.

As previously mentioned, OAuth 2.0 supports four grant types, also known as authorization flows:

- Client credentials
- Resource owner password
- Implicit
- Authorization code

Following a description of each of the flows.

Client credentials

Client credentials are used in scenarios where a client application requires access to a resource using its own credentials (also known as, a system account) and not the resource owner's. A simple example, an application that requires frequent access to some sort of non-user related reference data.

In this flow, the client application, for example, a mobile application or a web application uses its own credentials to authenticate against the Authorization Server and obtain an Access Token, then used to access a protected resource.

 This type of flow is also referred to as a **two-legged OAuth**, mainly because a client application can obtain access to a protected resource without requiring authorization of the resource owner throughout the flow.

The flow is as follows:

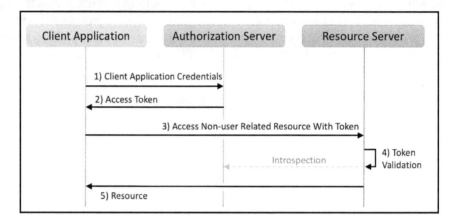

Client credentials grant flow

1. A client application authenticates against an OAuth 2.0 `/token` endpoint in the authorization server using HTTP Basic authentication. The client application's own credentials are used (not the user's).
2. If successful, a **JSON Web Token** (**JWT**) is returned.
3. The client application calls a protected resource, for example, `/songs` and passes the token in the header.
4. The resource server verifies that the token is valid. There are two ways this can be done:
    - The first one is by configuring the resource server (for example, an API gateway) to trust tokens generated by the authorization server. This requires obtaining a certificate and then configuring the resource server so it can trust tokens generated by the resource server.

> This is how Oracle API platform gateway works in combination with Oracle identity cloud. This will be described in detail later in the chapter.

    - The second one is to have the resource server introspect the token by calling back the authorization server and asking it to verify the token.

It's worth noting that this approach is less performant as it introduces another call as part of the process. For this reason, a large majority of API Gateways, including Oracle's APIP CS API gateway, don't perform introspection.

5. If token verification is successful, the resource server provides access to the resource and then returns the relevant information, for example, a JSON payload containing the songs collection.

When implementing this flow, it's important to bear in mind the following considerations:

- There is no resource owner in the flow; meaning that the password (in this case, a secret) is that of the client application and not a user. Therefore, credentials should be pre-configured and safely stored in the application.

Alternatively, a **Refresh Token** grant type can be implemented to avoid storing credentials in the client application, and rather store a refresh token that can later be used to obtain an access token. Although this grant is not covered in the chapter, further information can be found at https://oauth.net/2/grant-types/refresh-token/.

- It should be used in scenarios where a client application needs access to non-user related data such as reference data.
- The client application shall be a trusted application as otherwise the client application credentials could be compromised.

By trusted application we mean an application that is considered secured and thus not exposed to common vulnerabilities. For example, a client-side JavaScript application can't be trusted because all of its source code can be accessed from the browser, so any credentials stored can be easily accessed.

Resource owner password

The resource owner credentials are similar to the client credentials flow, with the difference being that, in this case, the resource owner credentials are used to access a protected resource owned by the resource owner.

In this flow, the resource owner exchanges credentials with the client application via a user-agent, for example, a mobile application or a web application. The application then uses the credentials to authenticate against the authorization server to obtain an access token, then used to access a protected resource.

 This flow is also referred to as a **two-legged OAuth** as even though a user-agent may be present to enter the user credentials, there is not authorization required by the resource owner for the client application to gain access to a protected resource.

The flow is as follows:

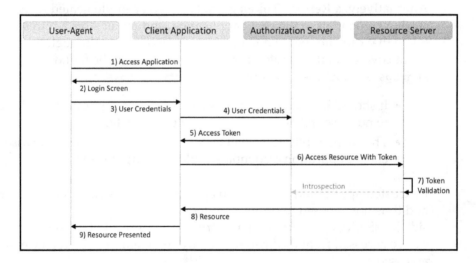

Resource owner password grant flow

1. A resource owner (the user) via a user-agent opens a client application, for example, a mobile or web application.
2. The client application presents to the user a login screen so the user credentials can be entered.
3. The user enters its credentials and submits.

4. Once the credentials are entered, the client application authenticates against an OAuth 2.0 /token endpoint in the authorization server by passing the user credentials in the HTTP POST.
5. If successful, a JWT is returned.
6. The client application then calls the protected resource the user wants to access, for example, /songs and passes the token in the header.
7. The token is validated by the resource server following a similar process as described earlier.
8. If token verification is successful, the resource server provides access to the resource and then returns the relevant information, for example, a JSON payload containing the songs collection. If verification is unsuccessful, a HTTP 401 (unauthorized) response will be sent back.
9. The resource is presented to the user via the user-agent.

When implementing this flow, it's important to bear in mind the following consideration:

- As the resource owner credentials will be entered in the application to subsequently obtain a token, the client application must be trusted otherwise the credentials could be compromised. This in turn could provide access the users protected resources.

Implicit

The main purpose of this flow is to completely prevent a client application from ever being exposed to the resource owner's credentials. To this end, the token can only be obtained by redirecting the user-agent to the authorization server, who then authenticates the user, and then redirects the user-agent back to the client application with a valid token.

This type of flow is also referred to as a **Three-Legged OAuth**, mainly because a client application alone cannot get access to a protected resource without the resource owner's consent. This means that the flow involves an additional whereby the authorization server obtains consent by the resource owner as part of the flow.

The flow is as follows:

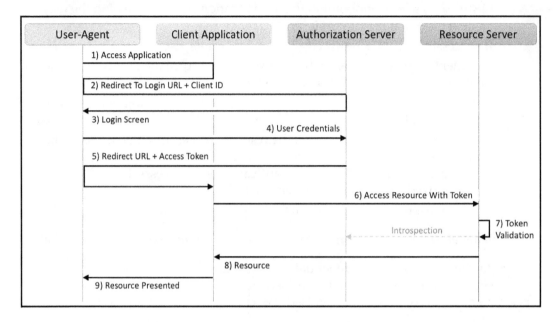

Implicit grant flow

1. A resource owner (the user) via a user-agent opens a client application, for example, a mobile or a web application.
2. The client application redirects the user-agent to the authorization server. A client ID is passed in the HTTP header.
3. The authorization server presents the user with a login screen so the user credentials can be entered.
4. The user enters its credentials and submits.
5. Once the credentials are entered, the resource owner authenticates the user and if successful, the user-agent is redirected back to the client application, with the JWT as a parameter in the HTTP GET URL.
6. The client application then calls the protected resource the user wants to access, for example, /songs and passes the token in the header.

7. The token is validated by the resource server following a similar process as described earlier.

8. If token verification is successful, the resource server provides access to the resource and then returns the relevant information, for example, a JSON payload containing the songs collection. If verification is unsuccessful, a HTTP 401 (unauthorized) response will be sent back.

9. The resource is presented to the user via the user-agent.

When implementing this flow, it's important to bear in mind the following considerations:

- The client application must be pre-registered with authorization server so a client ID is obtained.
- Access grants should be pre-configured during client application registration in the resource server.
- This flow is ideal for non-trusted client applications, for example, JavaScript client-side app, as credentials are never exchanged through the app.

Authorization code

This shares similar principles to the Implicit flow, as both are meant to prevent a client application from ever being exposed to the resource owner's credentials. However, in this flow, a client application stores a client secret in order to later obtain a token.

In this flow, the client application exchanges its client ID, secret, and a code with the authorization server in order to obtain the access token. This is ideal for server-side web applications where a client secret can be securely stored.

> This type of flow is also referred to as a **Three-Legged OAuth**, for similar reasons to the implicit flow, even this this grant requires additional steps.

The flow would be as follows:

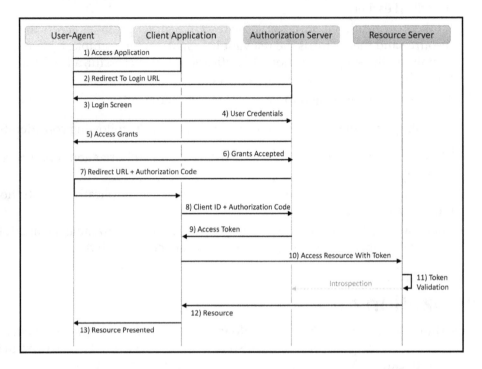

Authorization Code Grant Flow

1. A resource owner (the user) via a user-agent opens a client application, for example, a mobile or a web application.
2. The client application redirects the user-agent to the authorization server. A client ID is passed in the HTTP header.
3. The authorization server presents the user with a login screen so the user credentials can be entered.
4. The user enters its credentials and submits.
5. Once the credentials are entered, the resource owner authenticates the user and if successful, presents the user with the grants the client application requires in order to access the protected resources.
6. The user accepts or rejects the grants.
7. The user-agent is redirected back to the client application, with an authorization code as a parameter in the HTTP GET URL.
8. The client application uses the authorization code and client ID to obtain a JWT from the authorization server.

9. The authorization server verifies that the authorization code and client ID both are valid, and then responds with the JWT.

10. The client application then calls the protected resource the user wants to access, for example, /songs and passes the token in the header.

11. The token is validated by the resource server following a similar process to earlier described.

 At this point, the resource server will also verify that all required Grants are in place, as otherwise access will be denied.

12. If token verification is successful, the resource server provides access to the resource and the returns the relevant information, for example, a JSON payload containing the songs collection.

13. The resource is presented to the user via the user-agent.

Considerations when using this flow:

- Client application pre-registered with authorization server in order to obtain a client Id and client secret
- Client secret securely stored by client application
- Client secret shared with authorization server to obtain token
- Access token stored securely by client application
- Ideal for server-side web applications, not for client-side JavaScript or native apps

MRA use case

Given that MRA's Media Catalogue API is public and accessible, not just to registered partners but also to communities of developers in general, MRA wanted an authorization mechanism that is flexible yet robust. Although OAuth 2.0 was broadly accepted as the way forward in terms of authorizing users, the question remained as to what OAuth 2.0 is to implement. After careful consideration, MRA made the following conclusions:

- The API gateway should act as resource server and thus enforce policies such as only users with valid tokens and corresponding authorization grants could access an API.

- The API gateway as resource owner should be agnostic of what OAuth 2.0 flow is implemented by a given application.
- The OAuth 2.0 Authorization Server should be flexible enough to support in the long term multiple authorization flows. However, MRA felt that the **Implicit** grant would be the most secure option, however as MRA had no prior experience implementing OAuth, the internal teams would first try out **Resource Owner Password** to gain experience and then adopt Implicit.

 Note that this book describes how to implement the Resource Owner Password grant as it is considered a good learning path towards more advanced (but also more secure) grants such as implicit and authorization code.

- The authorization server should be capable of authenticating users against MRA's existing identify stores, mainly consisting LDAP's servers and be-spoke user repositories. MRA had also implemented a SAML Identity Providers (IdPs) to try and simplify access to identities specially during user authentication.
- **JSON Web Tokens** (**JWT**) should be adopted as standard for the tokens given its broad adoption industry wide.

Given that MRA had already opted for the Oracle API Platform Cloud Service, the natural fit was to adopt the **Oracle Identity Cloud** as not it would satisfy all of the identified needs, but also delivered very rich capabilities to handle identity and access management requirements in general-which was critical for MRA given the multiple identity stores available in the organization.

The solution in mind is the following:

1. Oracle identity cloud to act as:
    - OAuth 2.0 authorization server.
    - User interface to authenticate/authorize users during implicit and authorization code flows.
    - Register users based on existing identity stores and in the future self-service.

2. Use of the Oracle API platform API gateway to:
    - Apply OAuth 2.0 authorization policies to ensure only authorize with the right rights (scopes) in the token can call the API.

- Apply other relevant policies and route the call to the backend (micro) service.

- The user-agent could either be a web browser (for example, when accessing a web application) or a device (when accessing a native app).

- The resource owner would effectively be the party that has acquired rights to access MRA's API. In this case, the user of the application.

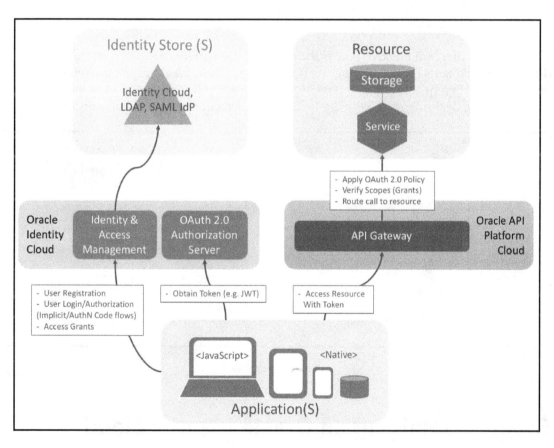

MRA's OAuth 2.0 solution components

The following section describes the steps followed to implement the aforementioned OAuth 2.0 solution.

Implementation steps

The steps can be broken down into six main steps:

1. Obtaining an Oracle identity cloud account
2. Configuring an Oracle identity cloud resource server
3. Configuring an Oracle identity cloud client application
4. Adding users and groups to client application
5. Configuring the API platform gateway
6. Applying OAuth 2.0 policy to APIs

The following diagram illustrates how the different implementation steps relate to the different components of the solution. As it can be seen from the diagram, the relationships between the different solution components is also described. This can be very useful when understanding dependencies and why the steps are executed in a particular order:

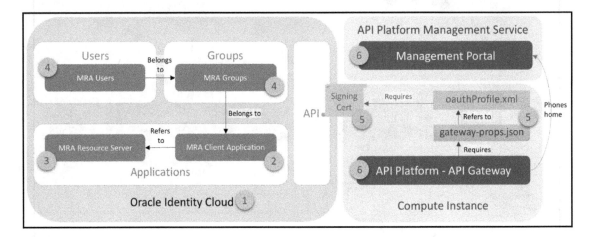

OAuth 2.0 configuration steps

Step 1 – obtaining an Oracle identity cloud account

Before any OAuth 2.0 configuration can be done, the obvious first step is to obtain an Oracle identity cloud account. For users with a **Universal Credits** (**UCM**) account, this step is not required as an Oracle identity cloud (foundation) instance is provisioned free of charge.

For further information on the different types of Oracle cloud accounts please refer to the following link:
`https://docs.oracle.com/en/cloud/get-started/subscriptions-cloud`
`/csgsg/types-oracle-cloud-accounts.html`

It is also important to understand that there are three different flavors of Oracle identity cloud: **foundation**, **basic** and **standard**. For the majority Oracle cloud, only OAuth 2.0 requirements, foundation tends to be enough. However, for more complex requirement such as multi-factor authentication or federation of identities from third parties is required, basic or standard account would be required.

For further information on the different types of Oracle identity cloud accounts and their differences please refer to the following link:
`https://docs.oracle.com/en/cloud/paas/identity-cloud/uaids/oracl`
`e-identity-cloud-service-pricing-tiers-and-features.html`

For users with a traditional Oracle cloud account, a one-month free trial of Oracle identity cloud may be obtained as following:

1. Browse to `cloud.oracle.com` then click on **Infrastructure | Oracle Cloud Infrastructure**:

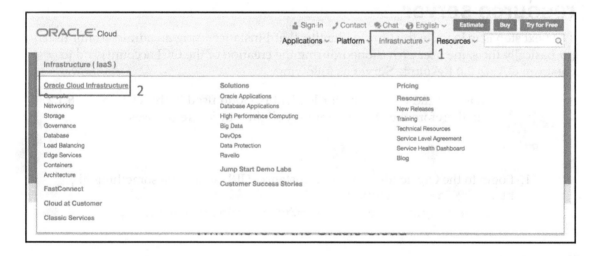

2. Click on **Try for free** and follow all the steps to create an **Oracle Cloud Infrastructure** (**OCI**) account. Once an OCI account is created, an Oracle identity cloud account will also be provisioned:

Step 2 – configuring an Oracle identity cloud resource server

The next step is to login to the Oracle identity cloud Instance using an administrator user (or basically the same user provisioned during the creation of the OCI account) and to create an **OAuth 2.0 Resource Server** as following:

 Note that the version of Oracle identity cloud used in this chapter is **18.1.2** and therefore the steps might vary slightly in future releases.

1. Login to the Oracle identity cloud Instance. URL should be something like, `https://idcs-<instnace id>.identity.oraclecloud.com/ui/v1/adminconsole`.

2. Once logged in, click on the **+** sign next to **Applications** to create a new application:

3. Select **Trusted Application**:

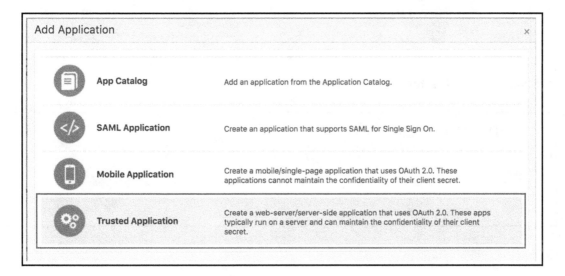

4. Enter the name of the OAuth 2.0 Resource Server (for example, `API Gateway Resource Server`), a **Description** and click **Next**:

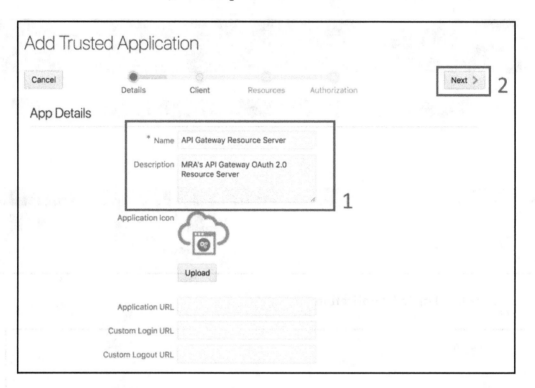

5. Select **Skip for later** and click **Next**:

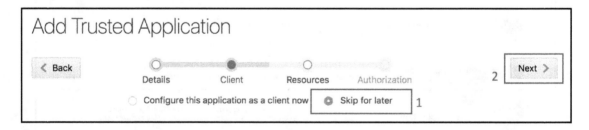

6. Select, **Configure this application as a resource server now** and enter details as indicated. Notice that **Primary Audience** is set to **MRAPublicAPIs** and that a scope named MRA Media Catalogue API has been added. This is a critical step in the configuration of the resource server as the scope can be used to determine what resources a user has access to:

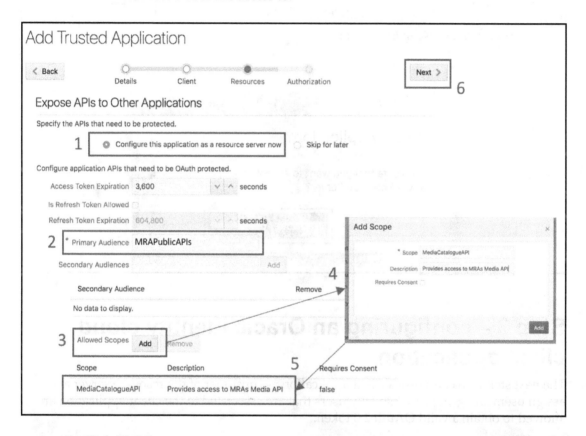

7. Click **Finish**:

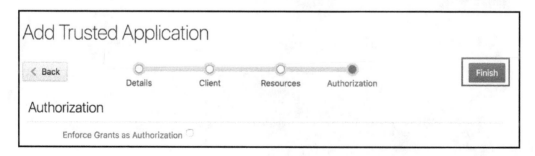

8. And lastly, to activate the application click on **Activate** as indicated:

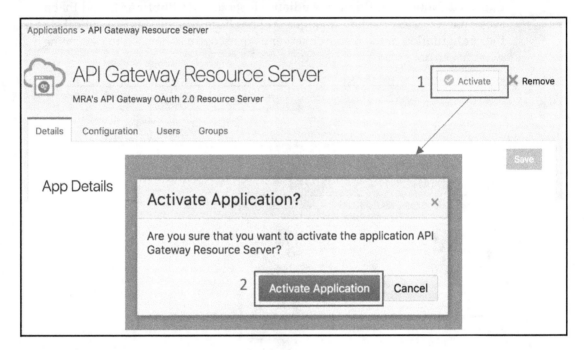

Step 3 – configuring an Oracle identity cloud client application

The next step is to configure a client application as consumer of the resource server and assign users and groups to it so only users that are associated to the client application are allowed to obtain a valid OAuth 2.0 token.

Follow these steps to accomplish the configuration:

1. From the main menu (top left-hand side), select **Applications** and once the **Applications** home page opens click on **Add**:

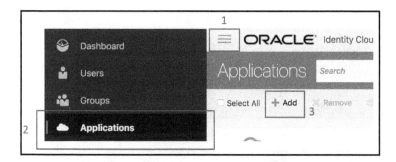

2. Select **Trusted Application** as this example describes how to implemented a resource owner password grant flow which assumes that a consumer application is trusted:

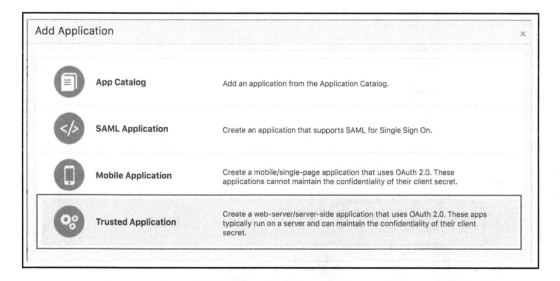

 Alternatively, it is recommended to use Mobile Application if implementing an implicit flow using a **JavaScript** based client application (for example, Oracle JET) however note that this example only describes how to implement Resource Owner Password.

3. Enter a **Name** of the client application, and a **Description**. Also select both of the shown **Display Settings** as indicated and click **Next**:

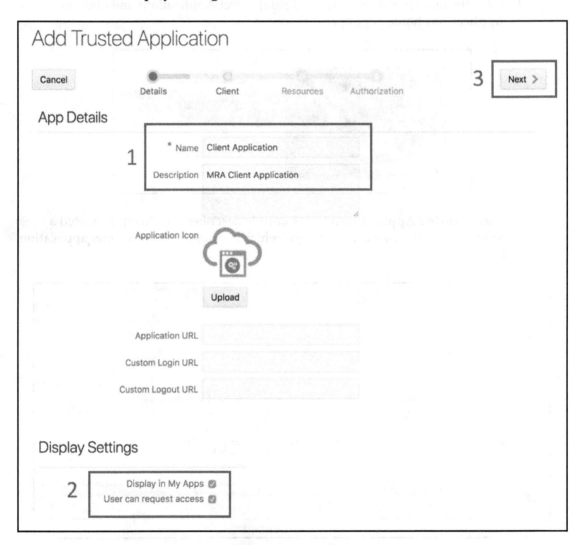

4. Select **Configure this application as a client now**, then select **Resource Owner** and **Client Credentials** as grant types to support in this client, also select both **Allowed Operations** options and click on **Add** under **Allowed Scopes**:

Note that grant type client credentials is just required for obtaining the **Signing Certificate** later on which is required for the API gateway configuration. So once the gateway is configured, this grant can be removed if desired.

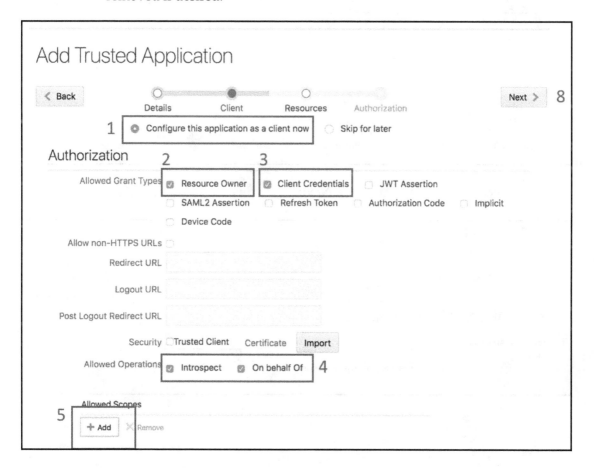

5. When the **Add Scope** window appears, click on the resource server and scope previously created. Then click **Add**, and on the main window **Next**:

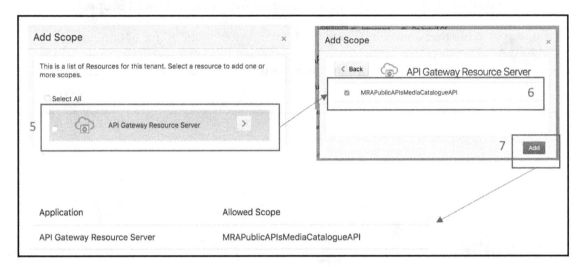

6. Select **Skip** for later and click **Next**:

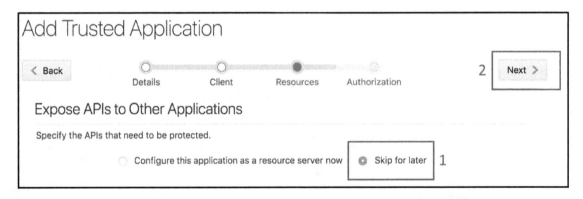

7. Select **Enforce Grant as Authorization** so only users or users with the roles assigned to the application can obtain a valid OAuth token. Then click **Finish**:

8. Take note of the **Client ID** and **Client Secret** displayed as it will be required later when obtaining the signing certificate:

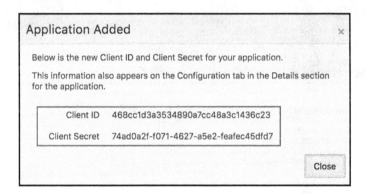

9. And lastly, to activate the application click on **Activate** as indicated:

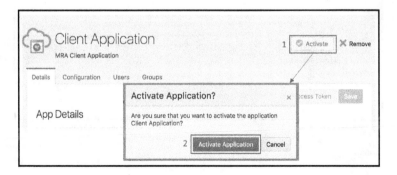

Step 4 – adding users and groups to client application

Now that the client application has been created and associated with the resource server, users can be created and assign to a group that should also be associated with the client application. Following are the steps to accomplish this:

1. Create a group by clicking on the **Groups** option from the main menu (top left-hand side) and then click on **Add**:

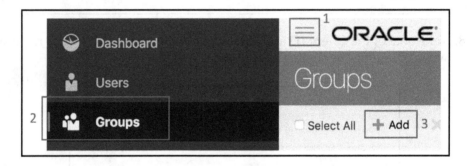

2. Enter a **Name** and a **Description** and then click **Finish**:

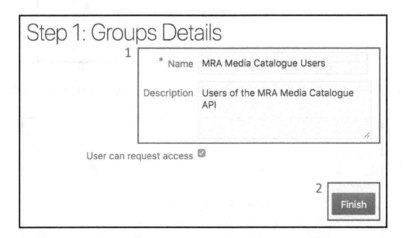

3. When the group details page opens, click on **Access**. Optionally also clicking on **Users** can request access to allow self-service request by users to belong to the group:

4. Then click on **Assign Applications** to associate the group with the recently created client application:

5. Select the previously created **Client Application** and click **Ok**:

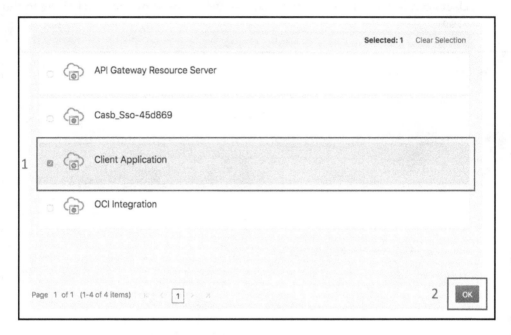

6. Now that a group has been created, users can also be created and added to the group. To do this, click on the **Users** option from the main (top left-hand side) and then click on **Add**:

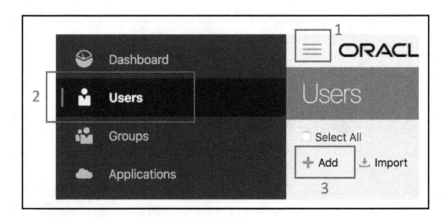

7. Enter the details for the user as indicated. You may choose to use or not email address as the user name. This is useful as many organizations don't use email as the username for most systems. Then click **Next**:

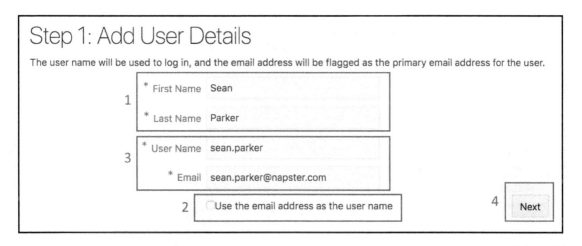

8. Select the previously created group and click **Finish**:

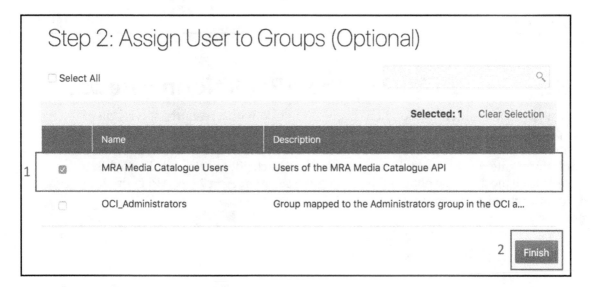

9. At this point the user should have received an account activation email. The user should click open the email and click on **Activate Your Account** to reset the password and activate the account. This step is required to obtain a valid OAuth token:

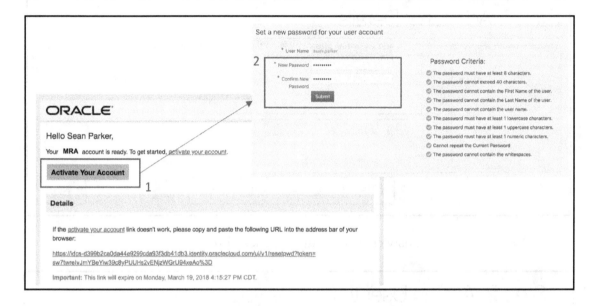

Step 5 – configuring the API platform gateway

Now that Oracle identity cloud has been configured with a resource server, client application and also users and roles that belong to the application (and therefore are authorized to obtain valid OAuth tokens), the next step is to configure the Oracle API platform gateway to trust tokens generated by Oracle identity cloud. To do this, a signing certificate most first be obtained by calling the `SigningCert/jwk` API endpoint in Oracle identity cloud as illustrated:

1) Install Postman

2) Obtain client_credentials Token

Access Token

3) Obtain Signing Certificate

Signing Certificate

Steps to obtain a signing certificate in Oracle identity cloud

1. Download Postman for your relevant operating system from
   `https://www.getpostman.com`. Then download the following pre-configured
   Postman collection from
   `https://github.com/luisw19/MRAMediaCatalogueAPI/tree/master/oauth` and
   import it into Postman. Finally set the following environment as indicated in
   steps (**1**), (**2**) and (**3**):

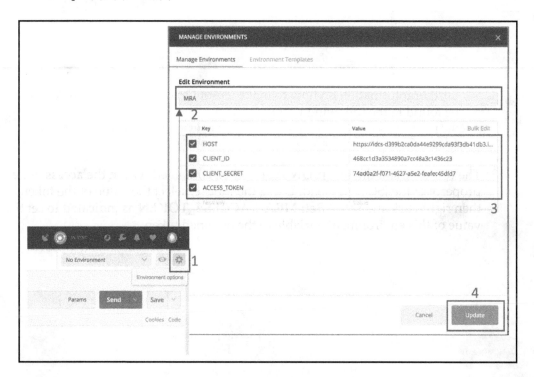

Note that HOST, CLIENT_ID and CLIENT_SECRET should be set to match the desired environment, the shown values are representative.

2. The next step is to obtain an access token for the client application. From the MRA OAuth config collection, select the **Obtain Access Token (for Signing Cert)** test. Make sure the previously created environment is selected, and then click **Send**:

Further information on how to make use of Oracle identity cloud APIs can be found in the following URL:
`http://www.oracle.com/webfolder/technetwork/tutorials/obe/cloud/idcs/idcs_rest_postman_obe/rest_postman.html`

3. The response should be a **JSON Web Token** contained within the **access_token** property of the JSON payload. Using the mouse, select the value of the token, then right-click and select **Set: MRA | ACCESS_TOKEN** as indicated to set the value of this environment variable to the obtained token:

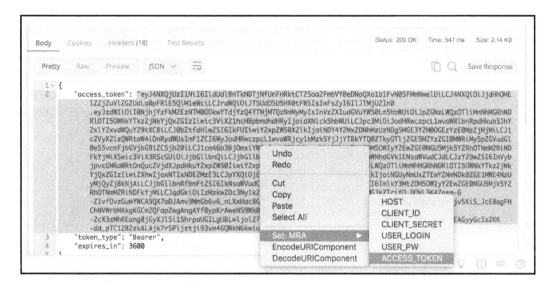

4. Now select the **Obtain Signing Cert** test and click **Send**. The response should be the signing certificate included in the first element of the x5c collection. Copy the entire JSON response as it will be used when configuring the gateway:

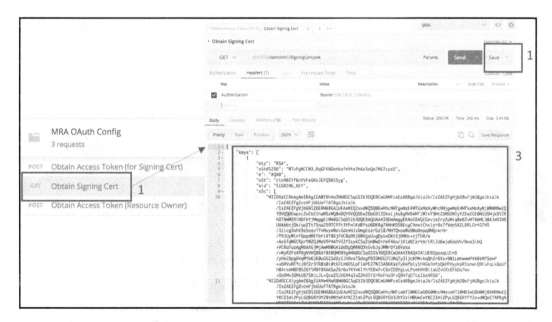

5. SSH into the API Gateway server and create a file called `oauthProfile.xml` under the same directory where the API gateway was installed. Use the following content but then replace the values of tag `<Audience>` to match the audience created in the resource server (`MRAPublicAPIs`). Set the value of tag `<JWKFormatPubKey>` to the previously obtained signing certificate. Lastly, set the value of tag `<AudienceRestrictionFromConfig>` to true so only tokens with the right audience are accepted by the gateway:

```
<OAuth2TokenLocalEnforcerConfig>
    <Name>DEFAULT</Name>
    <!-- Issuer of the token. In this case Oracle Identity Cloud -->
    <Issuer>https://identity.oraclecloud.com/</Issuer>
    <AudienceRestrictionFromConfig>
        true</AudienceRestrictionFromConfig>
    <!-- Audience should match the Primary Audience
        in the Resource Server in IDCS -->
    <Audience>MRAPublicAPIs</Audience>
    <PublicCertLocation useFormat='JWKFormatPubKey'>
            <JWKFormatPubKey>PASTE SIGNING
            CERTIFICATE HERE</JWKFormatPubKey>
    </PublicCertLocation>
</OAuth2TokenLocalEnforcerConfig>
```

Alternatively, download the following sample `oauthProfile.xml` from the following URL (for example, using `wget <URL>`) and modify accordingly:

```
https://raw.githubusercontent.com/luisw19/MRAMediaCatalogueAPI/master/oauth/
oauthProfile.xml
```

 Further information on how to configure OAuth providers in the Oracle API platform available in the following URL:
`https://docs.oracle.com/en/cloud/paas/api-platform-cloud/apfad/configuring-oauth-providers.html#GUID-0FFC0562-B6B1-4C91-8C62-D87BC85AF341`

6. Locate into the API gateway installation folder, locate `gateway-props.json` and edit it by adding the following property `"oauthProfileLocation":"<path>/oauthProfile.xml"`. Make sure that the path to `oauthProfile.xml` is correct as otherwise next step will fail.

7. Apply the OAuth profile by running the following command:

```
./APIGateway -f gateway-props.json -a updateoauthprofile
```

8. The outcome should be similar to:

```
[opc@apigw apigatewayinstaller17331]$ ./APIGateway -f gateway-props.json -a updateoauthprofile
Please enter user name for weblogic domain,representing the gateway node:
weblogic
Password:
2018-03-19 00:37:53,493 INFO Initiating validation checks.
2018-03-19 00:37:53,494 INFO validation complete
2018-03-19 00:37:53,494 INFO Install action logs are located in /home/opc/apigateway/logs
2018-03-19 00:37:53,495 INFO Logging to file /home/opc/apigateway/logs/main.log
2018-03-19 00:37:53,495 INFO Outcomes of operations will be accumulated in /home/opc/apigateway/logs/status.log
Please enter gateway manager user:
demo-gateway-admin
Password:
2018-03-19 00:38:43,164 INFO Performing update oauth profile step.
2018-03-19 00:38:44,617 INFO Update oauth profile step complete. Status = UPDATE_EXECUTED .Please refer log file for
 details.
2018-03-19 00:38:44,617 INFO Execution_complete.
```

Step 6 – applying OAuth 2.0 policies to APIs

Now that the Oracle API platform gateway has been configured to accept OAuth policies in accordance to the previously created resource server in Oracle identity cloud, we can apply the OAuth 2.0 Policy to the MRA Media Catalogue API and test that it works. Following are the steps to accomplish this:

1. Open the API platform management portal (`https://<API Platform Host>/apiplatform`), and click on the **MRA Media Catalogue API**. In the **API Implementation** tab, expand the **Security** policies and click on **Apply** over the OAuth 2.0 policy:

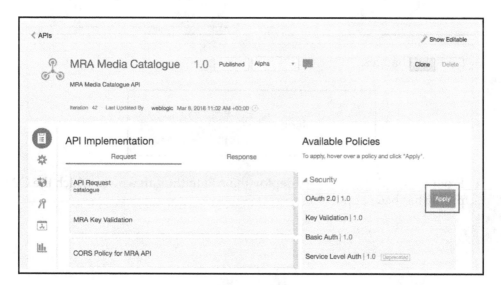

2. When the OAuth 2.0 policy wizard opens, click **Next**, select **At Least One** to enforce that at least one of the desired scopes is present in the token. Then enter the name of one of the scopes previously configured in identity cloud (for example, **MediaCatalogueAPI**). Only if this scope is present in the token, along with the right audience and signature, a user will be able to call this API. Then click **Apply**:

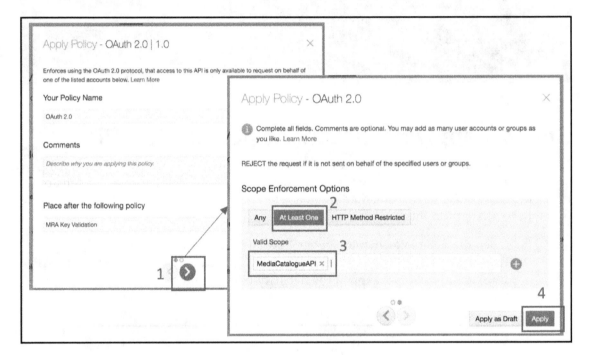

3. Save the changes:

4. From the **Deployments** tab, deploy the API to the gateway to which the OAuth profile has been applied to.

5. Using Postman or another tool of choice (for example, CURL) try calling the `/catalogue/artist` resource and notice that a 401 Unauthorized error is received. This is because the OAuth policy has been applied to the API, therefore the user must first obtain a valid token and add it into the **Authorization** HTTP header as a **Bearer** token:

6. Open the MRA OAuth Config Postman collection again and edit the MRA environment previously created. Add the variables USER_LOGIN and USER_PW and set them to the values of the user previously created in IDCS:

7. Open the **Obtain Access Token (Resource Owner)** test and click on **Send**. The response should be a JSON Web Token for the previously set user:

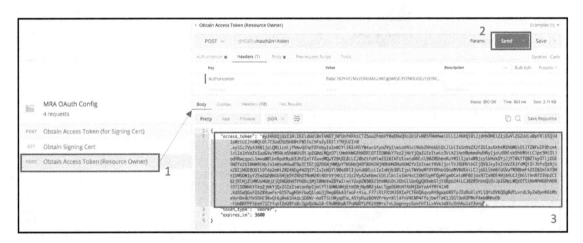

8. At this point, it may be desirable to check that the token contains the desired audience and scopes. This can be done by copying the token and pasting it the JWT debugger tool available in `https://jwt.io`:

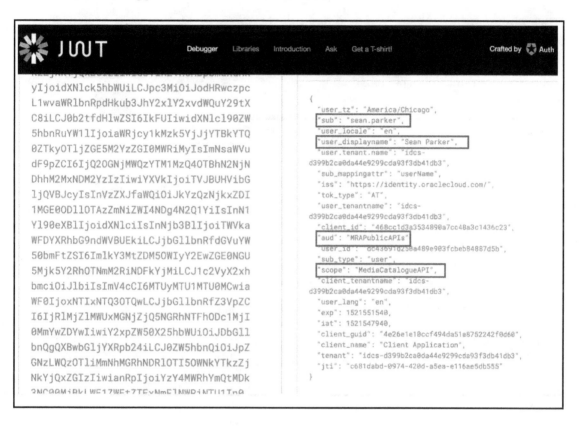

9. And lastly, call the MRA Media Catalogue API `/catalogue/artist` resource again, and notice that this time the response is successful given that a valid **Bearer** token is available in the HTTP header:

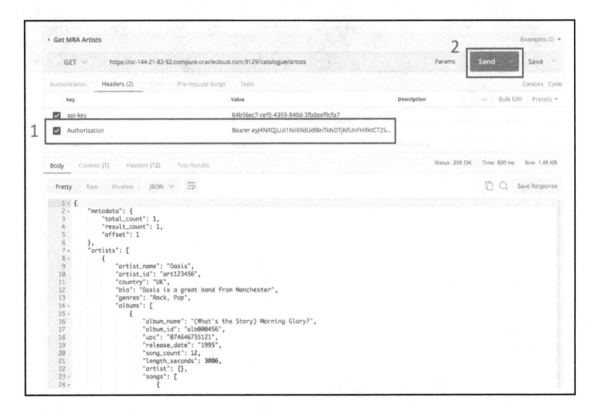

Summary

This chapter started off by covering key concepts around **OAuth 2.0**. It was emphasized from earlier in the chapter the criticality of understanding key concepts surrounding OAuth specially around the different **Grant Types** (otherwise known as Grant Flows) and when they are suitable for use.

The chapter then continued by elaborating how OAuth 2.0 could be applied in the context of MRA and MRA's Media Catalogue API in order to satisfy different authorization requirements. At this point, it was explained that given the nature of MRA's requirements, the resource owner password grant would satisfy in the short term MRA's requirements, however the solution should be extensible enough to support all other grants in the future.

The chapter then walked through all of the steps required in Oracle identity cloud and Oracle API platform in order to configure OAuth 2.0 end to end, including:

1. How to obtain a free (one month) trial of Oracle identity cloud
2. Configure a resource server and a client application in Oracle identity cloud
3. Configure users and groups in Oracle identity cloud
4. Configure the Oracle API platform API gateway with OAuth 2.0
5. Apply OAuth 2.0 policy to APIs

In the next chapter, we will describe in detail how custom policies can be applied in order to satisfy more complex requirements that cannot be addressed with standard out-of-the-box policies.

Implementing Custom Policies 9

There are occasions when out of the box policies won't be able to provide the behaviors required of the API platform as they are rather unusual or specific to the context in which the platform is being used. These scenarios maybe addressed through the use of a callout a policy that invokes a separately managed piece of logic. However, this approach could be cumbersome in some cases, such as:

- Applying special payload validation rules
- Routing based on runtime conditions, for example, using a microservice registry to handle help determine the URI of a service instance to call
- Dynamically segmenting the workload based on the attributes of an API call

Therefore, it becomes necessary to have the means to create a custom policy or in special cases even create a bespoke or use a third party provided policy.

Within the API platform, there is custom and customizable policies come in several flavors:

- **Logging policies** can be considered partially customizable (compared to other policies which are best described as configurable) as we can incorporate elements of the Groovy script to control what information is output to the logging and the formatting of the output.
- **Groovy policies** (which in this book are referred to as customs policies) where Groovy scripting can be applied within the UI to make a policy behavior customized to that situation.
- **Custom Java policies**, which could be argued as being a misnomer as these policies are built using the exact same framework that the out of the box policies use. To help with the differentiation an out of the box policy is often just referred to as a Java policy, rather than a custom one.

The level of complexity and sophistication from logging policies to full Java custom policies increases, but all are built on common foundations, which this chapter will follow to help introduce progressively some the sophisticated aspects of custom policies. To do that, this chapter will progress work through the following aspects:

- Firstly, a number of basic ideas need to be introduced before we can start by looking at the use of Groovy within logging policies
- Then addressing the full use of Groovy in creating custom policy capabilities
- To produce successful policies, an understanding of how the information in the presentation translates to efficient and quick execution as slow running policies will undermine the requirements of a good API platform
- With an understanding of how policies work, the chapter can progress into the Java custom policies and the aspect it brings around the design-time features of API policies

To help illustrate the different aspects of both custom Groovy and java policies the MRA use case will be used to present realistic applications of these product features. The chapter will obviously need a number of tools to allow certain aspects of custom policy work to be progressed. Rather than trying to introduce all the requirements at once, the tools will be introduced as they're needed making it easier to get started.

What is Groovy?

To understand how the gateway works with Groovy, an understanding of Groovy is first required.

Groovy is a scripting language which has been developed with the intent to make it easy for Java developers to write scripts. As a result, the language is very similar to Java but with some simplifications to make it easier, to create and run actions in a manner more like a Linux shell script. Groovy's commonality to Java comes not just from the objective of Groovy but also the fact that Groovy actually uses the Java virtual machine. This means that all the standard Java and Java extension libraries can be used by Groovy.

 The Groovy language syntax details can be seen at `http://groovy-lang. org/syntax.html`.

If Groovy is more like a shell script and purely interpreted then the obvious question is, will it not be affected by performance issues? After all, an interpreted language is never as fast as a compiled language. Oracle has overcome this issue by exploiting the fact that Groovy runs on the JVM and therefore it can be compiled into a class file just like Java. However, this does impose some constraints. The transformation of Groovy to class files occurs as part of the deployment process. This does mean that the validation of your code is left late in the process. But at least if the deployment process fails, you can assume that the problem is most likely the compilation of your Groovy script.

We can summarize our challenges in developing Groovy-based policies in the form of:

- Certain expressions in Groovy that can be handled by the interpreter through inference can't be dealt with during the compilation process. These constraints will be described in a little more detail later.
- The policy editor is not equipped to be a syntax-aware editor, as a result, there are no visual indications of whether the script is incorrect.

This leads us to two questions:

1. How do I know when my Groovy script is wrong, and what is wrong with it?
2. Is there an easier way to edit my code?

These questions will be addressed in this part of the chapter. Before these questions are tackled it is better to understand the framework in which Groovy will execute.

Why provide Groovy for logging?

The availability of a limited use of Groovy (the limitations will become clear shortly) is necessary as when it comes to logging and recording of API message content several considerations need to be accounted for, particularly:

- The payloads for an API maybe large but only a small part of the content needs to be logged, remembering writing contents to disk is a lot slower than the cost of executing logic to reduce what needs to be written to logs.
- API payloads may contain sensitive data (for example, personal data, passwords, and so on) which should not be included into log files as the log files are written in plain text and not encrypted in their standard configuration. For example, if the API is handling credit card transactions, logging the card information would conflict with the **Payment Card Industry** (**PCI**) rules.

The full rules for PCI compliance can be read at `https://www.pcisecuritystandards.org/pci_security/`. While the rules go beyond just software considerations, PCI is recognized as a good practical set of security guidelines to apply in a wider context if you viewed personal data in the same manner as card data.

To address these factors, it is possible to apply Groovy expression(s) to selectively log elements of the payload. The following example shows how a Groovy expression can be applied to log the contents of an API call:

```
Header=${header}
Payload=${payload}
```

This expression would result in the contents of the HTTP(S) header and the message body being written into the log file with the content prefixed with the text `Header=` and `Payload=` respectively. This works because Groovy recognizes the use of `$` operator (see Groovy string interpolation `http://groovy-lang.org/syntax.html#_string_interpolation`).

In addition to this Groovy also allows a dot based notation that allows the contents of objects to be traversed (`http://groovy-lang.org/operators.html#_object_operators`). This means it is possible to reduce the content logged, for example, part of the GetSong API payload would be:

```
{
    "song_name": "Wonder wall",
    "song_id": "son003456",
    "isrc": "GBAAW9500189",
    "release_date": "1995",
    "audio": {
    "format": "mp3",
    "length_seconds": 259
},
```

However, the logged information could be reduced to just showing an HTML formatted fragment containing the song name and year using the following:

```
<p>${payload.song_name} (${payload.release_date}) - Playtime
${payload.audio.length_seconds} in seconds</p>
```

As the example shows the text outside the Groovy notation `${payload.song_name}` is treated as simple text and written to the log unaltered. Note that the notation allows the reference to navigate into nested objects.

To allow access to different parts of an API, the platform provides access to a number of predefined objects, the details of which are shown in the following table:

Groovy Object	Description
headers	Provides access to all the HTTP and HTTPS header values.
queries	Provides access to the query part of the URL.
payload	The expression can be used to retrieve the body payload from the API call, as well as the Response. Also, it can be used to retrieve the body that has been set in the objects `ServiceRequest` and `ApiResponse`. Therefore, its usage is wider than just the API call.
msgProperties	Currently a reserved object, but not currently in use.

How Groovy custom policies work?

Custom policies work by providing a means for the policy to incorporate some Groovy code that is then executed by the gateway. The Groovy policies have the means to interact with the gateway engine through some language interface classes. The use of Groovy is also subject to some constraints due to the way that the language is optimized for runtime. In the following sections, the interface layer and then constraints will be explained and illustrated with a real example.

APIs to access call data

For the Groovy policies to be of value, they obviously need to be able to access the information relating to the API call. This is solved by providing several java interfaces that can be invoked by Groovy without needing an import statement. These APIs are common to both the Groovy approach and the Java approach for building the API policies.

The following table describes the roles of the key interfaces and classes and how they can be used:

Class/Interface	Description
Interface `ApiRequest`	The `ApiRequest` object. Defines an object to provide information about an incoming API request. The `ApiRequest` object provides data including parameter name and values, attributes, the body of the message, as well as additional protocol-specific data (for example, HTTP method).
Interface `ApiResponse`	The `ApiResponse` object. Defines an object to assist a policy runtime in sending a response to the client.
Interface `ApiRuntimeContext`	The `ApiRuntimeContext` object can be used to access and manipulate the request and response of both API and service, as well as application context associated with the API request. Also has methods to allow policy runtime to publish runtime EDR (event data record) statistics.
Interface `ApplicationContext`	If an API is associated with an application, this object allows retrieval of application related information.
Interface `Body`	An interface to an object that contains the body of the request or response message. There are different implementations of this interface tailored to different use cases. For example, a body object from incoming API request maybe backed by an `InputStreamBodyImpl` instance. Another example is a policy runtime that wishes to set the body of an outbound service request to a given string, in which case an instance of `StringBodyImpl` may be used. The goal of this abstraction is to keep the body in its original state (for example, a stream) without buffering, materialization or parsing the payload unless it is required.

Interface `IncomingMessage`	Contains information about the message incoming to API platform runtime. This could be an inbound API request or outbound service response. The interface `IncomingMessage` includes methods for examining the body (payload) of the message as well as the metadata, such as transport-level headers.
Interface `OutgoingMessage`	Defines an object with information about the message outgoing from API platform runtime. This could be an outbound service request or returning API response. The interface `OutgoingMessage` includes methods for setting the body (payload) of the message as well as the metadata, such as transport-level headers.
Interface `ServiceRequest`	Extends `OutgoingMessage`. Defines an object to assist a policy runtime in setting up an outbound request to a service
Interface `ServiceResponse`	Extends `IncomingMessage`. Defines an object to provide information about an outbound service response.
Class `PolicyProcessingException`	Thrown when a policy runtime fails to continue to process the request. As a result, the provided HTTP code will be returned to the client. The provided ID will be logged as part of the EDR.
Interface `PolicyRuntime`	This is an SPI and will be implemented by Policy provider for each supported policy type. The interface contains one operation of boolean execute (`ApiRuntimeContext` context). Where the boolean indicates whether the policy chain should continue to be executed.
Interface `PolicyRuntimeConstants`	Provides the definition of enumerations including: • APIP_REROUTED • APIP_SERVICE_ACCOUNT • APIP_SERVICE_ID • APIP_USE_PROXY
Interface `PolicyRuntimeFactory`	A Factory for creating policy runtime objects. The implementation of this class needs to be registered in the metadata JSON associated with the policy implementation.

Interface `PolicyRuntimeInitContext`	Provides contextual information about the gateway, API, or other API-related artifacts while building the policy execution pipeline.
Interface `ServiceRequestPolicyRuntime`	Provides the means to retrieve runtime information regarding the policy being executed.

The javadoc for the API Policy interfaces can be found at `https://docs.oracle.com/en/cloud/paas/api-platform-cloud/api-platform-javadoc/index.html?overview-summary.html`.

Not all of these interfaces are required to be able to produce Groovy polices. To better understand which interfaces offer what operations, look at the interface relationships shown in the following diagram:

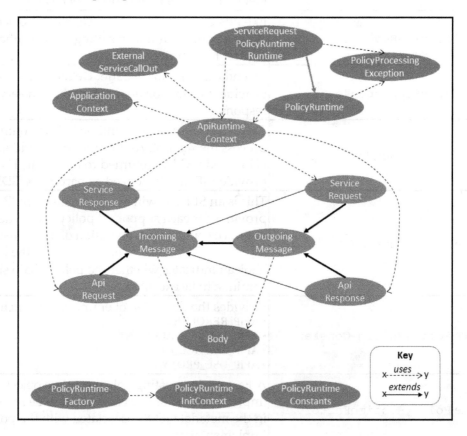

Interface relationships

In the preceding diagram, the interfaces that are central to interacting with API calls have been highlighted in red.

In terms of understanding which interfaces need to be used, it is helpful to see them in the context of an API invocation. The following diagram shows the follow in and out of an API call:

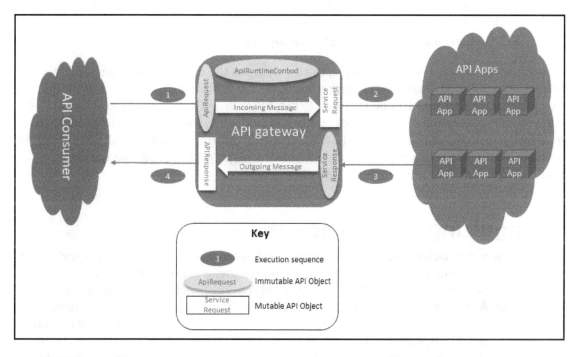

Policy interfaces

For a Groovy policy to interact in the inbound (API invocation/request) as shown by (**1**) then it can make calls using the `ApiRequest` interface to retrieve the API call's HTTP header and body. To change or add the downstream call to an API invocation (shown by (**2**) in the diagram) including setting the end-point to call the Groovy code needs to use the `ServiceRequest` interface. Then conversely in the API response, the response object can be read (but not changed) using `ServiceResponse` and the final outcome sent by manipulating `ApiResponse`.

The restrictions that make the object representing the original request and the original response immutable are shown in the preceding diagram by using oval rather than a rectangular shape.

How to reject an API call in a Groovy policy?

The custom policy may need to terminate the API invocation for various reasons; for example, the script is validating the payload and it doesn't comply with the rules. The termination needs two things:

1. Defining the response information, such as the HTTP status code (the full set are defined at `https://www.w3.org/Protocols/rfc2616/rfc2616-sec10.html`)
2. Throwing a `PolicyProcessingException`

As with any other Java or Groovy code, the throwing of the exception will immediately result in the policy steps stop executing. Hence, set the HTTP status code first. With the exception of a string that will be returned to the API user indicating the failure. So, the content of the exception needs to be carefully handled—too much information and it will give insight into the platform to an attacker. Too little information and it will be impossible to diagnose the issue. It is in this scenario where the response is just an internal error that code can be a very effective way forward.

Recognizing Groovy errors

As the UI, which provides the means to define the Groovy policy, does not incorporate the features of an IDE such as syntax highlighting and testing, it is possible, even likely, that eventually an error in a script will occur, so the hallmarks of such an issue need to be understood. As previously explained, the Groovy gets translated into Java for runtime execution. During the policy deployment, any script errors will show up at this stage. From a management UI perspective, a failed deployment will be reported. To understand in more detail as to why the script failed the API gateway logs need to be examined. The specific logs needed can be found at `./domain/<gateway name>/apics/logs`.

Finding the error in the log files can be solved in many different ways depending on how the utilities are available, and whether there is a preference to use a command line approach or work through an editor. The following steps have yielded results easily, and can be trusted to work on just any flavor of Linux:

1. Locate the appropriate log file hopefully the latest `apics.log` file in your gateway deployment. The location will be something like `./domain/gateway1/apics/logs` depending on your configuration, but this will depend on how long ago the deployment was executed, and the precise configuration of the gateways logging configuration.

2. Open the log file with `vi` and either search forwards taking advantage of the fact logs usually, include a timestamp and search for the timestamp in hours and minutes, for example, 10:47, or navigate to the bottom of the log file and search backwards for either `codehaus.groovy` or `MultipleCompilationErrorsException`. For more on search and using `vi` try `http://www.linux-tutorial.info/modules.php?name=MContent&pageid=40`.

The following screenshot will give a sense of what can be expected to be found when such an error is located:

Groovy script error

The specific error shown in the preceding screenshot can be seen in more detail in the following fragment of output:

```
org.codehaus.groovy.control.MultipleCompilationErrorsException: startup
failed:

script15162878541891973240339.groovy: 16: [Static type checking] - Cannot
find matching method
oracle.apiplatform.policies.sdk.context.ServiceRequest#setHeader(java.lang.
String, long). Please check if the declared type is right and if the method
exists.

@ line 16, column 1.

context.getServiceRequest().setHeader("spanId", generator.nextLong())
```

As the example shows the line that causes the failure is highlighted. In this example, the cause is fairly easy to understand. The compilation process has failed to match the types to the `setHeader` call. This is because the object `generator` has a method that is by its name returning a `Long`. However, we know that the `setHeader` is expecting two strings. More complex code examples can provide misleading errors though when braces, brackets or commas are out of place. In an IDE or text editor where all the surrounding code is visible, the editor can highlight pairs of brackets, and so on, it becomes easy to spot such errors.

Each gateway that gets the policy deployed will manifest the same errors.

Groovy policy illustration

Having examined how a Groovy policy works, how to isolate any issues and so on, it is best to put this into practice by developing a couple of Groovy policies. As `Chapter 7`, *Testing APIs with API Fortress* introduced many of the standard API policies we won't go down into every little detail.

In the next couple of sections of this chapter, we will go through the process of building an API with a Groovy policy as shown in the following screenshot:

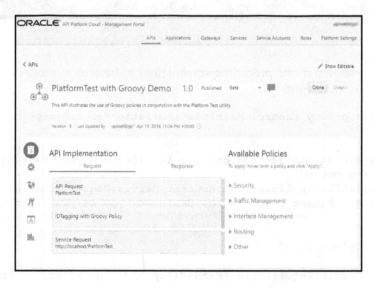

API including a Groovy policy script part

It is often useful, when developing API policy configurations, to have a stub back end that either simply reflects back to the caller what was received or a dummy payload. This helps verify that the policy configurations such as the Groovy script behave as expected. In many respects, this is like using a mock in unit testing. So as we build this policy a suitable tool will be deployed.

Addressing a problem with a simple Groovy policy

Before working through the steps to create and execute this policy the purpose of the Groovy script needs to be understood. In `Chapter 2`, *Use Case*, the fictional company MRA was introduced. The approach to delivering the functionality for MRA have followed a microservice approach as illustrated by `Chapter 4`, *Building and Running the Microservice*. MRA have now reached a stage that they have a number of microservices and tracking how things are being executed is starting to become a challenge as microservices cascade API calls. This is not a new problem for IT and has existed for as long as we've had distributed systems.

A common approach to tackle this problem is to add to the HTTP header a recognizable tag, then as the API call is routed around the header tags are carried with the payload of the call. Then at an appropriate point, the header tags are recorded to logs. When the logs are brought together it becomes possible to trace the journey of an API call through different systems by tracking the header attributes. Zipkin (`https://zipkin.io/pages/instrumenting.html`) does this using several header Ids prefixed by X-B3; **Spring Sleuth supports** the Zipkin approach or the use of Baggage tags (`https://cloud.spring.io/spring-cloud-sleuth/single/spring-cloud-sleuth.html#_baggage_vs_span_tags`).

Looking back further Oracle's SOA suite engaged with the issue by using ECIDs (`https://www.capgemini.com/2015/05/oracle-soa-suite-metadata-repository-performance-management/`). The ideas and terminology are best represented and embodied through the OpenTracing (`https://opentracing.io`) specification which has now come under the umbrella of the **Cloud Native Computing Foundation** (**CNCF**), `https://www.cncf.io/blog/2016/10/20/opentracing-turning-the-lights-on-for-microservices/`.

Ideally, the identifier is applied as early as possible. As it increases the ability to trace through the end to end process. This could include tracking how routers, switches, firewalls, and so on. handle messages. Given this, then using the OpenTracing terminology the application of `TraceId` and `SpanId` at the earliest point is ideal. Therefore, why not check for the Id's existence on the API platform and apply values if they don't exist. That way anything that handles the call that records information will create an audit trail of the call.

The following Groovy script does this very task of determining if a header value exists or not and if not generating values in accordance with the definition of `TraceId`. As a result, anything logging header attributes from the gateway onwards will create a trail that can be followed:

```groovy
// determine if the traceId has been provided in the
// API Call header
if (!context.getApiRequest().getHeaders().containsKey ("X-B3-TraceId"))
{
  // use the current time in milliseconds as a seed to
  // the random number generator
  def instant = java.time.Instant.now()
  def random = new java.util.Random(instant.getEpochSecond())
  // take 8 bytes aka 64 bits from the random
  // number generator
  byte[] b1 = new byte[8]
  random.nextBytes(b1)
  // convert the bytes into a lower case hex
  // representation as per definition of TraceId
  final Writable printableHex = b1.encodeHex()
  final String traceId=printableHex.toString()
  context.getServiceRequest().setHeader("X-B3-TraceId", traceId)
  context.getServiceRequest().setHeader("X-B3-SpanId", traceId)
  // record that header has been set
  final String log = "apply header change - traceid " + traceId
  println (log)
}
```

The preceding Groovy script checks the header for the existence of the `TraceId` value. If the definition of the `TraceId` value is a 64-bit value represented as a string. To create this, the Java random class is used, which requires a seed value. The seed value for `Random` is being created using the seconds from epoch using the `Instant` object from the Java time package.

With the `Random` object seeded, the appropriate number of bytes can be obtained and then converted to a string attribute and applied to the `ServiceRequest` header. Note, how the script utilizes the APIs provided by the framework to interact with the header object. The code also illustrates how some of the Groovy constraints such as not allowing imports, classes, and so on, are handled.

Building our API

1. The first step is to sign into the management portal and then access the **API** tab and use the **Create API** button to start the processes of creation. We would suggest using the following values to complete the initial set of required details:

Field	Value
Name	PlatformTest with Groovy demo
Version	1.0
Description	This API illustrates the use of Groovy policies in conjunction with the platform test utility

2. With this information entered we can get the API created with the **Create** button.

3. Before concentrating on the Groovy policy, we should complete the API request and `ServiceRequest` policies. So, click on the **Edit** button for the API request and we would recommend completing the fields with the following values:

Field	Value
Your Policy Name	Leave this at its default value of **API Request**
Comments	Place the comment: A simple endpoint accepting either HTTP or HTTPS
Configuration-Protocol	**HTTP & HTTPS**
Configuration-API Endpoint URL	PlatformTest

4. This can be completed using the **Apply** button.
5. Repeat the same steps to start editing the Service Request and complete the configuration using the following values:

Field	Value
Configure Headers	Leave this at its default value
Service	Set the **Enter a URL** as selected
Service URL	In this field, we will enter the following URL: http://localhost/PlatformTest
Service Account	Leave at its default of None

6. This can be completed using the **Apply** button. The implementation of the back-end solution will be explained shortly. As a result, the policy should appear like this:

Policy preparation

7. We can start setting up the **Groovy** policy now, by selecting it from the **Other** menu, this will launch the policy configuration UI. Complete the fields with the following values:

Field	Value
Your Policy Name	`IDTagging with Groovy Policy`
Comments	`This policy exists to illustrate how Groovy can be used to manipulate API calls and responses. It includes the TraceId. The response is expected to be provided via the PlatformTest utility.`
Place after the following policy	**API Request**

The UI should now look like:

Creating a Groovy policy-info page

8. We can use the arrow button to then move to the second panel which provides a text field for the Groovy script. Paste in the script previously illustrated. The Groovy script can also be retrieved from `https://github.com/APIPlatform-Book/GroovyPolicies/blob/master/spanId.groovy`. With the script insert the UI should appear like:

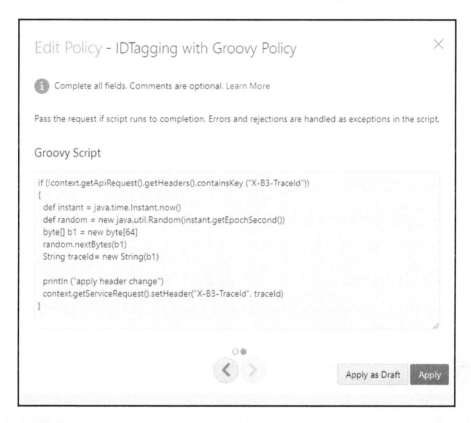

The Groovy script within a Groovy policy

As can be seen, by the preceding screenshot the policy UI doesn't support any form of IDE capability, so it is best to at least take advantage of syntax checking from another tool such as Atom, Sublime, Eclipse, JDeveloper, and so on.

9. The Groovy policy can be saved using the **Apply** button. We now have a completed policy as shown in the following screenshot:

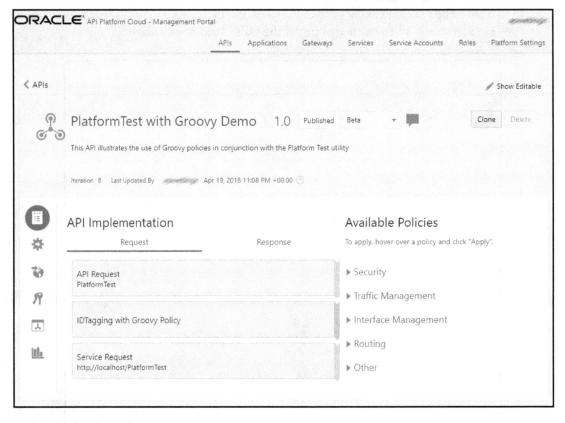

A Groovy policy within an API

10. From here we can deploy the policy to the API gateway as previously done. By navigating to the deploy view on the policy (icon is a cog with an embedded arrow).

11. Then click on the **Deploy API** button. When the dialogue is displayed select the gateway and click on the **Deploy** button. The API should deploy, error in the cut and paste process will manifest itself by failing to deploy as previously described.

12. In setting up the policy service request we've assumed that our test tool will be co-deployed with the API gateway. The test tool we will use will reflect back to contents of the API in the response body.

It is possible to find many implementations of this kind of logic as it is a common means to help illustrate REST. The implementation that has been adopted in this case is based on Node.js and can be freely obtained from `http://bit.ly/PlatformTest` (more information on this implementation can also be found at `http://bit.ly/PlatformTestDoc`). You might also consider implementations of this idea such as `https://httpbin.org/get`. As Chapter 4, *Building and Running the Microservice* goes into detail on how to setup Node.js and run Node functionality, we will assume that you will know how to deploy the `PlatformTest` node solution ready to be used.

Run the test

13. The Policy can be tested by invoking the inbound endpoint: `http://<Gateway address>/PlatformTest`. This can be done by simply pointing a web browser at a URL or using Postman by just adding the URL and setting the operation to **GET** and clicking on **Send**.
14. When tested with Postman then the result should appear something like this:

Groovy sets the SpanId

Note the existence of the `SpanId` attribute that was not part of the original HTTP invocation.

With this, we have completed the incorporation of a Groovy script into a policy. If the approach to using the policy development includes the temporary use of a mock, then now would be the time to change the service request or other routing policy to point to the real back-end service.

Implementing a Groovy policy for an API response

The API response can also work with a Groovy script. However, the objects which can be manipulated as the earlier diagram is shown are different. Rather than `APIRequest`, the entity will be `APIResponse`, correspondingly `ServiceRequest` is now `ServiceResponse`.

While the API platform offers a redaction policy it maybe more desirable to use Groovy to manipulate the response and mask values by replacing the specific with `xxx` for example. This is something commonly seen in websites handling credit cards. Using the same test framework for manipulating headers and the test tool, the response previously shown can be changed and have the `x-b3-traceid` masked out, using the following Groovy script:

```
// get the body of the response as text
String strbody = (String)context.getServiceResponse().getBody().asString()
def headerStr = "";
try
{
  int spanPos = strbody.indexOf("x-b3-traceid")
  int fstquote = strbody.indexOf(":", spanPos)
  int sndquote = strbody.indexOf(",", fstquote)
  headerStr = strbody.substring(0, fstquote) + ":\"xxx\"" +
strbody.substring(sndquote)
}
catch (Exception err)
{
  headerStr = strbody+ "doh";
}
def aBody = new StringBodyImpl(headerStr, " application/json")
context.getApiResponse().setBody(aBody)
```

Note how a new body object is created to create the response in the preceding example script. This is done because the original payload either from the originating call or the response object is immutable.

It should be noted that the approach shown here is simple and while being used with a small payload not too demanding, but with a large payload, it would prove to be fairly costly as it involves parsing the body to and from a JSON representation. Within the Java framework is a class called `oracle.apiplatform.policies.sdk.util.PayloadIntroSpector` that provides a means to more effectively manipulate this kind of payload, the Java approach will be addressed later in this chapter.

The steps to apply the response Groovy script are as follows:

1. Log into the management portal and then access the **API** tab, and then find and click on our policy `PlatformTest with Groovy Demo`. Then click on the **Response** tab so the API response is shown as follows:

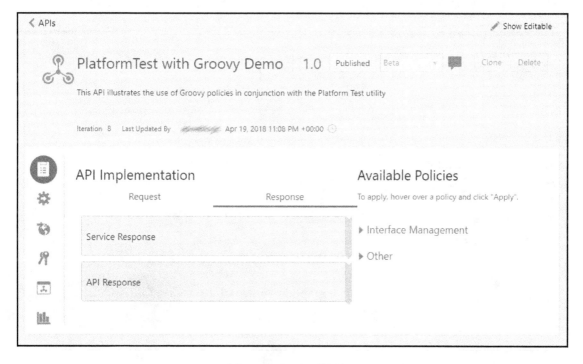

API response configuration with its Groovy

2. We can start setting up the **Groovy** policy now, by selecting it from the **Other** menu, this will launch the policy configuration UI. Complete the fields with the following values:

Field	Value
Your Policy Name	Leave defaulted this time as **Groovy Script**
Comments	`The script will mask out part of the returned values from the PlatformTest utility`
Place after the following policy	**Service Response**

3. Next, move the second part of the Groovy policy, where the previously shown Groovy script can be pasted into the text field. The script can also be retrieved from `https://github.com/APIPlatform-Book/GroovyPolicies/blob/master/basicMask.groovy`.

4. Once the script has been applied to the text field. The policy can be completed using the **Apply** button. The response part of the policy will now look like:

Groovy script applied to an API response

5. From here we can deploy the policy to the API gateway as previously done. By navigating to the deploy view on the policy (icon is a cog with an embedded arrow).

6. Then click on the **Deploy API** button. When the dialogue is displayed select the gateway and click on the **Deploy** button. The API should deploy, error in the cut and paste process will manifest itself by failing to deploy as previously described.

7. Testing the revised policy is precisely the same invocation as before except, the result of the API using this script in the response results in the value of the ScanId becoming xxx as shown in the following screenshot:

Groovy script manipulated response

A closer look at Groovy language limitations

Having examined the framework in which a custom policy works, the final step before any scripts can be written is to understand the language limitations in more detail. As previously mentioned the Groovy gets converted to a Java class, specifically the innards of a Java method. This means that the Groovy code can only reflect what Java allows syntactically inside the method. The common errors as result of this are:

- **Use of imports**: An import statement is not possible. So, any class that needs to be used can only be addressed using the full name. For example, using a HashMap must be referred to as `java.util.HashMap`.
- **Classes**: Classes can only be defined as inner anonymous classes in the following manner:

```
def customMap = new java.util.Map(<String> <Object>) {
  @Override public String getKey() throws IllegalStateException {
    return null;
  }
}
println customMap
}
```

> The Groovy limitations are also explained in an article by the Oracle A-Team
> at `http://www.ateam-oracle.com/everything-you-should-know-about-t he-apip-groovy-policy/`.

As a rough rule of thumb, if the Groovy script is starting to use classes outside the core language for anything other than accessing existing information such as environment variables, dates, and so on. it is likely that the policy being developed may warrant a different approach such as a callout to a separate service or a custom Java policy. For example, the following language features will cause issues:

- Implicit parameter (`http://groovy-lang.org/closures.html#implicit-it`)
- Method pointers (`http://docs.groovy-lang.org/latest/html/documentation/core-operators.html#method-pointer-operator`)

> The Groovy documentation of differences to Java which will help understand where things might become an issue `http://groovy-lang.org/differences.html`.

Custom Java policies

As previously introduced, the API platform can support the development of custom Java API policies. The rest of this chapter will focus on this subject. There are many ways that this can be approached as a developer.

As the different aspects of build a policy are addressed, the steps that are recommended to be taken are identified.

Rather than including all the code for the custom Java policy in these pages, the source has been provided at `https://github.com/APIPlatform-Book/GeoIPJavaPolicy`. The rest of the section will include fragments of code to help illustrate and highlight specific details of the way custom policies work.

Composition of a custom Java policy

It is worth noting that all interfaces and how they relate to API calls apply equally to the Groovy policies as they do to the custom Java policies. This means understanding how Groovy works will provide a good foundation to understanding the Java approach.

As custom Java policies use the same basic framework that normal policies use as provided by Oracle as part of the platform there are a number of different pieces. The following list identifies the core groups of elements:

- UI to display and capture the policy configurations.
- Design time data validation to ensure the UI values are valid before deployment.
- Configuration covering a range of areas including:
    - Localization
    - Metadata influencing behavior such as handling versions
- Runtime code that creates Java objects ahead of the execution to optimize performance (factory)
- Policy execution class.
- The means to build and deploy the policy.

As the different parts of a custom policy are examined it is worth keeping in mind a couple of questions, as they will help in the understanding of how the different elements fit together:

- How configuration values are accessed
- How the policies are deployed to the gateways
- How configuration values are provided to a custom policy, in the same way, it is possible to provide values to an out of the box policy
- How to understand what version of a policy is being deployed?

To help understand how the custom Java policies works, the following sections will look at a custom Java policy needed for our MRA use case.

Creating a custom policy for MRA

Returning to our fictional company MRA, as described in `Chapter 2`, *Use Case*, while being multinational don't trade in every country, and therefore want to limit their API use to countries where they have business interests. This is as a result of legislation set by in countries in which it operates and organizations like the United Nations. For example, in the past, countries have been subject to trade embargoes. Countries may include:

- North Korea
- Yemen
- Syria

To meet this requirement MRA have decided that it would be beneficial to have a custom API policy that can be used on all of its public-facing APIS. The API needs to be able to accept named countries during the configuration of the policy and then at execution time determine whether the API call can be accepted based on the determined origin of the call and what restrictions have been applied to the policy configuration.

The custom policy will work by using the API configuration to identify where the data for mapping from the network or IP addresses to a location (more on this shortly) and the configuration expressed as a comma-separated list of countries that are should be blocked.

The IP for the origin will be retrieved from the HTTP header attributes. As faking the origin IP is going to create a lot of unnecessary effort, we'll include a test switch that when set will retrieve an HTTP header attribute that contains an IP we can set during testing. This means we can confirm the filter is working by reversing the process, choosing a country that will be configured to be excluded and determine an IP that originates in that country.

Getting geolocation information

A number of businesses collect data from companies providing internet infrastructure which map IP addresses to the physical locations. Depending on the services provider, this can be identified down to very specific locations in some cases this can be unique addresses, in others it will be the local phone exchange to the individual or company allocated the IP. These are companies such as `IP2Location.com` and `IPLocation.net`.

IP2Location provides their course grained (IP mapped to a country or region) data set for free. As course grained accuracy is all that is needed the free dataset from IP2Location and having a downloaded local data set means that MRA can ensure that the API gateway performance is not impacted by needing to invoke someone else's API.

The first steps are, therefore:

1. To get the data, it will be necessary to register freely with `IP2Location.com`.
2. After this, download the CSV for the Country Lite dataset (`https://lite.ip2location.com/database/ip-country`). From the downloaded dataset, the policy makes use of two configuration files:
   - `GeoLite2-Country-Blocks-IPv4.csv`: This describes an IP mask using CIDR notation (Classless InterDomain Routing: `https://www.rfc-editor.org/info/rfc4632`) along with a couple of network characteristics such as either it belongs to a satellite-driven network (so can't be reliably attributed to a country based location) along with a `geoname_id` which allows the network information to be linked to the second file. This has been deployed simply as `country.csv`.
   - `GeoLite2-Country-Locations-en.csv`: This takes a defined Id and provides the country and related attributes. This has been deployed simply as `country-locations.csv`.

These files presently need to be manually deployed into the environment. To use the policy in an enterprise way some consideration should be given to how this is done for example,

- Gateways can all read a shared file system (limits the deployment options – but simple to deploy the updated files)
- A deployment tool or script such as Chef, Ansible, or Puppet is used to push out the file from a central location to a predefined part of the file system on each gateway

As the data is provided in a CSV format it becomes very easy to distribute. Additionally, the policy should not be impacted by any performance overheads of calling a central location to determine the country based on the IP. One way to address this is a scheduled copy from a defined location. Another approach is that the data is provided by the Policy user interface. There are some drawbacks to this in addition to benefits.

Simplifying the development process

While it is possible to build a custom Java policy from scratch, doing so can result in small errors that can be difficult to tease out and fix. As a result, the Oracle A-Team have built and made available a Python script which will simplify the process greatly by taking the name of the policy to be developed and then generating:

- Template code for the UI assuming that one text block called **script** will be used to pass configuration from the UI to the backend
- Provides templated internationalization files supporting the basic UI view
- Runtime code including a basic factory and execution class
- A build file based on the path used for the build process-this uses **Ant** in conjunction with Groovy to include the means to perform the build and deployment-addressing the need to create correctly structured JARs through to handling SSL and invoking the API management platform REST services to perform the deployment
- A configuration file to provide the properties that will enable REST API calls to be made to the management portal
- Pre-populated metadata file
- Template validation classes
- An Eclipse project file that can be loaded into Eclipse to complete the development

From release 18.1.5 of the API platform, the Python script will be included in the gateway installer. As an interim solution, the Python script has been put into the GitHub repository (`https://github.com/APIPlatform-Book/PolicyTemplateTool`) that goes with this book. When the Python script is published and maintained, the GitHub entry will replace the script and provide details with where the latest maintained/supported version of the script can be retrieved.

To utilize the Python script a recent version of Python will need to be installed (versions 2.7.13 and 3.6.2 have been tested but any recent version of Python 2 or 3 can be reasonably expected to work). The tool has been tested in both Windows and Linux environments.

These prerequisites can be downloaded from:

Python: `https://www.python.org/downloads/`
Ant: `http://ant.apache.org/bindownload.cgi?Prefer` (for the ant build command to work from the command line)
Eclipse: `http://www.eclipse.org/downloads/`

The next steps needed to help prepare for development are:

3. Download and install Python from
   `https://www.python.org/downloads/release/python-2714/`

4. Ensure Python is on your `PATH` so the installation location doesn't impact your scripts

5. Retrieve the Python tool from a gateway deployment if available or pull it from the book's GitHub repository at `https://github.com/APIPlatform-Book/PolicyTemplateTool`

6. As the framework is encapsulated in a number of JAR files, we need to gather them together into a single location to make life easier when it comes to `classpaths`. The JARs needed are:

   - `groovy-all.jar`
   - `json-20160212.jar`
   - `oracle.apiplatform.policies.sdk.jar`
   - `oracle.apiplatform.shared.jar`
   - `oracle.apiplatform.utils.jar`

   The locations of these jars have changed over time in earlier versions of the gateway node the jars can be found in the file system relative to the installation of the gateway `./domain/<gateway name>/lib` with the exception of the Groovy jar, which can be found at `./GATEWAY_HOME/ocsg/httpclient`. Since 18.1.5 version of the gateway they can be located at `$GATEWAY_INSTALL/oracle.apiplatform.sharedlib.ear` file. Inside the `APP-INF/lib` folder.

   The location of these jars can always be found using the `command find . -name <filename>` for example `find . -name groovy-all.jar`.

   We collected these into the folder. `/home/oracle/apics/labs/policy-develop/policy-sdk`.

7. Python in place, the script and the dependencies the utility can be used to generate our skeleton. Before using the tool, lets look at the options available:

   ```
   python PolicyTemplate.py -t <targetDirectory> -p <policyName>
   -s <sdkDirectory> [-S|--style] [-h|--help]
   ```

Parameter	Description
-t <targetDirectory>	must be a non-existent directory on your filesystem where your Custom Policy project will be generated, for example, -t /home/oracle/policydev.
-p <policyName>	An alphabetic name that will be part of certain Java class names, directories, and files. Therefore, it is important that this string is going to be valid in both the Java class naming and folder creation contexts. For example, -p GeoIP.
-s <sdkDirectory>	The sdk directory is the location of the SDK jars copied. This needs to be an absolute path, for example, -s /home/oracle/policysdk.
-S|--style	The style is an optional feature that changes the case of the policyName such that in the Java context it will become uppercase but in the context of directory naming, it will be lowercase. In the example implementation, this was not used.
-h|--help	Displays the help information.

To generate the skeleton we have run the script with the following options:

```
python PolicyTemplate.py -t GeoIPPolicyDev -p GeoIP -s
/home/oracle/apics/labs/policy-develop/policy-sdk
```

Using an IDE

The Python utility in addition to generating the classes, scripts and properties also generate an Eclipse project file. As developing Java code is always easier with an IDE it makes sense to take advantage of this. There the next steps should be:

8. Download **Eclipse** from http://www.eclipse.org/downloads/ and install it
9. Start Eclipse and import the project file

Build properties

Alongside the Eclipse project file is the build.properties providing us with the relevant properties needed to execute and the building and deployment of the custom Java policy as shown here:

```
policyName=GeoIP
jarPrefix=oracle.apiplatform.policies
policy-sdk=/home/oracle/apics/labs/policy-develop/policy-sdk

autoRevision=true
autoDeploy=true

### If either 'autoRevision' or 'autoDeploy'
### properties are set to 'true', then the
### properties below must be set as well.

mgmtServerHost=http://apics.oracle.com
mgmtServerPort=7201
mgmtServerUser=weblogic
mgmtServerPass=welcome1
```

The following table describes the value and purpose of the property:

Property Name	Explanation
policyName	The name of the policy being created-should only contain alphabetic characters as this will impact.
jarPrefix	The base part of the URL path and used to prefix the relevant jars. While this could be changed to be a non-Oracle path as it is unlikely to have been extensively tested for other names. Any concerns over the implications of the copyright of the developed policies can always be offset through including copyright declarations in the files.
policy-sdk	This provides the path to where the jars are that form the SDK as previously described. For simplicity, we would recommend that these jars are copied to a convenient location and referenced here.
autoRevision	For a custom policy to be pushed out to the gateways for execution, the policy needs to have its revision incremented. Without such a change, the policy will be assumed to be the same as the previous deployment and no further action is taken. It is recommended that this is left set to true.

Property Name	Explanation
policyName	The name of the policy being created-should only contain alphabetic characters as this will impact.
jarPrefix	The base part of the URL path and used to prefix the relevant jars. While this could be changed to be a non-Oracle path as it is unlikely to have been extensively tested for other names. Any concerns over the implications of the copyright of the developed policies can always be offset through including copyright declarations in the files.
policy-sdk	This provides the path to where the jars are that form the SDK as previously described. For simplicity, we would recommend that these jars are copied to a convenient location and referenced here.
autoRevision	For a custom policy to be pushed out to the gateways for execution, the policy needs to have its revision incremented. Without such a change, the policy will be assumed to be the same as the previous deployment and no further action is taken. It is recommended that this is left set to true.
autoDeploy	The build process, once it has successfully built and packaged the relevant artifacts can use the provided credentials to then push the artifacts to the identified management server immediately afterward, is set to use.
mgmtServerHost	The URL of the management server. No resource elements need to be provided.
mgmtServerPort	The port that can be used to communicate to the management server. This is initially set to the default port when a management portal is instantiated.
mgmtServerUser	The username part of the credentials needed to be able to invoke the appropriate REST APIs. We would recommend this be an admin user.
mgmtServerPass	The password that is needed by **mgmtServerUser**.

10. As the file is partially templated, and some of the values have been derived from the parameters provided. This means that some of the properties need to be configured to work with your specific API platform management cloud instance. The following attributes need to be addressed:

- `mgmtServerHost`
- `mgmtServerPort`
- `mgmtServerUser`
- `mgmtServerPass`

The last consideration in our setup is the utilization of a source code configuration tool. For the book, GitHub has been used. But this is down to a preference, so the next action should be:

11. Install and integrate a configuration management tool such as Git, SVN, and so on.

Build process

The build process needs to assemble the different parts and then stitch them together into a single deployment artifact. The deployment artifacts in a JAR file comprising of:

- The runtime Java classes need to be incorporated into a JAR file that is expected to be called `GeoIP.jar`
- The HTML and JavaScript along with the internationalization data need to be a bundled together in a ZIP file called `ui.zip`
- The management portal backend Java also needs to be generated into a `config.jar` file
- The `manifest.json` file which describes the policy

Finally, the jar should adopt the naming convention of `<policy-name>.jar`.

With the build properties, and Ant incorporated into it is possible to drive the build process everything including deployment can be done from within the Eclipse environment as shown in the following screenshot:

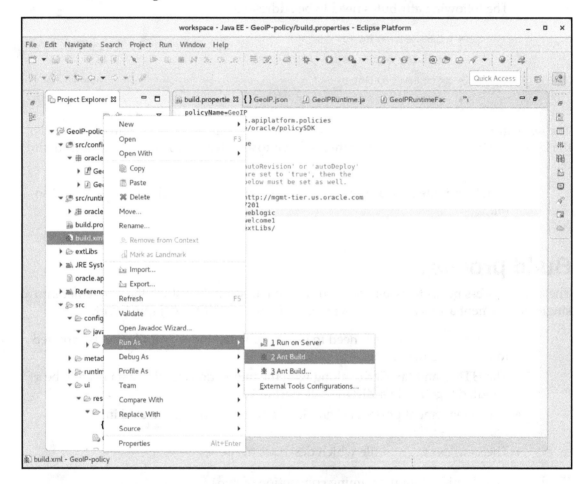

Eclipse environment with Ant build command

The full set of artifacts involved in a policy and the folder layout of the content can be seen with the following Eclipse tree:

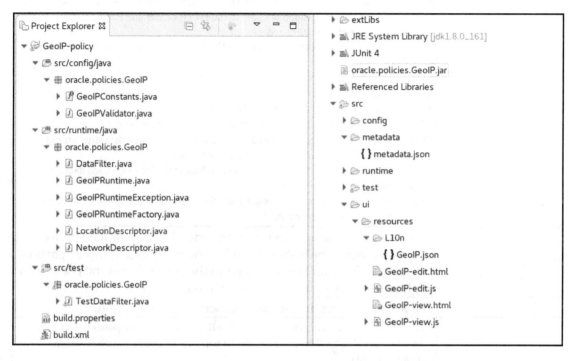

Code tree for a Java policy

The following table provides some additional information on each path of the preceding screenshot:

Path	Content
/src	• `Build.properties`: The build information. • `Build.xml`: The Ant build which includes Groovy.
src/config/java	• `GeoIPConstants`: Constant strings for the names of configuration elements in the REST structure. • `GeoIPValidator`: Validation of UI values.

src/runtime/java	• DataFilter: Abstracts the understanding of the data structures from the execution class. So if we replace Ip2Location with a different data set provider, the data structures are hidden. The GeoIPRuntime.execute includes the call to retrieve the location for the provided IP. The location is added to the HTTP header and evaluates if the location appears in the exclusion list. • GeoIPRuntime: The class created and contains the execute method used to process an API call. • GeoIPRuntimeException: Exception class that extends the standard PolicyProcessingException. So we can differentiate between as runtime error and a deliberate API call rejection. • GeoIPRuntimeFactory: Factory class for the runtime object (GeoIPRuntime). Used to prebuild the network IP to location data structures in memory ready. Created as part of the template mechanism. • LocationDescriptor: Class created to handle the location-based data file from IP2Location. • NetworkDescriptor: Class to handle the Network and IPs which then reference the LocationDescriptor.
Src/test	This part of the file system is not provided by the template utility. But added to contain the test cases built to help validate complex parts of the policy. This won't get included in the packaging of the policy and deployment as it should never go into the production environment.
src/metadata	The folder holding the metadata describing the API policy.
src/UI	• GeoIP-edit.html: The edit view HTML for collecting the policy configurations. • GeoIP-edit.js: Model side of the UI handling UI events and displaying/retrieving configuration data. • GeoIP-view.html: The display only view HTML for collecting the policy configurations. • GeoIP-view.js: Model side of the UI handling UI events and displaying configuration data.
src/ui/L10n	• GeoIP.json: JSON file containing the localization labels for the UI.

Having examined the accelerator tool, code structure, the development and build mechanisms we can now start to look at the policy implementation itself.

Presentation definition

The presentation layer needs to be provided in two versions, one which provides the means to edit the information needing to be supplied in the policy and the other for read-only views. The read-only views are used to allow the API policies to be viewed from the gateway. You can see examples of the read-only view by following the following steps:

   a. Select the **Gateways** tab and this will show you all the logical gateways.
   b. Select from the list of logical gateways a logical gateway known to have policies deployed, this will display details of the gateway.
   c. Click on the **Deployment** (cog icon) and this will result in a list of APIs deployed to this gateway.
   d. Click on the title of one of the policies, and the policy will open to show the policy details with both the **Request** and **Response** pipelines.
   e. Click on one of the policies and the read-only view will be displayed.

The key difference typically between the edit version of the HTML and the view version of the HTML is that UI elements will be configured such that they are disabled (that is, drop downs can be opened, text fields can't be edited) through the inclusion of attributes such as disabled: true being included in the HTML. The following HTML example illustrates an edit version of a policy UI.

Note that the default element name is called *script* and this will also be the default name of the element in the JSON configuration object. The following illustrates the default version of the edit HTML:

```
<div id="policy-ui-content" class="oj-form">
  <div class="oj-row">
    <span data-bind="text:l10n()['label.condition.phrase']"
      class="condition-field-label-2"></span>
  </div>
  <div class="conditions-container-div"></div>
  <div>
    <label class="policy-dialog-field-label" for="script"
      data bind="text:l10n()['label.field.header']">
    </label>
    <textarea id="script" rows="10" style="resize: vertical;"
        data-bind="ojComponent: {
        placeholder: l10n()['placeholder.script'],
        component: 'ojTextArea',
        value: script,
        rootAttributes: {style:'max-width:100%; resize: vertical;'} }">
```

```
        </textarea>
      </div>
    </div>
```

To satisfy the requirements the templated code for `GeoIP-edit.HTML` has been altered to:

12. Provide three text fields called:

- **country**: This will hold the comma-separated countries that should be excluded
- **GeoFilename**: This is the country to network mappings file provide by IP2Location

- **NetworkFilename**: This takes the network address list

13. In addition to adding the field, the call to get the correct localization label needs to be altered so the relevant UI label text is retrieved.
14. The view only versions of the policy also need to be created.

The naming convention for the HTML is `<policy-name>-edit.html` and `<policy-name>-view.html`.

Oracle are adopting the use of their open source JET UI toolkit for UI development. Note how the components are prefixed with `oj`-confirming that the UI is here is also using standard JET. This means in any UI development all the standard JET features can be leveraged for our custom API interfaces.

To help understand how the UI works it is worth noting that JET works by bringing together a number of well-proven open source components, this includes `Knockout.js` (`http://knockoutjs.com/`), `Requires.js` (`http://requirejs.org/`), and JQuery (`https://jquery.com/`). These are used together supporting the **Model View View Model** (**MVVM**) pattern (`http://bit.ly/JET-MVVM`).

For more information on Oracle JET, you can go to:

```
https://oraclejet.org
http://bit.ly/YouTube-OracleJET
http://bit.ly/OracleJETOLL
https://www.packtpub.com/web-development/oracle-jet-developers
```

Supporting JavaScript

To support each HTML file is a corresponding JavaScript file. The JavaScript implements the process of initializing the page and handling events occur such as when the UI is closed. The code needs to follow the same pattern to allow it to be effectively injected into the framework. To modify the templated content of `GeoIP-edit.js` and `GeoIP-view.js`, the following steps are needed:

15. Change the references to script to cover the three fields needed. Including setting up the observables for the UI elements, retrieving and setting the UI values and initializing the REST representation of the configuration.

The following code is the modified version of the template-`GeoIP-edit.js`:

```
function PolicyConfigurationModel(ko, $, oj, config,
additionalParams) {
    self = this;
    self.config = config;
    self.country = ko.observable("");
    self.GeoFilename = ko.observable("");
    self.NetworkFilename = ko.observable("");
    self.l10n = ko.observable(additionalParams.l10nbundle);
    self.disableApplyPolicyButton =
additionalParams.disableApplyPolicyButton;
    self.initialize = function() {
       if (self.config) {
          self.country(config.country);
          self.GeoFilename(config.GeoFilename);
          self.NetworkFilename(config.NetworkFilename);
       }
       self.disableApplyButton(false);
    };
    self.getPolicyConfiguration = function() {
       var config = {"country" : "", "GeoFilename" : "",
"NetworkFilename" : ""};
       config.country = self.country();;
       config.GeoFilename = self.GeoFilename();;
       config.NetworkFilename = self.NetworkFilename();;
       return config;
    };
    self.disableApplyButton = function(flag) {
       self.disableApplyPolicyButton(flag);
    };
    self.initialize();
}
```

The UI framework relies on two callback methods that the JavaScript implementation must provide:

- `self.initialize = function()`
- `self.getPolicyConfiguration = function()`

The first of these is called upon the UI open, while the other is executed after the user clicks on the **Apply** button as can be observed in the previous piece of code. In addition to this, in the previous code example the declaration of the config variable-`var config = {"country" : "", "GeoFilename" : "", "NetworkFilename" : ""}`. This is creating the JSON object that will be incorporated into the configuration data provided to the runtime elements. This means that all the values passed should be initialized here.

The JavaScript will ensure that the values provided in the UI elements are copied into the JSON configuration that is then eventually passed to the Java runtime code (remember the gateway *phones home* to retrieve its configurations).

The following example shows the view only version of the JavaScript in its pure template form:

```
    function PolicyConfigurationModel(ko, $, oj, config,
additionalParams) {
        self = this;
        self.config = config;
        self.l10n = ko.observable(additionalParams.l10nbundle);
        self.conditions = ko.observableArray();
        self.script = ko.observable();
        self.initialize = function() {
          if (self.config)
          {
            self.script(self.config.script);
          }
        };
        self.initialize();
    }
```

16. In the same way, `GeoIP-edit.js` was changed the `GeoIP-view.js` file needs to be amended, the difference between the two here is there is no requirement to handle amending the values.

Localization of the UI

Within in the HTML, there are a number presentation labels referenced. For example:

```
<label class="policy-dialog-field-label" for="script"
databind="text:l10n()['label.field.header']"></label>
```

The label values are provided by the common pattern of pulling the actual display text from a localization file. This means the UI can quickly be switched to different language representations by simply swapping the localization files. These values can be seen in a JSON file (called `<policy-name>.json`) in a child folder to the HTML and JavaScript called `L10n` (short for Localization). The example values can be seen here:

```
{
  "l10nBundle" : {
    "policy.name" : "example",
    "policy.description": "<Policy description>",
    "#helpInfo" : "Complete all fields. Comments are optional.",
    "label.field.header": "PolicyName",
    "label.condition.phrase" : "Pass the request/response
      if code runs to completion. Errors and rejections
      are handled as exceptions.",
    "placeholder.script" : ""
  }
}
```

The code looks up names of the labels can be seen on the left side of the name-value pairs and will correlate to the references to in the JavaScript. When developing a policy, if additional fields need to be added, and therefore new labels will be needed, it is recommended that the last part of the label corresponds to the field/value making it easy to understand the purpose of the values.

The following annotated screenshot illustrates how the HTML and linkage to the JSON bundle impact the UI. This screenshot is taken from the custom policy example which will be explored later in this chapter:

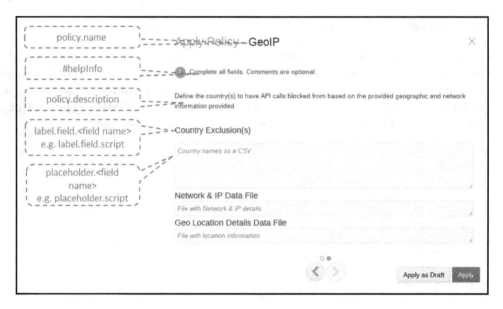

Mapping of the localization file to the UI

To align the GeoIP.json file to the HTML and reflect the purpose of this policy, the following steps are needed:

17. Replaced the default scratch field with country and added additional field labels into the l10n file that has been generated and called GeoIP.json (found in the folder GeoIP-policy/src/ui/resources/L10n) as part of the template tool.

18. Modify the default title labels to suit the use case such as the policy description (policy.description).

UI Backend for validating configuration

Any UI should have the possibility of validating the data before being used. The generated class `oracle.apiplatform.policies.GeoIP.GeoIPValidator` could be implemented to verify the file paths as being legal, but remember as the UI is in the cloud onto where gateways will be deployed it isn't possible to test the path as actually being valid.

The final UI aspect to draw specific attention to is the illustration of the edit Javascript called `GeoIP-edit.js`. Previously we mentioned that the values to be passed across the need to be initialized, as can be seen in the code this has been modified to be:

```
var config = {"country" : "", "GeoFilename" : "", "NetworkFilename" : ""};
```

These values can also be seen in the class `oracle.apiplatform.policies.GeoIP.GeoIPConstants` that has been generated using the template tool and then modified. This interface can then be used to reference the names in the configuration JSON payload passed into the factory. Therefore:

19. The `oracle.apiplatform.policies.GeoIP.GeoIPConstants` class will need updating to cover all the relevant configuration values
20. Review the HTML, JavaScript, JSON properties and Java code to ensure naming is consistent, otherwise, there will be mismatches as a result errors

This highlights the importance of consistency in the naming conventions.

Backend implementation

As previously described the logic run by the gateway relies on two classes, which when generated for us get called `GeoIPRuntime` and `GeoRuntimeFactory`. To keep these classes purely focused on the runtime processes rather than reading and transforming the file data into usable data structures several additional classes have been added, these are:

- `DataFilter`: This class is exposed to the runtime layer and provides the services that the execution of the GeoIP runtime will need. By abstracting away from the runtime, we can if necessary rework the way the GeoIP data is used. For example, replacing the processing of files with a local database.
- `LocationDescriptor`: This handles the location side of the data, breaking up a file into its constituent parts and using a map data structure to access the information.

- `NetworkDescriptor`: Performs the same basic task as `LocationDescriptor` for the network data. However, as we can't use the CIDR record structure as a key this is just held in an array-list structure which we could iterate over. The matching process then stops at the first valid match. As we need to determine whether an IP matches a CIDR definition, we have taken advantage of the implementation of logic from Apache commons and extended the Apache commons class `org.apache.commons.net.util.SubnetUtils`. This means we need to exploit the external lib packaging logic to ensure that this is available at deployment.

- `GeoIPRuntimeException`: Allows us to differentiate between a `PolicyProcessingException` exception which is used to reject an API calls vs an error that is specific to the operation of the GeoIP logic.

21. These elements will need to be created, or retrieved from the GitHub repository to recreate the GeoIP functionality.

As a result of `GeoIPRuntimeFactory` implementation is very simple with the constructor initializing a static object which is the `DataFilter` and returning the `GeoIPRuntime` class. To make this extremely easy to test the initialization process is actually performed by a separate method.

The `GeoIPRuntime` then when executed extracts the origination IP from the HTTP header and if the test flag is set the test header called `Test.Host`. It then calls the `DataFilter` object to locate the correct appropriate location data. It then sets the outbound payload header with a value `Origin.Country` containing the country name if it is an accepted origin. Otherwise, an exception is thrown so that it feeds back the rejection.

The method always returns true, as this tells the gateway engine to call any subsequent policies which will do other tasks such as a log or determine the URI of the implementing functionality.

API runtime

The core of the Java policy is the implementation of a factory and several Java interfaces. The interfaces implemented aren't used in the Groovy policies explicitly but based on the description of the way Groovy works the role they play can be recognized.

The policy configuration values are provided through the policy factory as a `JSONObject`. By caching these values in the custom policy, they can be referred to at any time, although ideally all the data preparation is performed within the factory and held in memory if at all possible to ensure the policy will execute quickly. It is important to remember that the custom policy will need to be quick in execution, otherwise, it will have a significant impact on the number of API calls that can be handled. This will be illustrated when an example policy is built.

The following code shows the factory used by the Java policy framework the get an API Policy instance. Assuming that the policy being built is called Example. Note how the Factory is derived by implementing one of the defined interfaces provided by the SDK (`PolicyRuntimeFactory`).

```
package oracle.apiplatform.policies.Example;

import org.json.JSONObject;
import oracle.apiplatform.policies.sdk.runtime.PolicyRuntime;
import oracle.apiplatform.policies.sdk.runtime.PolicyRuntimeFactory;
import oracle.apiplatform.policies.sdk.runtime.PolicyRuntimeInitContext;
public class ExampleRuntimeFactory
  implements PolicyRuntimeFactory
  {
    @Override
    public PolicyRuntime getRuntime(
        PolicyRuntimeInitContext initContext,
        JSONObject policyConfig)
        throws Exception
        {
          return new ExampleRuntime(initContext, policyConfig);
        }
  }
```

22. Needs to be modified such that it can retrieve the configuration data and parse it into an in-memory structure so each the policy is executed the lookup to determine what needs to happen is very quick.

This factory class is instantiated by the gateway at startup or during deployment. If the factory constructor fails, then the deployment itself will also fail. This is the basis of the validation of Groovy policies.

In the same package as the factory, we also have the runtime object which is used when an instance of the policy is being executed.

```
package oracle.apiplatform.policies.GeoIP;
import org.json.JSONObject;
import oracle.apiplatform.policies.Example.GeoIPConstants;
import oracle.apiplatform.policies.sdk.context.ApiRuntimeContext;
import
oracle.apiplatform.policies.sdk.exceptions.PolicyProcessingException;
import oracle.apiplatform.policies.sdk.runtime.PolicyRuntime;
import oracle.apiplatform.policies.sdk.runtime.PolicyRuntimeInitContext;
public class GeoIPRuntime implements PolicyRuntime, GeoIPConstants {
    JSONObject policyConfig;
    public GeoIPRuntime(PolicyRuntimeInitContext initContext,
      JSONObject policyConfig) {
        this.policyConfig = policyConfig;
    }
    @Override
    public boolean execute(ApiRuntimeContext apiRuntimeContext)
      throws PolicyProcessingException {
        String header = policyConfig.getString("script");
        apiRuntimeContext.getServiceRequest()
          .setHeader("ExampleConfig", header);
        return true;
    }
}
```

The preceding code represents the template prior to the modification to meet the policy requirement. In the runtime class, the constructor is called with the `policyConfig` which is stored for later use as a member variable. The policy is then initiated through the `execute` method which provides the context to the API call. This is the same object that is referenced in the Groovy example that allows the policy to access the received call information and populate the outbound object. Which objects to work within the context depend upon whether the policy is being run as a result of an API request or the API Response. In this example, it is assumed that it is only going to be used in an API request.

The `execute` method is performing a very simple task of retrieving the configuration value provided in the user interface and adding it to a new HTTP header element called `GeoIPConfig`. The configuration value is assumed to be called script. However, the property could be called anything. The property name needs to be handled carefully so that the value created using the JavaScript deployed creates the JSON structure with the same names.

Note that the method has been hardwired to return `true`. This indicates that the subsequent policies should also be processed. If for example, this policy was to behave like the **Gateway Routing** policy where the alternate routing path can be defined, therefore other policies can be ignored, then a Boolean `false` need to be returned. Although releases after 18.1.5 this flag will have no impact. As with the Groovy policy example to terminate the API processing because something has been deemed illegal then the `PolicyProcessingException` exception needs to be thrown. The guidelines on what to provide when the exception is thrown are the same here as for the Groovy approach.

23. The execute method needs to be modified to become:

```
public boolean execute(ApiRuntimeContext apiRuntimeContext) throws
PolicyProcessingException {
  String originName = null;
  String originIP =
apiRuntimeContext.getApiRequest().getRemoteHost();
  if (test) {
    logger.info("will check for override");
    try {
      originIP =
apiRuntimeContext.getApiRequest().getHeader(TESTHOST);
      if (originIP != null) {
        originIP = originIP.trim();
        if (originIP.length() == 0) {
          // defer back to the default value
          originIP =
apiRuntimeContext.getApiRequest().getRemoteHost();
          logger.info ("couldn't override origin");
        }
      }
    }
    catch (IOException ioErr) {
      logger.error("getting origin. msg="
        +ioErr.getLocalizedMessage(), ioErr);
    }
  }
  originName = applyFilter (filter,
    apiRuntimeContext.getApiRequest().getRemoteHost());
  apiRuntimeContext.getServiceRequest()
    .setHeader(ORIGIN_COUNTRY, originName);
  return true;
}
```

This implementation of the `execute` method includes allowing for the test header value which means we can simulate a call from another country.

Metadata

Along with the source code, HTML and JavaScript some additional metadata is required to tell the API cloud and gateways how to manage the policies. The following table describes the key properties and the values. The metadata is defined in the form of a JSON file. The metadata for all the available policies can be examined through calls to the API management cloud REST API.

Key	Description and Value(s)
`type`	This should be the name of the policy without any space characters and prefixed with the value.
`name`	The name of the policy.
`version`	The version provides an identifier that can be displayed. The version number should only change when the functionality reaches a new release. The version number should be used to indicate compatibility. So, moving from a version 1.x to 2.0 would indicate a compatibility breaking change. Whereas 1.x to 1.y would indicate that there has been a major change which may impact the logical behavior.
`revision`	This indicates the smallest level of change and needs to be incremented each time the custom policy is deployed, otherwise, the managed process will not trigger the distribution of the change to the gateways.
`schemaVersion`	This value has been put into the configuration for future use.
`sdkVersion`	This reflects the version of the SDK being used—in this case, `3.0`.

category	This links the policy to the policies available to list displayed in the policy editor, as shown in the following screenshot:  Available Policies To apply, hover over a policy and click "Apply". ▶ Security ▶ Traffic Management ▶ Interface Management ▶ Routing ◢ Other Service Callout | 2.0 Service Callout | 1.0 Logging | 1.0 Groovy Script | 1.0 For example, `@implementations.policyCategory.other` would place the policy in the **Other** list. Note that the last part of the value correlates to the policy categories. Presently custom policies should only go to the **Other** category.
description	This is an internal description that allows others to understand the role of the policy. This information is provided if metadata on policies are retrieved.
constraints.direction	Some API policies can be applied to both API requests and responses, others are only appropriate to one direction. The options are: • REQUEST • RESPONSE • REQUEST_OR_RESPONSE

`constraints.requestZone`	These identify which parts of a sequence of policies the custom policy can be defined. These details are described at `https://docs.oracle.com/en/cloud /paas/api-platform-cloud/apfad /implementing-apis.html#GUID-8F6851FE -FA80-4AA3-9AE0-3227C18BD510`.
`constraints.responseZone`	The response equivalent to `constraints.requestZone`.
`constraints.singleton`	This indicates whether the policy can be used more than once within an API policy set. If set as a singleton then the policy can only be used once. For example, it maybe desirable to include the logging policy more than once in an API configuration, but a routing policy such as **Header Based Routing** should only ever appear once.
`ui.edit.html`	This identifies the bundled HTML file within the policy that should be used to render the editor for providing configuration data.
`ui.edit.js`	This identifies the JavaScript that supports `ui.edit.html`. This includes populating the metadata payload.
`ui.edit.helpInfo`	To be used to provide a UI hyperlink to the supporting documentation for the policy.
`ui.edit.helpUrl`	This points to the web page that will provide the policy documentation help.
`ui.view.html`	This identifies the bundled HTML file within the policy that should be used to render the view only version of the configuration data.
`ui.view.js`	This identifies the JavaScript that supports `ui.view.html`.
`ui.view.helpInfo`	The view version of the UI will not have all the possibilities of the edit view, correspondingly it may be desirable to provide a link to different documentation compared to `ui.edit.helpInfo`.
`ui.view.helpUrl`	This points to the web page that will provide the policy documentation help.

`configuration.services[].type`	Part of an array of pairs of values-the other element being the service. This element defines the roles, for example: • `oracle.apiplatform.policies` `.sdk.validation.PolicyValidator`: Identifies the validation of values for the UI • `oracle.apiplatform.policies.` `sdk.runtime.PolicyRuntimeFactory`: Identifies the factory class for the runtime process
`configuration.services[].service`	This partners the type entity to provide the fully qualified class name of the object implementing the type of task defined.

Having described the elements of metadata, the following provides an example metadata file content:

```
{
  "type": "o:example",
  "name": "policy.name",
  "version": "1.0",
  "revision": "10",
  "schemaVersion": "1",
  "sdkVersion": "3.0",
  "category": "@implementations.policyCategory.other",
  "description": "policy.description",
  "constraints": {
    "direction": "REQUEST_OR_RESPONSE",
    "requestZone": "30,40,50",
    "responseZone": "150",
    "singleton": false
  },
  "ui": {
    "edit": {
      "html": "example-edit.html",
      "js": "example-edit.js",
```

```
      "helpInfo": "#helpInfo",
      "helpUrl": "http://www.oracle.com",
      "helpTopicId": "policies.example"
    },
    "view": {
      "html": "example-view.html",
      "js": "example-view.js",
      "helpInfo": "#helpInfo",
      "helpUrl": "http://www.oracle.com",
      "helpTopicId": "policies.example"
    },
    "l10nbundle": "L10n/example.json"
  },
  "configuration": {
    "services": [
      {
        "type":
          "oracle.apiplatform.policies.sdk.validation.PolicyValidator",
        "service":
          "oracle.apiplatform.policies.example.exampleValidator"
      },
      {
        "type":
          "oracle.apiplatform.policies.sdk.runtime.PolicyRuntimeFactory",
        "service":
          "oracle.apiplatform.policies.example.exampleRuntimeFactory"
      }
    ]
  }
}
```

The templating tool will configure many of these values correctly for as long as the conventions used are not deviated from. There some adjustments that are necessary.

24. Alter the `helpUrl` to `https://github.com/APIPlatform-Book/GeoIPJavaPolicy/blob/master/Help.html`.

Additional libraries

A custom API policy that performs tasks beyond fairly basic operations is likely to need external libraries (jars), for example **Log4J** or a database connector. As you may have observed in the `execute()` method, the provided implementation makes use of Log4J. As the custom policy also needs to determine whether an IP maybe within a network range the Apache common net package is also exploited.

To use libraries such as Log4J or Apache commons, for example, requires the jars to be either:

- Manually deployed and included into the gateway classpath.
- Be part of a standard WebLogic/gateway deployment.
- Incorporated into the policy deployment packaging.

This last option will in effect ensure that the jars get deployed into the gateway classpath, but without needing to do anything manually. To get the jars into the deployment it is necessary to:

25. Add the jars to an `extlibs` folder which should be picked up by as part of the packaging and deployment process
26. Amend the `build.properties` file so that it correctly references the `extlibs` folder created, the outcome would, therefore, be `bin.includes = extLibs/`

Deployment

Policies are deployed to the gateways using the cloud API management. The build process will have created a JAR file for the policy containing metadata, Java classes (and source), HTML and JavaScript. It is deployed to the API platform using a REST call to `<API management instance> /apiplatform/administration/v1/policies` as a POST call with a file stream.

 Presently once a Java API Policy is deployed there are no means to remove it from use. So before commencing the deployment of a custom API Policy, it is recommended that the decision to deploy a policy is agreed with all stakeholders.

The final step therefore is:

27. Deploy the policy by executing the Ant build (`build.xml`) which given the configuration compile, package and push to the management cloud the custom policy

It is possible to perform the build without automatically deploying the policy by changing the `build.properties` file. To see how this can be done refer back to the descriptions to identify the appropriate flags to change.

Current constraints

Currently, the API platform has a couple of constraints with the use of custom Java policies. As the product continues to mature and develop we can expect the constraints to be removed. But until the necessary refinements arrive, it is worth understanding the constraints and implications they have on custom policy development.

Probably the most significant of the current constraints come from the support of the custom policy lifecycle (like any typical piece of software a custom policy will go through a cycle of design-development-test-production-maintain-depreciate-undeploy).

The first constraint manifests itself during the development and test phases. As soon as a custom policy is deployed for the first time, it can be picked up and be used by anyone developing an API, not ideal while the API is being tested and not validated as production ready. There a couple of things that can be done to mitigate this, such as:

- Modify the UI so the messaging of the development state is obvious.
- In Chapter 5, *Platform Setup and Gateway Configuration*, the idea of having a small instance of the API Platform cloud management and a gateway. Such an environment would allow the development to be done without disruption.

The second part of the lifecycle that currently has a gap is the deprecation and withdrawal of the policy. The only way to remove a policy once deployed is to actually create a new clean environment, as the policy can't actually be undeployed. We can, however, limit the impact of not being able to undeploy a custom policy through the following actions:

- Deploy an update to the policy that means the UI clearly shows the policy is deprecated or redundant
- Change the underlying policy logic so that it generates warnings if used, and reduce the code so that it is purely a stub

The single issue that exists with the current lifecycle is that if a custom policy is developed as a stop gap until an enterprise-class implementation from Oracle or another 3rd party comes along is that if the policies have the same names you could see conflict, so think carefully about the policy naming.

The second consideration is that the supporting documentation for the SDK is limited at present. This in part comes down the fact that the SDK is largely being used by Oracle to build the standard API policies although some customers are known to be using the SDK.

Custom policies – which policy type to use?

Having been through the custom policies that can be created with both Java and Groovy, the question begs when to use which approach? To know which approach to use (Groovy or Java) means understanding the pros and cons of each approach. Why these pros and cons exist will become apparent as the chapter works through how custom policies work and are developed.

Java Pros:

- Will appear as a re-usable policy across all gateways and available immediately to all APIs (compared to Groovy which would require the logic to be cut and pasted every time the policy needs to be used in a new API)
- The policy is built using traditional development techniques, as a result, complex logic can be more easily developed (compared with a Groovy policy) with all the quality processes that go with this kind of development including:
    - Opportunity to include code analytics
    - Unit testing
    - Configuration management
    - Keep proprietary algorithms hidden

Java Cons:

- Requires greater investment in an effort to produce a policy.
- Logic can't be incorporated into other out of the box policies that support scripting, for example, logging.
- **Increased Operational Expenditure (OPEX)** as the code needs to be developed, tested and maintained. If an organization is not operating its own development teams and maintaining expertise this could carry greater costs.

Groovy Pros:

- Simple language to work with for basic manipulations
- Low level of investment to implement a one-off policy
- Doesn't require additional privileges to develop and deploy

Groovy Cons:

- Detecting issues in the script don't occur until deployment time and the error requires effort to determine
- Groovy policies can only be re-used through cutting and pasting
- Limitations of what packages can be used to implement features, for example, 3rd party libraries aren't an option

- The sophistication of the logic is constrained as functions and classes can't be created in the Groovy script

The underlying theme, between the two approaches, is re-use and complexity. We can approach the decision with a few guiding rules:

- If a Groovy policy requires more than 20 or 30 lines of code it is likely the limits of practical maintainability are being reached, use a custom Java policy
- The implementation needs to utilize classes and methods, and so on, it's getting too complex – better to use a callout and deploy the functionality elsewhere
- The policy needs to be used in multiple places-use the Java approach
- The logic depends upon classes outside of the JDK and the API SDK, then you need to use Java custom policies

Summary

In this chapter, the application of **Groovy** script to logging and Groovy policies was described and illustrated. With this the relationship to the framework in which policies were introduced, and how the framework enabled behaviors such as manipulating the API call payloads and headers.

With that foundation of knowledge, a couple of Groovy policies where configured to illustrate these ideas. The Groovy part of the chapter also drilled into more depth about using the language to build a custom policy. The idea of the `PlatformTest` service was introduced and an implementation was deployed to help test the example policies.

The second half of the chapter went on to the development of custom **Java policies**. This time rather than defining an API and applying and a little script applied, a custom policy had been taken and examined. As the policy and the tooling to accelerate the development have been examined the steps needed to be taken have been called out.

In both the Groovy and Java custom policies we looked at requirements from the perspective of our fictional company MRA and it's use cases.

If there is to be a singular takeaway from this chapter, it should be that neither the Groovy or custom Java policies exist to provide a means in which integration logic should be built. Trying to implement such functionality will undermine the value proposition of the API Platform.

The next chapter explores the factors and considerations involved in transitioning from earlier API based products from Oracle such as the API gateway 11g to this new product.

10
Moving from API Management 12c to APIP CS

This chapter discusses the transition from Oracle API management suite 12c to the new Oracle API platform cloud service (APIP CS). It sets out to discuss some of the architectural differences between the two products and maps the tool usage between the two platforms. It also discusses a recommended approach for API migration. Unfortunately, there are no automated tools as of the time this book was written to migrate APIs between the two platforms. REST APIs could be used to create a tool for such a purpose and while this is potentially possible it would be complex and subject to severe limitations. These limitations are discussed later in this chapter.

Oracle API management suite 12c

The previous incarnation of Oracle's API management suite, 12c, was made up of three products:

- **Oracle API Catalog 12c (OAC)**
- **Oracle API Manager 12c (OAPIM 12c)**
- **Oracle API Gateway 11g (OAG 11g)**

OAC helps organizations to catalogue existing enterprise and third-party services and APIs, thereby unlocking functionality and information, which would have been previously hidden. API catalog allows application and/or mobile developers and architects to discover and reuse assets rather than inadvertently re-creating them from scratch each time, thereby greatly reducing redundancy and maintenance overhead issues.

OAPIM 12c is installed on top of Oracle service bus and allows curators to take existing OSB proxies and use them to create APIs. These can either be managed APIs, where an API key must be used to access the API or non-managed, in which case a key is not required. Interested consumers and external developers use API manager to register applications and discover APIs.

OAG 11g is a standalone software platform that is deployed in the DMZ to guard against external threats such as denial-of-service (DOS) attacks, injection and malicious code (like SQL or XPath injection), confidentiality integrity (such as packet sniffing and parameter tampering), reconnaissance attacks (like directory reversal) and privilege escalation attacks (like race conditions and buffer overflow). It acts as the first line of defence for an organisation and virtualises actual service endpoints.

 Further details of the API Manager 12c and related products can be found in the book *Oracle API Management 12c Implementation* by *Packt Publishing* (`https://www.packtpub.com/application-development/oracle-api-man agement-12c-implementation`).

OAG 11g and OAPIM 12c are distinct and separate products that are separately installable.

The following diagram illustrates the high-level architecture of OAPIM 12c and OAG 11g:

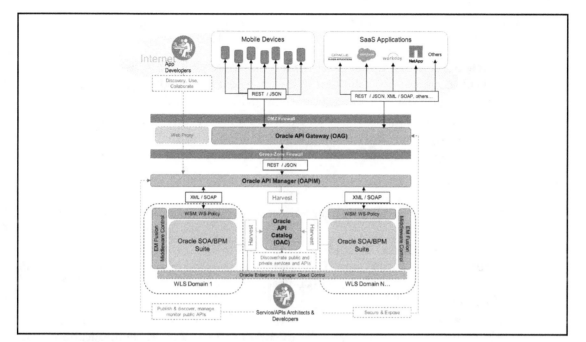

A high-level architecture for OAPIM 12c and OAG 11g

The following sections provide a brief overview of these products for those readers who may be unfamiliar with the older platform and tasked with determining how best to transition to APIP CS. It will provide the reader with some context for the rest of the chapter.

Oracle API manager 12c overview

Oracle API manager 12c (OAPIM 12c) facilitates the creation and management of APIs. From a user perspective, Oracle API manager consists of the following components:

- **Oracle Service Bus Console**: In order to promote OSB Proxy Services to APIs and subsequently publish them so they can be available through the portal, the **API Curator** must perform a series of tasks in this module.
- **Oracle API Management portal**: Once an API has been created and published via OSB, any other configuration or task will be performed through this interface. It is used by API Curators, API Administrators and API Consumers.

OAPIM 12c provides the following features/capabilities:

- **API Creation**: The API manager will take OSB proxies and use them to create APIs.
- **API Documentation**: Addition of metadata for APIs making it possible to document and classify them. This is a task performed by an **API curator**. The API metadata, together with the API contract, are then published via the **API Management portal**.
- **Search and Discovery**: API consumers and third party developers will access the API manager to search for and discover APIs. They can register applications that act as a vehicle for consuming the APIs.
- **Access**: Third parties will gain access to APIs via a URL and a security token, which will be used for authentication and identification. Third party details are also managed in API manager.
- **Analytics and monitoring**: API publishers will use these capabilities to understand the metrics and usage consumptions of the published APIs.

Oracle API gateway 11g

OAG 11g is used to publish and secure APIs for access by web and mobile developers. It virtualises service endpoints and implements security policies, protecting organisations from potential threats.

The following tools are used to develop, deploy and manage APIs in OAG 11g:

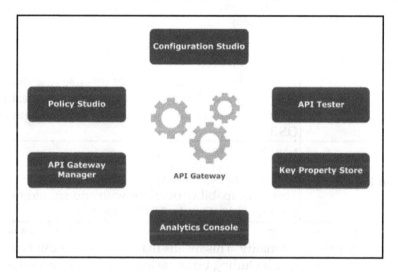

OAG 11g tools

Briefly, these tools can be described as follows:

- **Policy Studio:** Used to define policies for APIs. These are then deployed to the gateway where they were enforced as a first line of defence.
- **Oracle API Tester** is a graphical tool that enables testing of API performance, scalability, and security.
- **Configuration Studio** is a graphical tool used to promote API gateway configuration from development environments to upstream environments (for example, test or production).
- **API Gateway Manager** is a Web-based administration console that enables operational monitoring, management, and troubleshooting.
- **API Gateway Analytics** is a Web-based monitoring and reporting console that enables generation of scheduled reports and analysis of API use in multiple API gateways across a domain.

The following table shows the key features of OAG 11g for managing the lifecycle of protected APIs:

Feature	OAG 11g Offering
Quality of Service	• QoS monitoring, alerting and enforcement • Real-time and offline performance monitoring • Client-based policies
Dynamic Transformation and Routing	• Routing based on client and device identity, message type, network, condition and geography • Content and context based routing • Protocol bridging (for example, REST to SOAP) • Data Transformation The last three characteristics of this use case overlap with **Oracle Service Bus's 12c** functionality. The best practice from an architectural point of view is to handle them through **OSB**.
Monitoring and Reporting	• Auditing and logging • Real time monitoring and alerting • Analytics and usage statistics This last capability overlaps with and should be handled preferably by **Oracle API Manager 12c**.

As you can see from the preceding table, OAG 11g, which was an OEM, is a *heavy-weight* product that has very rich functionality. This means that the gateway can be used to implement a vast amount of logic including business logic, although this is considered a bad practice in modern architectures (we will revisit this point later in the chapter).

Oracle API Platform Cloud Service

Oracle API Platform Cloud Service (**APIP CS**) is a brand new third generation API platform that is built from the ground up to support Web APIs and modern API requirements such as API-first development, hybrid deployment models, elastic scaling and **Microservice** Architecture. It is designed to handle JSON end to end natively. SOAP APIs are supported from 18.1.3 using the REST to SOAP Policy.

The concept of third generation API platforms is discussed in Chapter 1, *Platform Overview*.

The following diagram shows the high-level architecture involved:

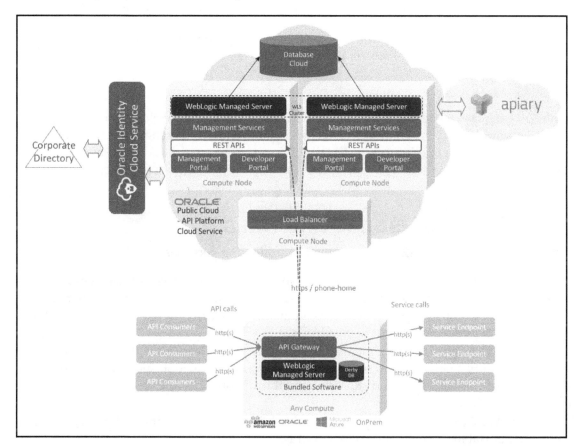

The APIP CS architecture

Briefly, APIP CS is made up of the following components:

- **My Services Console**: Used to provision new service instances, start and stop service instances, initiate backups, and perform other lifecycle management tasks.
- **Gateway**: This is the security and access control runtime layer for APIs. Each API is deployed to a gateway node from the management portal or via APIP CS REST APIs.
- **Management Portal:** This is used to create and manage APIs, deploy APIs to gateways, manage gateways, and create and manage applications. It is also possible to manage and deploy APIs and manage gateways using REST APIs.

- **Developer Portal:** Application developers subscribe to APIs and get the necessary information they need to invoke them from this portal.

Further details of the components that make up APIP CS can be found in Chapter 1, *Platform Overview*.

The API gateway can be deployed in the cloud (Oracle or any other cloud vendor) or on premise. Importantly, the gateway can be deployed in the closest geographical region to the API implementation that it protects. Details of how to configure the APIP CS and gateways is provided in Chapter 5, *Platform Setup and Gateway Configuration* of this book.

Mapping of personas and roles

Oracle API Management 12c Suite involved the following personas:

- **API Curator**: Responsible for publishing the APIs into the API management portal and documenting and maintaining the metadata associated with these APIs. The main responsibility is on maintaining the API metadata in the portal. This role is equivalent to the **OAC curator**.
- **API Administrator**: System administrator with full access to the system. Has the ability change system settings but also access information such as runtime metrics, analytics, and subscription information. This role is equivalent to the OAC admin.
- **API Consumer**: Third party or internal developers using the API management portal to discover and consume APIs.
- **Policy developer**: Virtualize APIs and develop security policies based on defined policy definitions. This may involve extending current policies or developing new ones as appropriate.
- **Deployer**: Promote policies and configurations among different environments.
- **Operator**: Uses the analytical and monitoring capabilities of the gateway to monitor the API gateway.
- **Gateway administrator**: Administer and troubleshoot the OAG 11g platform ensuring that it is always up and running. They are also in charge of stopping, starting and maintaining the gateway.
- **Key property store administrator**: Create specific key values that will be used by the policies. This user can modify these properties at runtime, providing agility and real time modifications for the APIs.

APIP CS uses the following personas:

- **API manager**: People responsible for managing the API lifecycle, which includes designing, implementing, and versioning APIs. Also responsible for managing grants and applications, providing API documentation, and monitoring API performance.
- **Application developer**: API consumers granted self-service access rights to discover and register APIs, view API documentation, and manage applications using the developer portal.
- **API Designers:** This role does not exist as such in the platform, but rather is a logical role to represent API managers and/or application developers that have access to Apiary and therefore can either produce API designs, participate in the API design process and/or associate Apiary documentation to a specific API in the APIs page.
- **Gateway manager:** Operations team members responsible for deploying, registering, and managing gateways. They may also manage API deployments to their gateways when issued the deploy API grant by an API manager.
- **Administrator:** System administrators responsible for assigning people to roles in the system. Administrators possess the rights of all other roles and rights to all objects in the system. They can also deploy custom policies.
- **Gateway runtime:** This role indicates a service account used to communicate from the gateway to the portal.

The following table shows the typical tasks performed when defining and consuming APIs and the mapping of personas between OAPIM 12c and APIP CS:

Task	OAPIM 12c	APIP CS
API Design	API Curator	API Manager
API Documentation	API Curator	API Manager
API Policy development	Policy Developer	API Manager
Discovery and Consuming APIs	Application Developer	API Consumer
API Administration	API Administrator	Administrator
Deployment	Deployer	API Manager
Gateway Administration	Gateway Administrator	Gateway Manager
Gateway Monitoring	Operator	Gateway Manager
Key Management	Key property store Administrator	Weblogic Trust Store

Architectural differences

OAPIM 12c and **OAG 11g** are second generation API platforms, based on monolithic technology stacks and derived from appliance-based technologies such as the Oracle service bus. They can perform many functions, from message routing and data transformation, to service orchestrations and even implementation of business rules. To deliver such diverse capabilities, the footprint of second generation platforms tended to be quite large. However, implementing logic and business rules in the gateway is not considered to be best practice in modern architecture design since it is better to keep the gateway lean. Service logic, including message and protocol transformations should be encapsulated in the service implementation itself. Services can then be scaled at the backend to meet required capacity levels. Thus, gateways should focus purely on API mediation requirements such as routing, authentication/authorization, throttling and rate limiting API access.

APIP CS by contrast, is a third-generation product, built almost entirely from the ground up to satisfy modern integration requirements, such as web APIs, monetarisation and hybrid deployment models. It fully supports **Microservices Architectures**, providing a lightweight, scalable, and affordable solution as compared to traditional, monolithic, heavy and invariably expensive second-generation API gateways.

A recommended read would be *3rd Generation API platforms: from proxies to micro gateways*:

```
http://www.oracle.com/technetwork/articles/soa/weir-3rd-gen-api-
mgmt-3787102.html
http://www.soa4u.co.uk/2017/11/2nd-vs-3rd-generation-api-platfor
ms.html
```

The following diagram summaries how API management suite 12c and API platform cloud service map to each other:

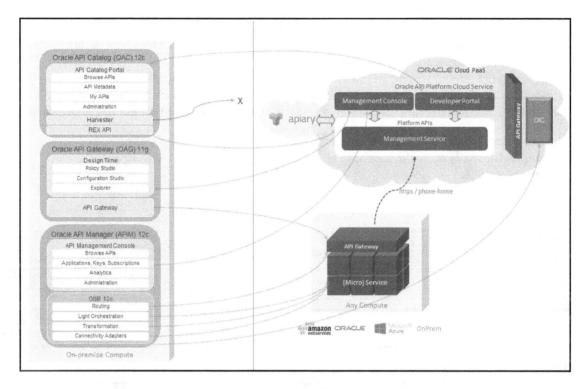

Mapping architectural differences between API manager 12c and APIP CS

As can be appreciated from the preceding diagram, OAC capabilities are now moved into the development portal, which allows developers to discover and consume APIs and designers to add documentation.

OAPIM 12c capabilities have been migrated to the management console in APIP CS. Here the emphasis is on defining and administration of the API-for example adding security policies. There are no harvesting capabilities in APIP CS. Oracle's strategy is to provide the ability to model APIs and services using the API Platform and to expose the REST APIs needed to create/manage both the API objects and services. The API manager is, therefore, responsible for entering all the required information into the API platform via the management portal or the platform APIs.

Oracle API gateway replaces OAG 11g and is a simpler product, focused purely on Web APIs. It provides authentication, authorization, throttling and security. There is no support for transformation and although protocol conversion from REST to SOAP is provided from version 18.1.3.

In an ideal world, organizations would re-write backend service implementations as fully encapsulated microservices. For example, on premise SOA Suite services exposed using OSB would be rewritten using microservice design principles. However, it is not always possible or cost effective to do so. So alternatively, the preceding diagram also shows that service implementations can be implemented in OIC, which is a more strategic product than SOA Suite. The decision on which approach is best will depend on the organization.

The following table shows the typical tasks that are performed when defining, consuming and deploying APIs and which products are used in OAPIM 12c/OAG 11g and the new API manager cloud service:

Task	OAPIM 12c /OAG 11g	API Manager Cloud Service
API Design (API Blueprint/Swagger)	Not available	Apiary
API Mock	Not available	Apiary
Define Publically exposed API	Policy Studio	Management Portal
Document the API	API Management portal	Apiary and Management Portal
Discovery and Consumption	API Management portal/OAC	Development Portal
Define security policies	Policy Studio	Management Portal
Test APIs	API Tester	API Fortress
API Validation	Not available	Dredd/Apiary
View API Details	API Management portal	Developer Portal
Deploy APIs	Configuration Studio	Management Portal
Manage Gateways	API Gateway Manager	Management Portal
Gateway Analytics	API Gateway Analytics	Management Portal
Key Property Store	Key Property Store	WebLogic trust stores

One of the things that you may notice from the preceding table is that with OAPIM 12c and OAG 11g it is necessary to register or amend an API both in API manager and in OAG 11g. The latter being used when the service is exposed externally. This meant that API curators had to potentially learn two separate tools and two separate user interfaces. The process is much more streamlined in APIP CS as there is just one tool used to identify, secure, and deploy APIs.

Strategy for transitioning APIs from OAPIM 12c to APIP CS

As discussed in the preceding section, the architecture of the two product suites is fundamentally different and unfortunately there are no automated tools to help with migration at the time of writing this book. The authors considered the possibility of using REST APIs to assist in the migration of APIs between the two environments but concluded that this would be challenging and the subject for a whole new book. For example, it would be difficult to cope with schema changes, such as those observed between the export from OAPM 12c and the required import schemas for the APIP CS platform. Indeed, it would be difficult to maintain the underlying data integrity when importing related entities due to fundamental differences between the metadata models of the two products.

 Further details of how to use APIP CS REST APIs can be found at `http://www.ateam-oracle.com/apip-rest-python/`.

Therefore, we would recommend that the first step in the process is to create an **API Re-Implementation Design Document** that details technical decisions about how APIs will be re-implemented and defined. The following steps are required when migrating APIs and these should be considered in detail as part of the migration design:

- API re-implementation design
- Service Implementation
- API definition and API-first design
- API creation/policy implementation
- API testing
- API switch-over strategy

The remainder of this section will consider some of the key issues that need to be addressed by this document.

API re-implementation design

One of the first steps in the transition process will be to assemble all existing service endpoints and consider a migration strategy for each. Depending on the degree of maturity of an organisation, this may be just a question of going into OAC or an existing UDDI registry to obtain the endpoint URLs. **Oracle Enterprise Repository** can be used to harvest existing services where these have not previously been documented and collated, but this product does not enable automated conversion of services to APIs.

A design authority, which should include business stakeholders, must decide which APIs and data will be exposed externally through the gateway and how. This is not a trivial task and careful consideration is required.

Depending on the decisions made, architects and API managers need to design API contracts which match the specified requirements, and this will also influence the degree of re-usability for service implementation logic between external and internal services. It will also dictate whether APIs are designed to be single purpose or multipurpose. Single purpose APIs are usually targeted to a single use case or task and indeed may be for a certain type of consumer. Multipurpose APIs on the other hand tend to perform a set of tasks and are designed to deliver everything that a consumer needs from on API call.

The API re-implementation may also coincide with a digital transformation programme, in which case new processes will be designed with a customer first approach. APIs should then be designed to support these new processes, and process automation where applicable, thus helping to streamline business processes and thereby improve customer experience. This would most likely be associated with a whole new enterprise architecture initiative and would be very costly.

Service implementation

The re-implementation design strategy needs to consider not just the API service endpoint itself, but also the backend service implementation. The architects may decide to completely redesign certain services, in which case, they may consider adopting modern architecture philosophies such as those proposed by the OMESA project and advocated by this book. The OMESA project defines a complete reference architecture for API implementations.

More details can be found at `http://omesa.io`.

Where there was previously a reliance on OAG 11g to perform protocol conversion, heavy-weight transformation, or business rules, the recommendation would be to redesign these interfaces from scratch, moving the heavy lifting logic to separate microservices or integrations. This will keep the gateway lean.

If the choice is made to maintain an integration layer within the organization, architects may simply mandate that services are re-implemented in more strategic toolset such as OIC. The choice will largely depend on the strategic direction of the organisation. Existing SOA services may simply be ported from on-premise SOA Suite to SOACS and the API repointed to the cloud implementation. This might, for example, occur when an organisation wishes to maintain its existing investments yet move to the cloud to reduce total cost of ownership.

Alternatively, existing backend services can be left as-is, such as on-premise SOA services, but exposed using new API endpoints in APIP CS. This will provide a much quicker approach in the first instance since it is more expedient than completely re-implementing backend logic. The new APIs will need to honour existing service contracts. This approach is especially true for key services that the organisation wishes to maintain in-house or for single purpose APIs which are targeted to specific use cases or single consumers and therefore it is not worth the cost of re-implementation. These services may be re-engineered and re-implemented later if time or budget permits.

The design strategy needs to consider all options and define the best approach based for an organisation, based on its chosen reference technical architecture.

API definition and API-first design

In all cases, new APIs will be created to front these services. APIs should be designed using an API first design approach, except where existing services are exposed and therefore the contract is maintained. **Apiary** should be the tool of choice to design and document all new APIs. Existing REST APIs, should also be documented in Apiary for consistency and to provide a single point of truth. Apiary has rich support for open standards such as OpenAPI and API Blueprints, which help define and mock APIs. Oracle Apiary also supports collaboration, documentation and testing. Multiple designers from within an enterprise can work together to design and test API concepts and a mock service can then be automatically generated for consumers and developers to provide their feedback.

The OpenAPI Specification (OAS) defines a standard, language-agnostic interface to RESTful APIs which allows both humans and computers to discover and understand the capabilities of a service without the need to access source code, documentation, or network traffic inspection. It was originally known as Swagger. Further details on OpenAPI can be found at https://swagger.io/specification/.

API Blueprint can be used to quickly design and prototype APIs or document and test already deployed mission-critical APIs. Further details can be found at https://apiblueprint.org/.

API creation/policy implementation

Mapping of policies from OAG 11g to APIP CS should also be covered in the re-implementation design document where existing APIs are exposed in APIP CS. The design document should stipulate which policies should be created and in what order. Further details of recommended policies and their order can be found in Chapter 6, *Defining Policies for APIs*, which also discusses the security policies required for both internal and external use. This is considered in more detail in the section *Defining API Policies* later.

While SOAP to REST policies are introduced in APIP CS 18.1.3, REST enabling existing SOAP services is still likely to be a key issue where existing services are exposed using APIP CS. This is because in most cases, the protocol transformation should not be done in the gateway to keep it light and highly performant: except of course in cases where integration is into a third party with no middleware installed. One option is to use Oracle service bus to expose SOAP services as REST APIs. Alternatives are available such as APIMATIC which can achieve the same conversion. Alternatively, protocol and message transformation could be achieved either by a service callout in APIP CS.

Further details on APIMATIC can be found at https://apimatic.io/transformer.

API testing

A detailed testing plan should be created to enable full regression testing of migrated APIs. API testing should be performed using API Fortress as this will fully exercise the functionality of ported APIs. More details can be found in Chapter 7, *Testing APIs with API Fortress*.

API switch-over strategy

An API switch-over strategy also needs to be formulated and this will largely depend on the organisation. The best policy would be to gradually migrate APIs to the new platform, targeting logical units of APIs that can be migrated together. This, however, requires a high level of control and communication with API consumers so as not to interfere with business processes. There is always the chance that a consumer forgets to re-point to the new API endpoint and therefore retirement of old APIs is important issue here.

For those organisations looking to reduce license costs, this may not be the approach as they would have to maintain licenses for both the old and new API platforms. The degree of coordination required for a *big bang* switch over, however, will be very high and an organisation may believe that the reputational damage of getting this wrong outweighs the cost of maintaining parallel licences.

A roadmap should be created to show a high-level plan of what capabilities will be delivered and when.

Defining API policies

Once the specifications for the APIs have been documented and agreed with consumers using Apiary, the APIs will need to be created in the management portal and policies defined that match as closely as possible with existing policies. A policy is a network of message filters that processes a message. A message can traverse different paths through the policy, depending on which filters succeed or fail. Policies were previously configured in OAG 11g using a tool called Policy Studio. In APIP CS, policies are implemented in the API management portal itself and so there is no separate product to consider. Further details on how to create policies can be found in Chapter 6, *Defining Policies for APIs*.

While OAG 11g has a very rich set of policies, this makes the product inherently difficult to use. Policies are much easier to implement in API cloud and are provided out of the box for the following areas:

- Security
- Traffic Management
- Interface Management
- Routing

The following table shows how policies in OAG 11g map to APIP CS:

OAG 11g	Oracle API Platform Cloud Service
Authenticate API Key	Key Validation
IP Address Authentication	IP Filter
HTTP Basic Authentication	Basic Authentication
CORS Profiles	CORS Policy
New to API Manager CS	API throttling-delay policies
Throttling	API Rate Limiting Policies
	Application Rate Limiting policies
Validate REST Request	Interface Filtering Policies
	Method Mapping Policies
	Redaction Policies
Routing Filter	Header Validation Policies
	Header based routing Policies
	Gateway based routing policies
	Application Based Routing Policies
	Resource Based Routing
Execute External Process	Groovy scripts and custom API policy development framework

Those familiar with OAG 11g will note that the set of policies available is much greater than those available in APIP CS. However, the latter does provide the ability to create custom policies that can be implemented in Groovy (this is similar to the utility filter *Execute External Process* in OAG 11g). Chapter 9, *Implementing Custom Policies* describes how to create and apply custom policies.

As discussed previously, the APIP CS Gateway should be used as a light weight component in the DMZ. Its main function is to enforce authorization and authentication and prevent malicious attacks. It should not be used for message transformation and payload enrichment. A better approach, and one advocated by OMESA, is that the service itself should be responsible for payload transformation and enrichment. Alternatively, a callout could be used to encapsulate the message transformation, which again can be implemented in a separately scalable microservice.

> Further details on OMESA can be found in `Chapter 1`, *Platform Overview* or at `http://omesa.io`.

Adding API documentation

In addition to the APIs themselves, the API manager will need to port documentation that describes how to consume the API. This is achieved using the **Publication** page of the **Management Portal** in APIP CS, which is used to provide general details about an API and links to detailed documentation. It is also possible to link directly to Apiary to import Swagger or API blueprint documentation. This is done be selecting the **Apiary** button as shown in the following screenshot:

Adding API documentation

API managers can then publish the documentation to the developer portal allowing application developers to discover, evaluate, register, and consume published APIs.

> Further details on how to define and publish API documentation can be found in Chapter 3, *Designing the API* and Chapter 4, *Building and Running the Microservice* of this book.

Deploying endpoints

Once all the policies have been defined and metadata created for the new APIs, the endpoints can be deployed to the required gateways. APIP CS is a much simpler tool to use than OAG 11g, having been architected as a leaner *third-generation* API product. The deployment in OAG 11g is a relatively complex affair involving registering the API and defining a wealth of security policies, transformation polices and integrity policies. Deployment in APIP CS is much simpler by contrast. The API's and their security policies are contained in one cloud-based tool and it is just a question of deploying to one of the configured gateways. APIP CS gateways can be deployed to any infrastructure; cloud (any vendor) and/or on-premise. It is also architected with federation in mind, supporting deployment to multiple data centers, which can be in different geographies.

> For more information on configuring the gateways, please refer to Chapter 5, *Platform Setup and Gateway Configuration* of this book.

Testing the API

In OAG 11g, administrators would test the APIs using the API tester tool. This is a graphical tool used to test API performance, scalability and security.

Testing in APIP CS can be facilitated using **API Fortress**. API Fortress helps developers to test and validate APIs, including message structures. Changes to the API implementation can be trapped and generate alerts to reduce the risk of modifications breaking access to consumers. Furthermore, Oracle Apiary is integrated with API Fortress meaning that designers can build and test designs directly from Apiary.

API Fortress is covered extensively in `Chapter 7`, *Testing APIs with API Fortress*.

Publication of the API

Once endpoints are deployed to gateways they can be published to the developer portal. Application developers can then discover and subscribe to APIs. API publication is covered in more details in `Chapter 3`, *Designing the API* and so the reader should refer to this for more information.

Analytics

OAG 11g Analytics was a separately installable product available as part of the previous OAG 11g release. APIP CS ships with a wealth of reports for those users with the correct privilege (Manage API or view all details API grant to view analytics for that API) and these can be viewed in the API management portal. After provisioning an API platform cloud service instance and configuring the gateway node domains, analytics can be enabled for each node in the domain.

Analytics charts in the API platform cloud service management portal show critical information, such as API usage and details of errors.

Analytics are covered in more detail in `Chapter 6`, *Designing Policies for APIs*.

Summary

APIP CS is designed from the ground to help organizations create and expose APIs in a secure, agile environment, while monitoring key performance indicators for every aspect of the life cycle. It is a new *third generation* API management platform that has been architected specifically for web-based APIs. It can be used to handle authentication, authorization, throttling and prevent malicious content. It is a superior product to the previous OAIPM 12c and OAG 11g releases, with a single browser-based interface, which makes it inherently easier to use. Heavy weight transformation and protocol conversion tools have been dropped since services themselves should ideally perform these functions, leaving the gateway as light weight and unobtrusive as possible.

While OAG 11g provided much of the same functionality as APIP CS gateway, it required on premise installations on separate machines in the DMZ. By contrast, APIP CS is cloud based and gateways can be deployed both in the cloud and on-premise.

Transitioning from OAPIM 12c and OAG 11g is not a simple task as there are no automatic migration tools available. Equally, there are no harvesting tools currently shipping with APIP CS making migration a manually intensive task. For new APIs being exposed for the first time, the recommendation is to use the rich functionality provided by APIP CS for the design and documentation of APIs using Apiary. For existing interfaces, it is a question of creating APIs and applying policies that match as closely as possible with existing policies.

Another book You May Enjoy

If you enjoyed this book, you may be interested in these other books by Packt:

Implementing Oracle Integration Cloud Service
Robert van Mölken, Phil Wilkins

ISBN: 978-1-78646-072-1

- Use ICS to integrate different systems together without needing to be a developer
- Gain understanding of what a number of technologies and standards provide – without needing to understand the fine details of those standards and technologies
- Understand the use of connectors that Oracle provide from technology based connections such as file and database connections to SaaS solutions ranging from Salesforce to Twitter
- Enrich data and extend SaaS integration to route to different instances
- Utilize a number of tools to help develop and check that your integrations work before connecting to live systems
- Introduce and explain integration concepts so that the integrations created are maintainable and sustainable for the longer term
- Provide details on how to keep up to date with the features that Oracle and partners provide in the future
- Get special connections developed to work with ICS

Leave a review - let other readers know what you think

Please share your thoughts on this book with others by leaving a review on the site that you bought it from. If you purchased the book from Amazon, please leave us an honest review on this book's Amazon page. This is vital so that other potential readers can see and use your unbiased opinion to make purchasing decisions, we can understand what our customers think about our products, and our authors can see your feedback on the title that they have worked with Packt to create. It will only take a few minutes of your time, but is valuable to other potential customers, our authors, and Packt. Thank you!

Index

www.ingramcontent.com/pod-product-compliance
Lightning Source LLC
Chambersburg PA
CBHW060639060326
40690CB00020B/4458